HUMAN PREHISTORY

More than 3 million years ago in Africa, our early ancestors began to systematically modify rocks into usable tools, thus inventing the first technologies that eventually permitted humans to dominate all life forms on the planet. In this book, Deborah Barsky offers a long-term evolutionary perspective on human culture and its relationship with technology. Using scientific information and examples from the global archeological record, she follows the remarkable human journey from the early phases of prehistory and shows how it has led humans to a dangerously uncertain future. Her archeological approach offers a fresh perspective regarding important issues that plague contemporary society, such as racism, the digital revolution, human migrations, terrorism and war. Written in an accessible style, Barsky's book demonstrates how insights into the distant past serve as a tool for understanding the present and building a sustainable future for all life on planet Earth.

Deborah Barsky is a lithic specialist, archeologist and researcher at the Catalan Institute of Human Paleoecology and Social Evolution (IPHES-CERCA) and assistant professor with the Open University of Catalonia (UOC) in the History and Art History Department at the Rovira i Virgili University (URV) in Tarragona, Spain. Engaged in research projects on archeological sites throughout the world, she has published numerous works in books and scholarly journals.

HUMAN PREHISTORY

Exploring the Past to Understand the Future

Deborah Barsky
The Catalan Institute of Human Paleoecology and Social Evolution

CAMBRIDGE
UNIVERSITY PRESS

University Printing House, Cambridge CB2 8BS, United Kingdom

One Liberty Plaza, 20th Floor, New York, NY 10006, USA

477 Williamstown Road, Port Melbourne, VIC 3207, Australia

314–321, 3rd Floor, Plot 3, Splendor Forum, Jasola District Centre, New Delhi – 110025, India

103 Penang Road, #05–06/07, Visioncrest Commercial, Singapore 238467

Cambridge University Press is part of the University of Cambridge.

It furthers the University's mission by disseminating knowledge in the pursuit of education, learning, and research at the highest international levels of excellence.

www.cambridge.org
Information on this title: www.cambridge.org/highereducation/9781316515426
DOI: 10.1017/9781009025492

© Cambridge University Press 2023

First published 2023

Printed in the United Kingdom by TJ Books Limited, Padstow Cornwall

A catalogue record for this publication is available from the British Library.

Library of Congress Cataloging-in-Publication Data
Names: Barsky, Deborah, 1962– author.
Title: Human prehistory : exploring the past to understand the future / Deborah Barsky, The Catalan
    Institute of Human Paleoecology and Social Evolution.
Description: First Edition. | New York : Cambridge University Press, 2022. | Includes bibliographical
    references and index.
Identifiers: LCCN 2021035078 (print) | LCCN 2021035079 (ebook) | ISBN 9781316515426
    (Hardback) | ISBN 9781009011990 (Paperback) | ISBN 9781009025492 (ePub)
Subjects: LCSH: Antiquities, Prehistoric. | Prehistoric peoples. | Archaeology.
Classification: LCC GN740 .B377 2022 (print) | LCC GN740 (ebook) | DDC 569.9–dc23
LC record available at https://lccn.loc.gov/2021035078
LC ebook record available at https://lccn.loc.gov/2021035079

ISBN 978-1-316-51542-6 Hardback
ISBN 978-1-009-01199-0 Paperback

For you, Dad, for inspiring me throughout my life and helping me to express how learning about the distant past is valuable for understanding the present situation of humankind.

CONTENTS

FIGURES

TABLES

ACKNOWLEDGMENTS

I sincerely thank my talented colleagues at the Catalan Institute of Human Paleoecology and Social Evolution and the Rovira i Virgili University and the Open University of Catalonia (IPHES-CERCA and URV and UOC, in Tarragona, Spain), in particular Xosé Pedro Rodríguez, Palmira Saladié, Andreu Ollé, Manuel Vaquero, Jordi Rosell, Ruth Blasco, Florent Rivals, María Gema Chacón and Marina Lozano, as well as the director of the IPHES-CERCA, my friend and colleague, Robert Sala Ramos. I extend warmest acknowledgments to my colleagues at the National Research Center on Human Evolution (CENIEH) (Burgos, Spain) and the Atapuerca Foundation (Eudald Carbonell and José María Bermúdez de Castro). All of these wonderful people have guided me with their friendship and constant support to my research, including photographic contributions and valuable scientific advice. I am also very grateful for constructive comments from the respected and kind Juan Manuel Jiménez Arenas, at the University of Granada, director of the Orce research project. I am privileged to be able to include artwork from my talented friend and colleague Oriol Oms who has shared his passion for geology with me over the years. I also thank my friend and teacher Henry Baills for his constructive advice on the text and photographic input. I also pay tribute to my dear friends and associates in France, especially in Tautavel (Centre Européen de Recherches Préhistoriques EPCC-CERPT) with whom I spent my formative years and shared so many experiences. I would also like to acknowledge the helpful input from Leore Grosman of the Computational Archeology Laboratory (CAL) at the Hebrew University of Jerusalem and my dear friend Gonen Sharon from Tel Hai College in the Upper Galilee. I acknowledge my treasured friends – the talented artist Sacha Barrette, who contributed the image for the book cover, and his wife, Veronica Zuniga, with whom I have shared ideas over the years about the importance of prehistory for understanding the present and future of humanity. Sacha has generously provided the image for my book cover from his collection of paintings *Homo urbanus*. This book could never have ripened without contributions from all of the volunteer excavators, students and aspiring researchers with whom I have had the privileged opportunity of sharing and exchanging experiences and ideas over the years; they are the ones holding the future! I am forever indebted to my wonderful family for their constant support and love. I thank my life partner, Denis Dainat, for his unswerving devotion and wonderful photographic talent. Finally, I thank my beautiful daughter, Celeste, who is my life.

A WORD ABOUT THE BOOK COVER

The book cover is a detail of the original painting by the Canadian artist Sacha Barrette. The work, entitled E (130 cm × 146 cm), is part of the *Homo urbanus* series of paintings and sculptures commemorating the importance of studying the past to better understand our present condition and the human trajectory into the future. Painted in Collioure, France, on May 30, 2018, sachaimages@gmail.com.

INTRODUCTION

The aim of this book is to introduce the basic notions of prehistoric archeology, discussing the important role it plays in our understanding of the modern-day human condition and considering how lessons learned from the distant past can be useful tools for preparing the future of our species, *Homo sapiens*. As a specialist in stone tool technologies, I have been involved in the field of prehistoric archeology for one-quarter of a century, focusing the gist of my work on the origins of first technologies made from stone and observing how they evolved through time. Most of my own work has focused on African and Eurasian archeological sites and their stone tool collections because these areas of the world up to now have yielded the oldest technologies known to humankind. My inspiration in writing this book comes from a deep-seated need to substantiate an old adage, in the words of Carl Sagan: "You have to know the past to understand the present."[1] Indeed, I set out on this project because it seemed to me that this idea, although not new, is not, in fact, so easy to materialize from data gleaned from the prehistoric archeological record. Finding links that will enable us to understand lessons learned from the remote past and using them to guide our species toward a brighter future may seem particularly nebulous for those estranged from the world of scientific investigation that is the very foundation of work in prehistory. It seems to me that so much of the information that is amassed by prehistoric archeologists remains inaccessible to many people simply because (more often than not) it is lost in complex methodologies, intricate graphic representations and statistical analyses of data sets whose meaning appears far removed from our daily lives. The information processed in archeology requires a wide knowledge of elaborate concepts of human evolution that can be grasped only after years of training in the specialized disciplines linked to prehistory (paleontology, geology, geochronology, to name just a few). In spite of this, I have found that the public maintains overall a keen interest in topics relating to human evolution even as it grapples with comprehending the long-term chronological frameworks and complex foundational cultural divisions, which tend to be diachronic and increasingly multifarious as we move through time. The main aim of this book, therefore, is to provide a synthetic, long-term view of the emergence and evolution of our species and to afford some answers as to how and why we came to be what we are in order to gain a clearer vision of what we might become in the future. To do so, I have based this book on my own experience as an archeologist and on my knowledge of prehistoric archeology, focusing my discourse on a number of key archeological sites situated mainly in the Old World.

The first part of this book (Chapters 1 and 2) outlines just what "prehistory" is and describes the different disciplines that are included within this vast and composite field of knowledge. I provide an overview of some of the foremost anatomical and cultural milestones that have contributed to defining humanity, bringing us to the point that we find ourselves in today's world. Obviously, it would be impossible to include every single element affecting the human evolutionary pathway (anatomical, climatic or other) that has fortuitously guided human development from ancient hominin forms up to the present-day hegemony of the single species of Homo: Homo sapiens. Rather, I concentrate my discourse on what I feel is the main influencing factor in the human evolutionary sequencing: the invention and evolution of technology. We shall explore together how and why the first stone tool technologies were invented, looking at the social and cultural implications of this groundbreaking event in the so-called hominization process. We shall see how, over time, toolmaking came to be the single, most important defining criterion for our species, today even affecting all other life forms with which we share the planet. Undeniably, and perhaps surprisingly, it is precisely these ancient stone and bone tools that have provided up to now the only foundation with which prehistorians have defined the human cultural succession throughout the entire Paleolithic Period.

In the next chapters (Chapters 3–5), I follow through on defining what it means to be human, taking a look at how we evolved and differentiated ourselves from other types of primates by developing innovative technologies and, by extension, heavily investing in the expansion of culture. I further explain how procedural evolutionary forces developed from within the first stone tool assemblages would eventually lead the ancestral members of the Homo lineage to unprecedented reliance upon their tools, surpassing by far that demonstrated by any other of the known tool-using species. I guide you, my readers, along this fascinating pathway as we observe together how early humanoid forms carved out the unique destiny that would eventually lead us to ultimate planetary domination. Beginning with the first bipedal hominins some 7 million years ago, we will explore the emergence of first technologies as the utmost distinguishing feature of our species. Following a timeline leading from the remote past to our present-day situation, this evolutionary overview throws light on the major stages of our uniquely human story, even as we seek, especially today, to better understand what we are and what we might yet become. Increasing our knowledge about the different evolutionary phases of past human cultures as they are interpreted from the archeological record sharpens our ability to adopt an informed and long-term perspective that, in turn, is helpful for dealing with the major challenges facing the survival of our species today: climate change, racism, immigration, intolerance, terrorism, pollution, and so on. We can only hope that this perspective will contribute in some way to helping humanity to assume worthily the new role we have ourselves carved out for our species: a role of *responsibility* – not only for ourselves and for our children – but also for the planet Earth and all of its life forms.

During the later phases of the Stone Age, anatomically modern humans (AMH) came to be the sole extant species of the genus *Homo* (Chapters 6 and 7). In the spiral of human innovations following up to this situation, we shall see how the technosocial evolutionary processes developed by humans through acculturation have contributed to connecting us so intimately with one another in the process of globalization. As we are melding into our machineries through invented – and often imposed – cultural norms, we feel that we are losing grasp of the very technologies we invent(ed) as they too evolve toward ends we dare not fathom. Through the special lens of prehistoric archeology, I explain what I believe to be some of the reasons for the many incongruities we observe in modern human societies (Chapters 8–12), such as global inequalities, racism and the unprecedented rise of compartmentalized nationalisms. Putting to use some of the data obtained from the study of our ancestral populations and their lifeways, I discuss why humanity maintains such strong ties to religious thought and institutionalized practices, even in a world where scientific advancements might long ago have annulled their credibility. We will examine why humanly driven climate change is today a reality that we must all face together and how we can predict that, in the near future, dwindling resources, such as basic foodstuffs and water and the future global migration crises these will engender will most certainly worsen.

Taking a close look at our present-day situation from a long-term perspective allows us to examine more thoroughly how, when and why humans came to rely on imaginary, symbolic and now virtually created realities in the rapidly changing planetary scenario we are experiencing today. Our actual posture with respect to nature results, inevitably, from a long chain of complex evolutionary processes of biological and technological reactions to real and created pressures that acted (and continue to act) as triggers for change. In today's world, so many of us are feeling the distance we have taken from our "original" and (we suppose) more balanced natural configuration as our journey into the future continues toward unknown pathways. In writing this book, I invite you to partake on this journey through time and space as we demystify some of the secrets held deep within our ancestral past. My intention is to make the past more accessible by revealing data obtained from prehistoric archeology that I consider highly relevant to the challenges that we humans are facing today (Chapter 13). As each of us gains a clearer understanding of where we came from, then we shall be better equipped to build a sensible and sustainable future for ourselves, our children and all life forms as we step together into the future.

1

A BRIEF INTRODUCTION TO PREHISTORIC ARCHEOLOGY

WHAT IS PREHISTORIC ARCHEOLOGY?

Prehistoric archeology, or prehistory, is a composite field of science that explores the physical features and lifeways of all members of the human lineage and the environments in which they lived. The prehistory of the human lineage encompasses the time frame that witnessed the emergence of the first humanoid forms recognized in the archeological register and follows their developments up to the time when writing became a widely used means to record events affecting human lives. Of course, the widespread use of complex writing systems did not happen all at once, nor did it occur at the same time all over the inhabited world. For this reason, there is a distinction between prehistory and proto-history, the latter being the discipline dealing with the (somewhat elusive) boundary between the invention of simple pictograms to convey messages and the extensive use of phonemic orthography as a common communication strategy. Proto-history separates, therefore, the Prehistoric and Historic Ages when peoples who possessed at least some basic form of writing established the first large-scale urban civilizations. In its nascent stages, "writing" was generally used for commerce and record keeping or for relating some outstanding event affecting specific societies among peoples who did not yet express themselves by writing with highly complex systems of signs and symbols. That said, it is clear that the geographical and temporal context that we call "prehistory" differs throughout the world and that, in fact, in some remote areas, people are still said to be living, by definition, in the Prehistoric Age. The setting up of prehistory as a respected science has been a rocky road indeed, marked most notably toward the end of the nineteenth century by the scientific revelations ensuing from the publication of Darwinian evolutionary theory. Human archeological consciousness prior to this time was concerned more directly with pro-tohistoric or historic evidence (monumental or classical archeology) simply because relics relating to these time frames were – at least in many parts of the world – relatively abundant and easily recognizable in the landscape (and had been so for a very long time).[2] Some obvious examples are the ancient Egyptian monuments of North Africa, Roman and Greek ruins from the Mediterranean basin and the megalithic structures of Britain. In contrast, Paleolithic archeological sites, the focus of the present work, are not ubiquitous in the landscape, nor are they easily recognizable to the untrained eye. The awareness of their existence and the acceptance of their great antiquity, therefore, occurred relatively later in global human perception. Furthermore, their recognition as a part of the human inheritance was often hindered, as we shall see, by popular trends in socially accepted thought processes, which, in turn, are directly related to dominant cultural norms.

In Europe, where prehistory was born and matured as a scientific discipline, the identification and recognition of the human Paleolithic record was given special impetus after the intense intellectual upheavals of the Age of Enlightenment (seventeenth and eighteenth centuries), when societies moved away from religious-guided beliefs, embracing the progressing universe of scientific information. Still today, in many low- and middle-income countries (parts of Africa and Central Eurasia), monumental and classical archeological remnants are more popularly researched and information from them more commonly shared through public venues compared to Paleolithic ones. This is not because they are more interesting but rather because fields of ruins or majestic temples are more immediately attractive to the public eye than museums or Paleolithic sites with stone tools and animal fossils whose meanings are only partially decipherable even to the trained eye. Even in Europe, many countries are only just beginning to recognize and exploit the global value of prehistoric archeology. In the very near future, we can expect that archeologists will continue to make new discoveries of ancient prehistoric sites in areas that have been only sparsely explored so far, further kindling the public's keen interest in this topic that has already been stimulated in regions where prehistory has more strongly taken root. To be sure, many countries where prehistory is still only in its embryonic stages are sure to have played a key role in the ancient evolutionary stages of humankind (for example, Sudan, Egypt, Turkey, Armenia). In some cases, politically or socially prompted crises (war, poverty) inhibit both the making of prehistoric discoveries and the possibility to scientifically develop the ones that have been made on a satisfactory level (Iraq, Iran, Libya and Syria are some examples). For the moment, many parts of the world are still lacking in infrastructure and educational facilities needed to bring about the archeological consciousness necessary to impulse prehistory forward and do justice to developing its full potential in contributing to our understanding of the emergence and evolution of modern civilization.

The word *archeology* comes from the Greek *arkhaios* (ἀρχαῖος), meaning "ancient," and -*logia* (λογία), meaning "knowledge of," and it touches on interests that I believe are common to all of humankind, seeking out answers to such questions as these: Who are we? Where do we come from? Prehistoric archeology progressively gained coherency throughout much of the Old World (especially after the sixteenth-century in Western Europe) as the deeply influential clutch of religion subsided and the foundations for many of the modern scientific disciplines were laid down. This tendency was reinforced further by the so-called antiquarians, who amassed personal collections of artifacts, providing a basis for their formulation of ideas about the past. In order to understand why it is so important to study prehistory, we must look to some of the most noteworthy historical developments that shaped its present-day conceptual agenda. It is therefore appropriate here to review briefly some of the milestones formative to the emergence of modern-day evolutionary theory: the cornerstone of prehistory. To do so, it is important that we recall some of the many key figures who contributed to its difficult birthing process, for they are the players underpinning the "coming out" of prehistory and its maturity into a true scientific endeavor, even in the face of difficult and even dangerous sociopolitical impediments. It is beneficial to remember that modern-day prehistoric archeology was made possible only through sacrifices by individuals who struggled to overthrow restrictive trends dominant in their own specific time frames and social contexts. In this sense, the evolution of prehistory as a science must be considered for its revolutionary quality. The essence of its maturity is a reminder to those individuals who are still reverting to alternative (outdated) modes of understanding human and animal evolution, or who preach religious explanations as mechanisms responsible for evolutionary change in the natural world, that they are doing so in blatant contempt for science and the battles raged to throw off the shackles of closed-mindedness and surrealistic interpretations of the universe.

SOME HISTORICAL LANDMARKS IN THE BIRTH OF THE DISCIPLINE OF PREHISTORY

It is only through upheavals that the consciousness of a very ancient existence for humans (going well beyond the biblical time frame) was eventually accepted and explored scientifically. Once condemned as heresy, acknowledging evolutionary theory has matured into a shared human passion. The (relatively new) awareness of human procedural evolution (or the so-called hominization process)[3] has progressively given way to intense archeological explorations, coupled with inventiveness and modern technological development, contributing to our capacity to understand (or at least reasonably hypothesize about) human ancestry by way of purely scientific methods. The word *hominization* refers to the diachronic achievements made by hominins as they climbed up the rungs of the evolutionary ladder of life (the word *hominin* is used throughout this book to refer to humans and their close extinct ancestors). This process is presently seen to have begun in Africa some 7 million years ago, in the Chadian desert west of the East African Rift Valley, with the emergence of the first bipedal hominins (*Sahelanthropus tchadensis*, fossil finds known as "Toumaï," meaning "life hope").[4] This change in primate locomotion, from quadrupedal and arboreal gaits to bipedal stature, was to give way to significant anatomical and later even cultural developments, marking human evolution in very significant ways. Indeed, this locomotor shift is viewed as foundational to a whole series of interrelated evolutionary events marking the human trajectory, such as higher success rates in competing against other large carnivores for obtaining food and even the invention of stone tools.

Today, thanks to historical documents, we trace the advances made in prehistory back through the centuries with the consciousness of their implications in relation to the dictates prevailing in each of the time frames within which they occurred – and then spread. In the seventeenth century, a book entitled *Praedamitae* (meaning *Men before Adam*) was written by a French theologian named I. de La Peyrère (1596–1676), who claimed that the biblical Adam was not the "first Man" and that other humans must have inhabited the Earth before him, thus founding the so-called pre-Adamite hypothesis. Of course, when it was published, the book was outlawed as heretical and La Peyrère was duly imprisoned until he accepted revocation of his claims.[5] The French naturalist G. Buffon (1707–1788) was another influential figure in the "coming of age" of prehistory as a science. He argued that science must be founded only on observable facts, consequently disengaging the laws of Nature from theology.[6] In the meantime, the Swedish naturalist C. Linnaeus (1707–1778)[7] developed deeply influential systems of scientific classification whose denominations (class, order, genus, species) are still in use today in all domains of natural history. His work *Philosophia Botanica* (1751) constitutes such a major achievement in science because it provided a means by which empirical realities could be converted into intelligible communicative systemic that minimizes subjectivity. Furthermore, Linnaeus observed species' plasticity, even before Darwin, introducing the notion of anatomical change over time. Perhaps most significantly, in his 1758 edition of *Systema Naturae*, Linnaeus "classified" humans as members of the primate order alongside the other Great Apes, thus opening the way for the subsequent works of Lamarck and Darwin.

Another remarkable landmark in the maturing science of prehistory was reached when the French naturalist J.-B. Lamarck (1744–1829)[8] established an evolutionary theory (called "transformism") as a model postulating the existence of an internal dynamic acting in accordance with environmental pressures that triggered anatomical change. According to this model, changing environmental conditions play a key role in driving biological change, therefore providing an explanation for the unusual species' morphologies that were being observed from the ever-increasing bulk of fossil finds. According to this scheme, species undergo modifications (behavioral and physical) to

Figure 1.1
Charles Darwin portrait (1809–1882) best known for his contributions to evolutionary
theory with natural selection as the central precept. (Walter William Ouless, Public Domain,
via Wikimedia Commons)

"adapt" to changes in their environmental settings. Certainly, by Lamarck's time, it was
becoming urgent to adequately address the fossil finds of species whose anatomic
features were markedly different from those known in the actual world. Lamarck's
precepts were awkwardly fitted with the dominant theological point of view that flatly
refuted any idea of extinction on the basis that it would imply that God's creation was
imperfect. In order to do so, theologians argued that since the environment is in
constant flux, so too were species required to be in a permanent state of transformation
in order to survive. In his time, Lamarck supported the theory of "spontaneous
generation," claiming that simple life forms suddenly appeared and then progressed
toward more complex forms, the ultimate of which was thought to be Man. Currently,
these ideas are still upheld by Creationists, who stubbornly continue to postulate that
God produced life in accordance with a divine plan, following some linear and
progressive notion of a move toward greater complexity, ultimately culminating in
human perfection.

A major turnover occurred following the publication of Darwin's landmark work *On
the Origin of Species* in 1859 (Figure 1.1).[9] Darwin not only proposed an evolutionary
model but also convincingly buttressed it with empirical evidence collected during his
five-year sailing voyage (1831–1836) around the world as a naturalist aboard the *HMS
Beagle* (notably along South America's coastline). During his travels, Darwin collected
information about geological formations as well as plant and animal life. Also running

hard against the predominant and restrictive biblical beliefs of his age, Darwin argued that all species evolved from previously ancestral forms through a special process that he named *natural selection*, thus explaining how anatomical change occurs through a discriminatory procedure. In natural selection, physical features are "selected" from within a range of possible morphologies that are specific to each species (today referred to as the *gene pool*). Natural selection refers to an adaptive process that acts within a species-specific range of potential, selecting those features that are most favorable to the survival of a given species by enhancing its reproductive success under changing circumstances. Because some traits are selected in accordance with their suitability for individual reproductive success, natural selection favors, ultimately, the "survival of the fittest." Darwin's theory of natural selection is based on the observation that heritable traits advantageous to a species' survival become more common in successive generations of a reproducing population, while unfavorable traits tend to be effaced due to differential reproduction. Natural selection acts on the phenotypes (the observable characteristics) of an organism, such that individuals with favorable phenotypes are more likely to survive and reproduce, while those with less favorable ones will tend to disappear. The morphology (anatomy) associated with the favorable phenotype will increase in frequency over the following generations. Over time, this process will result in adaptations that best outfit organisms to survive in specific ecological niches. In some cases, this procedural evolutionary scheme can eventually give way to changes that are so radical that they lead to the emergence of new species. In other words, natural selection is the mechanism by which evolution occurs within a population of specific organisms. It is noteworthy that A. R. Wallace (1823–1913),[10] another British naturalist, had concurrently proposed the concept of natural selection (he even coauthored the first paper on the topic with Darwin), but Darwin's book was the first complete and scientifically convincing work on the subject. It is incredible to acknowledge that, at the time of Darwin's writing, the scientific principles of genetic inheritance were virtually unknown. In fact, the foundations for modern genetics were finally laid only later in the early twentieth century, thanks largely to the works of G. Mendel (1822–1884).[11]

Of course, Darwin's work sparked intense debates between supporters of evolutionary theory and those upholding biblical interpretations to explain observed (and irrefutable) species' anatomical change over time. One major point of contention was, of course, the proposition that modern humans are *biologically* related to the Great Apes, a key notion leading to important developments in paleoanthropology and in the ways that human prehistory came to be viewed later. It is important to remember that the scientific community only progressively accepted Darwin's theory and that its basic evolutionary repercussions continue to be debated even today. Darwin also published other important works, including *On the Descent of Man* (1871)[12] in which he discussed the social, racial and religious implications of his theory in matters relating to the evolution of human beings. Many of Darwin's writings were later adopted by other thinkers, for example K. Marx (and his followers), contributing to the formulation of socioeconomic ideologies to explain the dynamics of class conflict and the likelihood of its eventual eradication in a classless society.[13,14]

Relating the Darwinian evolutionary model to prehistoric archeology, the English geologist Sir C. Lyell (1797–1875) was among the first Europeans to ponder fossilized animal bones in light of the newly developing principles of geology, stratigraphy and chronology.[15] The French pharmacist P. Tournal (1805–1872), credited with coining the word *prehistoric* (Fr. pré-historique), was also acquainted with Darwin's work. He was interested in species' origins and their migration patterns over time.[16] While excavating a Middle and Upper Paleolithic succession in the Bize cave complex (in southern France), Tournal was intrigued by his findings of extinct animals in apparent association with human fossils.[17] Another Frenchman considered to be one of the founders of prehistory is J. Boucher de Crèvecœur de Perthes (1788–1868),[18] who described a so-called Anti-diluvial Man (Fr. l'Homme anti-diluvien) to explain findings of stone tools (especially flint handaxes) associated with extinct animal fossils in gravel deposits at Abbeville (Somme Valley, France). And so, prehistoric archeology continued to advance amid the intensely heated intellectual debates and social upheavals of the nineteenth century, centered largely around human origins and human relationships with the animal world and, more especially, with the Great Apes – while the first Neandertal skulls were being brought to light in Europe. Indeed, significant Neandertal specimens were being discovered during this early period, such as at Engis (Belgium) in 1829 and Forbes Quarry (Gibraltar) in 1848. But it was a fossil find from the Neander Valley, near Düsseldorf in Germany (1856), that was to give a name to this enigmatic hominin – *Homo neandertalensis* – presently the closest known ancestor to modern humans. The eponymous appellation (place or context from which a name is derived) in fact originates from the family name of a local pastor: *Neuman*, meaning *new man*.

THE QUATERNARY PERIOD: FRAMEWORK FOR HUMAN EMERGENCE AND EVOLUTION

Since these tumultuous times, prehistoric archeology (or prehistory) has effectively matured into a respected discipline now commonly integrated into curriculums of universities worldwide on the same academic footing as other branches of science. The undertaking of research in prehistory requires the incorporation of data from a good many other fields of knowledge, which are unhesitatingly absorbed into its comprehensive research strategy. The agenda of the prehistorian is to explore the geo-archeological record of the Quaternary Period, a division of the geological timescale beginning some 2.588 million years ago. Its extension into the Holocene Epoch englobes more recent cultural phenomena relating to our species. The Quaternary Period follows the Tertiary Period that ends with the Pliocene Epoch (5.333–2.588 million years ago [Ma]). It is divided into two major geological epochs: the Pleistocene and the Holocene, which are in turn, subdivided into "stages." The limits of each stage within the Pleistocene were established mainly in accordance with patterns of faunal species turnover, coupled with geological data. We are currently living in the Holocene Interglacial that began some 11,650 calendar years ago before the present time. Compared to other geological timescales, the Quaternary Period denotes a very short moment in time (for example, the Cretaceous Period that saw the extinction of the dinosaurs some 65 Ma lasted some 80 million years and the Neogene Period at the end of the Tertiary spans some 20 million years). Because the Quaternary Period is the stage on which most of the evolution of human life has been played out, it is imperative for us to understand its meanings and contexts. From 1948 to 2009, the International Commission on Stratigraphy (ICS, founded in 1974)[19] had situated the beginning of the Quaternary Period (the Lower Pleistocene Epoch) at 1.8 million years ago.[20]

> The International Commission on Stratigraphy is the largest and oldest constituent scientific body in the International Union of Geological Sciences (IUGS). Its primary objective is to precisely define global units (systems, series, and stages) of the International Chronostratigraphic Chart that, in turn, are the basis for the units (periods, epochs, and age) of the International Geologic Time Scale; thus setting global standards for the fundamental scale for expressing the history of the Earth.[19]

The International Chronostratigraphic Chart (ICC) is a nonarbitrary age frame established based on information obtained from geological deposits and geomorphological type areas. Some of the common sources for this information have been major Western European river systems (alluvial accumulations) and mountain formations correlated with additional data acquired from paleontology (e.g. faunal turnover, anatomical change, migration patterning) and paleo-landscape contexts. Toward the middle of the eighteenth century, the Italian geologist G. Arduino employed the term *Quaternary* as a referent to specific rock formations located in sections of the southern European Alps, establishing one of the foremost geological classifications. Somewhat later, in the early nineteenth century, the French geologist J. Desnoyers used the denomination to describe Seine River alluvial accumulations in France known to postdate Tertiary Period rock formations. Subsequently, the French geologist C. Lyell designated the Pleistocene and Holocene as "epochs" dividing the Quaternary Period, establishing its basal chronology of 1.8 million years ago, in agreement with biostratigraphic evidence. Ongoing ICS meetings gradually came to favor more climate-based criteria, however, until its members decided, in 2009 to push back the age of the Quaternary Period to 2,588 million years ago, a time limit coherent with the establishment of cyclical glacial-interglacial events (of around 100,000 years) that remains in vigor to this day. Global climate change and the (cyclical) glacial and interglacial events of the Quaternary Period are guided by astronomical phenomena called *Milankovitch Cycles*.[21] The model designates astrophysical phenomena affecting the Earth's orbit around the Sun as causal to cyclical changes in the Earth's temperature (see Figure 1.2). First, its polar inclination relative to the Sun, or axial tilt, intensifies or weakens the Earth's hemispherical exposure to the

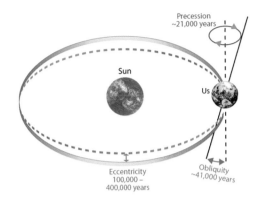

Figure 1.2

The Milankovitch cycles. Orbital parameters (after the Serbian geophysicist and astronomer M. Milanković) define astronomic patterns in the Earth's orbit around the Sun, influencing the solar impact on our planet and affecting climate over time at a known rate. (©Thomas Laepple, Alfred-Wegener-Institute, Germany. https://biocycle.atmos.colostate.edu/shiny/ Milankovitch/)

Sun's rays. Second, fluctuations of the planet relative to its own axis (or wobble) affect seasonal contrasts (precession). Third, changes in the shape of the elliptical path that the Earth makes as it orbits the Sun (eccentricity) modify its distance from the Sun, thus also affecting climate. The Milankovitch model is, therefore, especially relevant to cyclical changes in the expansion and retreat of the massive ice sheets covering the polar regions of the planet. As changes in the extension of the polar ice caps impulse important climatic fluctuations on the planet, they also regulate important geophysical events, including temperature and precipitation and the ebb and flow of the world's oceans and seas, thus dictating the faunal and vegetal composition in landscapes and their bioresources. All of these constitute the basic elements that have shaped human evolution (biological and behavioral) throughout the Quaternary Period. Indeed, these forces have constrained *all living species* to adapt, migrate or die out in the face of Nature's vicissitudes. Because the Earth's environments continue to be maintained in this state of endless transformation, only by familiarizing ourselves with the timing and intensity of these (Quaternary) cyclical climatic changes can we contextualize the events that have shaped human evolution through time (see Table 1.1).

CONSTRUCTING THE ARCHIVES OF PREHISTORY

To reconstruct the changing environments of the Quaternary Period and the unfolding of evolutionary changes undergone by past life forms, including humans, archeology has come to rely on a vast network of methodologies, incorporating modern technologies applied today in each of the different contributing fields of knowledge. Certainly, given the paucity of evidence left behind by prehistoric civilizations and the exceptional

Table 1.1

Geological denominations and the basal ages for the major time phases discussed in this book

Era	Period	Epoch	Stage	Basal Stage Age
Cenozoic	Quaternary	Anthropocene	To be determined	
		Holocene		11,650 BP
		Pleistocene	Upper	126 Ka
			Middle	780 Ka
			Lower	2.58 Ma
	Neogene ↓	Pliocene		5.33 Ma

BP: Before present
Ka: Thousand years ago
Ma: Million years ago

nature of its preservation in most cases, the absence of written documents renders this task particularly arduous. In addition to problems relating to preservation, other restrictive qualifiers limit the chances of discovering prehistoric archeological sites. When artifacts are brought to light, interpreting their concealed meanings with accuracy constitutes a major challenge for the specialists working in each different discipline. For the earliest periods of our shared prehistoric existence, evasive archeological "documents" are limited essentially to stone tools, fossilized animal or human bones and remnant structures that may be located (or described) thanks to alterations they cause in the natural configuration of geological or geomorphological contexts. Nevertheless, the science of prehistory endeavors to extract whatever precious information can be collected from such elusive sources, including the sediment enclosing the artifacts and the tiny indices it may contain (pollen, micromammal bones). The further we go back in time, the less likely it is for evidence to be preserved or – much less – discovered, and the more difficult its interpretation will be. As our knowledge advances in pace with the rhythm of each new archeological find, we must constantly adjust our interpretations of prehistory, so that what appears today as a factual explanation may dramatically change tomorrow, following even a single new discovery.

Prehistorians and archeologists are necessarily accustomed to this constant data flux. This factual flexibility often affects the chronological framework within which we place the different stages of human evolution and, more often than not, the tendency is to increase the age evaluations of each evolutionary landmark. Prehistoric archeology pursues investigations into the evolution of humans and their material culture, situating the artifacts within this flexible cultural template coherently with the larger framework of the cyclical climatic changes affecting the Earth during the Quaternary Period. Thus, different denominations are infused with chronological and cultural meaning (often in relation to specific regional contexts). Examples are the Paleolithic, Mesolithic and Neolithic Ages of Europe or the Early, Middle and Late Stone Ages of Africa. These wide categorizations also have multiple subdivisions, breaking them down into even more detailed chrono-cultural groupings (e.g. Lower, Middle and Upper Paleolithic) that also tend to vary in accordance with the geographical situation in question. These, in turn, are subdivided, enabling even more detailed descriptions of the cultural entities as they are perceived and classified in accordance with the specificities of the material culture found in the archeological register (typology of structures, objects, manufacturing techniques and the behaviors these reflect). However, the reality is that a growing body of archeological data indicates wide variations over time and space, which effectively hinder such generalizations and complicate attempts to fit early human culture into neat, successive chronological compartments.

Although we tend to use the word *culture* spontaneously in many disparate topics of discourse, it is paramount to grasp its true complexity, especially when we are looking at the oldest phases of the emergence of human-made objects and structures to formulate our ideas about their derived behavioral implications. In this book, I examine the many different layers of meaning encompassed by the word *culture*, bringing into perspective the complex social, structural and cognitive aspects that define both becoming and being human. This density of meanings forces us to temper our discussion when describing archeological materials or phenomena as representative of culture. To begin, we will look at how criteria assembled from the archeological record can allow us to recognize the first evidence of human material culture before following its evolutionary features through time and space. Once we have sketched the picture of some of the major cultural phases used to define human cultural evolution over time, then we will be prepared to discuss how and why this process affects our daily lives and in which ways it can help us to formulate viable hypothesis about where we, as a species, might be heading in the very near future. With all due respect to those who advocate the existence of culture in the animal kingdom, and for the sake of simplification, I forewarn that I shall be considering culture here strictly in relation to human behavior, as an aspect that has and continues to shape our situation in the universe through time. Over the millennia, humanity has developed complex social systems for effectively diffusing culture from one generation to the next. We will see how the acquisition, learning and sharing of cultural norms came to permeate the human social order throughout the different phases of the Quaternary Period, finally becoming an extremely powerful evolutionary force, most significantly after the emergence of the first anatomically modern humans (AMH), some 300,000 years ago in Africa.[22] Consequently, the massive diffusion of culture by humans, indelibly marked by intensely complex and symbolic forms of communication, has come to guide most behavioral facets of modern human lifeways.

Culture assimilates individuals into discrete social units and, in so doing, plays a vital role in the mental construction of both personal and shared identities. Without written documents, prehistorians turn to alternative types of evidence left behind by past humans. In fact, objects and/or structures from the prehistoric archeological record used to reconstruct former human lifeways actually provide only a very partial record (especially when we are dealing with the very distant past). Fragmentary evidence is all that remains for us to observe and interpret when, why and how different manifestations of human material culture emerged and developed. Therefore, the accuracy and the scope of scientific objectivity that our interpretations will have strongly depend on the validity of the archeological contexts from which the discoveries are taken as well as on the range and quality of the data recorded by archeologists. Archeologists actually generate a type of data bank composed of quantitative and qualitative descriptions of mute objects and structures that are often detached from their original contexts but that constitute human cultural heritage and move us beyond the biological sphere. We share culture from the moment we are born into the human family; throughout millennia, it has provided a binding fabric woven into the tissue of our existence. Culture is what we continuously transmit from generation to generation by means of specific processes developed by our human ancestors – consciously and unconsciously – establishing symbolism as an advantageous survival strategy. Over time, we humans have invented very intricate and time-consuming learning processes to transmit culture, underpinning its central role in our evolutionary expansion. The significant time investment committed by humans to the learning of culture indicates that it has been a systematically selected strategy over time, certainly, because it contributes adaptive advantages for the reproduction of our species. The human choice to invent and develop culture has affected not only our own evolutionary pathway but also that of all living beings with which we share the planet. Fossil finds from the Ledi-Geraru research area in the Afar region of Ethiopia have recently established the emergence of the genus *Homo* near the onset of the Quaternary Period, some 2.8 million years ago.[23] This time frame is closely coincidental with the appearance of the first (recognizable) stone tools in the African archeological record.[24,25,26] Today, an age close to 3 million years is generally considered likely for the emergence of what we call humanity. The hypothesis of transitional fossils providing a missing link between apes and humans is presently refuted by evidence pointing to a far more complex evolutionary framework for the human ancestral lineage. Although 3 million years may seem to be a very long time ago, consider by comparison that the dinosaurs, which reigned during the Mesozoic Era, survived for some 150 million years! Indeed, our story is truly just beginning – but will it end prematurely?

THE ANTHROPOCENE EPOCH: THE FIRST HUMAN-INDUCED SUBDIVISION OF GEOLOGICAL TIME

The term *Anthropocene* has been proposed to the ICS as a geologically viable referent for a new epoch of the Holocene derived from concrete, observable evidence of the influence of human activity on the Earth's atmosphere detectable in geological strata. This official designation of the Anthropocene represents the first time that a global geological epoch will be introduced based on measurable human interference on the Earth's atmosphere and reflected geologically (stratigraphically), ominously demonstrating the large-scale global influence that modern human activity has already had on the planet. Following ICS rules, the establishment of a new geological division must be founded only on solid empirical evidence perceptible in the Earth's geological layers. Originating in the Soviet Union, the term *Anthropocene* was used to refer to the final phases of the Quaternary. Coined in the year 2000 by the Dutch atmospheric chemist P. Crutzen and the American biologist E. Stoermer, the term refers to the time when evidence of human impact on the planet becomes clearly legible in the world geological record.[27] The reality of the degree to which anthropogenically driven change has impacted the planet today constitutes a subject of deep concern that led to the establishment in 2009 of the Working Group on the Anthropocene (WGA)[28] to comply with the request to formalize the Anthropocene as a geological epoch accepted by the IUGS. In order to do so, scientists must first agree on a date in the global geological record that human activity actually began to affect the Earth's biosphere, hydrosphere and atmosphere in ways significant enough to leave perceptible traces in the sedimentary record. While different periods were still under consideration (as of 2021) to determine the boundary for the beginning of the Anthropocene, all postdate the emergence of modern humans.

Different proposals for the timing of the beginning of the Anthropocene were still under consideration as of 2021[29] (Figure 1.3). Beginning with the oldest proposed age boundary, some suggest that the Anthropocene should begin during the last ice age (toward the end of the Upper Pleistocene, around 14,000 years ago), when many large-sized herbivores are thought to have been driven to extinction by intensive human hunting. Undeniably, there is strong evidence for correlations between the timing of the arrival of modern humans into virgin territories (northern Eurasia, the Americas, Oceania) and the disappearance of some species of fauna and vegetation from the archeological record. According to some interpretations, significant modifications to the landscape could have resulted from overhunting large grazers by modern humans, causing huge swathes of open grassland to be replaced by forest.[30] In addition, this situation would have affected the survival rates of other large carnivores as they found themselves facing a deficiency of large prey. However, other researchers have proposed that the Anthropocene begin closer the Upper Pleistocene/Holocene limit, some 12,000 years ago when the first semisedentary civilizations began to develop new survival strategies involving the domestication of some plants and animals. The result was significant niche construction[31] in affected areas, causing substantial changes to landscapes and modifying natural configurations. Perhaps looking to a more global consequence, other scientists argue that the most tangible shift to anthropogenic modification of the Earth (marking the start of the Anthropocene) began some 5,000 years or so later when large groups of peoples organized into settled sedentary units. After this time, civilizations practicing more intensive farming and animal husbandry would have

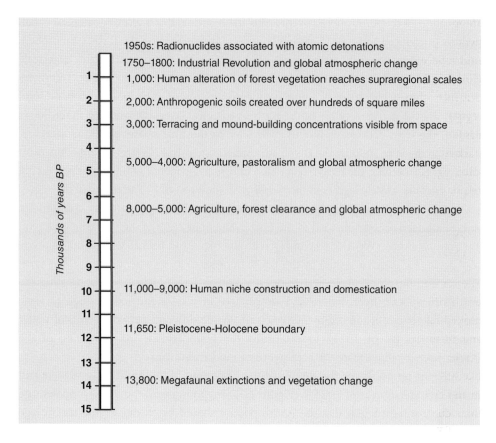

Figure 1.3
Temporal boundaries proposed for beginning the Anthropocene Epoch based on when global human interference on the planet becomes discernible in the Earth's geological record. (Adapted from Smith and Zeder [2013] and modified by Deborah Barsky after Braje and colleagues [2014])

caused significant amounts of methane gas emissions to be released, attaining levels high enough to be registered in the Earth's stratosphere.[31,32,33] It is also argued that a more fitting time for the Anthropocene boundary would be more recent, some 2,000 years ago when the first urban civilizations transformed considerable surface areas of the planet, creating huge areas of *anthropogenic soils* (in contrast with soils formed by natural processes).[33] In spite of this, others opine that the best indication for the onset of the Anthropocene is the Industrial Revolution (in Europe, 1750–1800 common era (CE) when pollutants from methane and carbon emissions were massively released into the atmosphere (for example, succeeding the invention of the coal-powered steam engine), becoming "registered" in a significant way in the Earth's strata.[27] Others suggest that the lower boundary of the Anthropocene be fixed even more recently, in the 1950s when artificial radionuclides associated with atomic detonations were released into the atmosphere[34] and humanity experienced the *Great Acceleration*.[35] Currently, as discussions among scientists from different fields of knowledge and environmentalists are still underway to resolve the issue, the ICS is closer than ever to officially introducing the Anthropocene into the geological timescale at some point in time within the Holocene.[36] Whatever the outcome of this debate, the fact remains that material evidence of past civilizations recorded indelibly in the world's archeo-stratigraphic register reflects the long process of human biological, social and spiritual evolution that has lead us to modify the natural course of the planet. Prehistoric archeology allows us to track the appearance and evolution of human culture reflecting the changes ultimately affecting our planet, making it necessary to find meaning in the Anthropocene and responsibly assume our newly acquired place in the world.

PREHISTORIC ARCHEOLOGY: A MODERN, INTERNATIONAL SCIENCE EMBRACING HUMANITY

The further back in time we go, the more unlikely we are to encounter archeological evidence and the more difficult it becomes to interpret the available data. Only a very limited range of artifact types is actually obtainable from earliest periods of prehistory and these include almost exclusively used/knapped stones and fossilized animal or (more rarely) human bones. Objects made by early humans from perishable materials like wood, bone or skins rarely preserved from the very remote past are generally found in more recent contexts (for example, after the Middle Paleolithic)[37] although exceptions do exist (e.g. a 1.4 million-year-old bone handaxe reported at the Early Acheulian site of Konso in Ethiopia[38]). Artifacts left behind by past civilizations have long been contemplated, collected or displayed, appreciated for their scarcity or safeguarded as precious treasures, or even (unfortunately) sold for lucrative motives. Fortunately, a more mature *archeological consciousness* has progressively emerged along the way, notably after the early nineteenth century, engendering the important notion of patrimony that now underlines the collective value of archeological relics as worldwide inheritance. In many societies, this growing awareness has led to the strengthening of the concept of cultural wealth and to the integration of prehistory as a comprehensive discipline fitted into modern-day university curriculums within the natural sciences. Overall, humanity has come to realize that the value of cultural heritage surpasses subjectively attributed limits, embracing a limitless wealth of tangible and intangible human creations that, regardless of time and space, lend specificity and cohesion to each society. In this way, prehistory is the mirror in which we can observe the exteriorization of our inner selves, and archeology is the tool that allows us to discover, analyze and understand this representation. Cultural heritage constitutes the legacy of material and immaterial properties distinguishing populations and justifying (at least symbolically) their grouping into distinct social units. Even though it is often regionally specific, cultural heritage is, in its entirety, the property of all humanity. Prehistoric archeology, as the means by which we access past cultural heritage – beyond regional boundaries – is therefore, by its very nature, *international*. Furthermore, by adopting a multidisciplinary approach, prehistory allows archeological research to advance through cooperative enterprises that, whenever possible, feasibly move beyond and even overcome geopolitical boundaries.

The methods used in prehistoric archeology to access data are also in a constant state of developmental flux as new techniques are constantly being invented and improved, enabling archeologists to more efficiently (and more responsibly) find, recover and preserve relics from the ancient past. In today's world of fast scientific progress, prehistoric archeology stands out as a rapidly evolving multidisciplinary science. Contributing to the expansive nature of this archeological consciousness is the effective use being made by the discipline of the ever-widening range of communication networks available in our modern society that are currently providing incredibly rapid (or even immediate) dissemination of information, thus favoring its development on a global level. From time immemorial, relics from the past have been displaced from their original contexts or even removed and covertly guarded by their discoverer or their referent collective social units. In some cases, archeological finds may be hidden away and prized for their beauty or scarcity or even (inopportunely) for their market value. Because of this selfish mentality, invaluable archeological sites are continuously being looted and precious artifacts disconnected from their original frames of reference, forever effacing their valuable contextual information. Often, important discoveries made by amateur plunderers are mistakenly deemed worthless and even discarded, their real significance lost forever to all humanity. Today, thanks to advances in prehistoric archeology and the large-scale dissemination of knowledge, many have come to recognize the importance of prehistoric archeological finds. This knowledge constitutes an essential prerequisite to the founding of a working ethics in archeological methodologies, underpinning the importance of accurately registering each and every artifact prior to its removal or separation from its context. Working with these fragile relationships reinforces the importance of adopting meticulous recording procedures and strict scientific analytical methodologies taking into account not only individual finds but also their enclosing or surrounding settings. Eager to unravel and reconstruct the pieces composing the puzzle of our past, contemporary archeologists apply the strictest procedural tools to create systematic methodologies for use in both the field and the laboratory. Indeed, different types of objects carry with them the potential to reveal information about the people who made or used them, their level of manual dexterity or the techniques they mastered. Studying them allows us to reconstruct the different phases of human technocognitive evolution and to visualize bygone pathways to global perception crystallized into material culture and expressed as regional traditions. Important information can be harvested from the contexts that artifacts are collected from, thus allowing specialists to determine how they were used, establish chronology and/or evaluate production motives. By placing each piece within a regional and then larger-scale geographical and chronological picture, guidelines are established over

Table 1.2

Approximate ages for first appearance of human material cultural complexes in the prehistoric Old World (as of the year 2021)

Cultural complex denominations	Africa	Near East	South and East Asia	Western Europe
Metal ages	5,000 BP	7,000 BP	5,000 BP	5,000 BP
Neolithic	10,000 BP	10,000 BP	8,000 BP	8,000 BP
Mesolithic, Epipaleolithic, Early Neolithic	25 Ka	20 Ka	20 Ka	15 Ka
Late Stone Age, Upper Paleolithic	70 Ka	50 Ka	40 Ka	40 Ka
Middle Stone Age, Middle Paleolithic (Mousterian)	350 Ka	350 Ka	350 Ka	350 Ka
Early Stone Age, Lower Paleolithic (Acheulian)	1.8 Ma	1.6 Ma	1.5 Ma	1.0 Ma
Early Stone Age, Lower Paleolithic (Oldowan)	2.6 Ma	1.6 Ma	1.9 Ma	1.4 Ma
Lomekwian	3.3 Ma	–	–	–
Mode 0 (?)	>3 Ma	–	–	–

Note: The dates indicated here provide only a general picture and are subject to change in keeping with new discoveries and improvements in technologies applied in archeology. It is important to keep in mind that the different cultural entities indicated in this table may or may not be present in a given region and that their representation – or not – depends on multiple factors. The overall outcome is diachronic with uneven events of ebb and flow of the different cultural complexes, accentuated by increasing cultural complexity with accelerating replacement events occurring more frequently as we move through time.

space and time that are useful for observing evolutionary change as a (diachronic) succession of customs, habits and abilities developed at different points in time throughout the world by thousands of generations of individuals composing the human family.

Such categorizations are used in prehistory to help archeologists pinpoint discoveries in time and space (see Table 1.2). Over time, generations of specialists have used their knowledge to create detailed descriptions of the types of artifacts and their modes of fabrication as elements indicative of culture. The particularities derived from artifact descriptions allow us to grasp regional-specific features of human activity forged over time in intervals characterized, as we have seen, by specific landscapes and climates. It follows that the style of a ceramic decoration or the morphology of a stone tool can reveal a regional tradition or perhaps even reflect bygone trade or migration routes. This enables archeologists to elaborate hypotheses helping to decode the behaviors and interactions of ancient human populations. Today, modern, fine-tuned methodologies are allowing archeologists to gain efficiency in their search for significance hidden in the archeology by contextualizing each find within established chrono-cultural frameworks that are, in fact, in a constant state of refinement. This exercise aims to reveal the meaning of archeological discoveries and their effect on the larger picture of human societal developments (economic, cultural, artistic, political). Detailed documentation, restoration and preservation of archeological finds and their contexts are thus vital to accomplishing this type of inquiry. Therefore, when an archeological discovery is made, the first steps are oriented toward the selection, adaptation and implementation of the most suitable excavation or fieldwork procedures. These strategies will differ in accordance with the types of archeological sites – their specific contexts and artifact types – that are widely variable. Obviously, strategies employed to excavate an open-air monument such as megalithic tombs will be different from those used to exhume stone artifacts buried deep within a cave's deposits. Nevertheless, some basic notions are common to all archeological investigations: meticulous documentation during the excavation process, spatial coordination of the objects within a preestablished grid, description of the enclosing geological context, and so on. These unifying strategies continue to be developed and reinforced by evermore precise methodologies and modern technologies specifically designed to achieve optimal preservation of every fragile and ephemeral archeological occurrence. Today, prehistoric archeology safeguards the vast time range of our species' evolution, exhuming, analyzing and exhibiting to the public the huge store of information composing our cultural heritage. Stemming out from shared roots, each domain connected to prehistoric archeology is recognized within its own scientific realm reflecting methodological rigor. All share a keen awareness of the importance of preserving the past and of developing the public's archeological consciousness.

THE RISE OF ARCHEOLOGICAL CONSCIOUSNESS

History tells us that human awareness of the precious nature of ancestral material remnants existed even in the distant past, especially those with long survival records.[2] Formerly, this "awareness" or "consciousness" belonged to a preliminary or *speculative* phase when significance was attributed to ancient artifacts or structures but truly systematic archeological methods had not yet been invented for their adequate study and conservation.[39] This begs the question of when archeological consciousness really began to take shape. When does it becomes possible to discern some type of awareness of the past in the archeological record? Indeed, this question can be explored even from the later phases of the Lower Paleolithic[40,41] when populations cyclically occupying single dwellings would logically have encountered objects left behind by previous inhabitants.[42] Up to now, this appreciation of the "object" as instrumental to gaining knowledge about the past is passively evoked in some archeological contexts relating to the Middle and Upper Pleistocene by the presence of unusual or exotic objects at some sites, without any clear functional role, or raw materials coming from considerable distances away. At some multilevel sites dating to the Middle and Upper Paleolithic, evidence for the reuse (or recycling) of previously discarded tools, giving a "second life" to some items, is also considered to denote some type of consciousness of the past–present continuum.[43]

Certainly, some of the earliest advancements in archeological methodologies were made from observing relics standing out in the landscape, such as megalithic structures or other types of monuments built up by past civilizations. Some obvious examples are the pyramids and temples of ancient Sudan, Egypt and Mesoamerica and the Roman cities of Herculaneum and Pompeii, miraculously (if tragically) preserved under a blanket of volcanic ash spewed out from the volcano Vesuvius in 79 CE. Such remnants were most certainly contemplated by successive civilizations who have even been documented as having performed some restoration activities on them.[2] Early on, mega monuments caused the focus of early archeological consciousness to be centered on these most visible vestiges of past human material culture and their iconography (megalithic tombs, temples, altars, memorial structures, etc.). These relics are therefore highly relevant for their contributions to our understanding of numerous tangible (architectural, technological) and nontangible (spiritualism, religious beliefs, social hierarchy) aspects of past societies. From the point of view of prehistory, such monumental structures are associated with the more recent periods from the Neolithic to the Metal Ages (expansion of urban constructions) and beyond into later protohistoric and historic societies. Inscriptions on stele or other types of representational artistic creations commonly associated with monumental archeology can be used to reconstruct past events. Thus, by examining both the physical and documental record of a site, archeologists working on these periods gain insights into how past populations lived and died. As evidence from different civilizations is accumulated, it is fitted into broader frameworks of social development on regional and then global scales.

Because they were established earlier, the branches of archeology dealing with the more recent time frames pioneered the development of systematic archeological field and laboratory strategies (for example, classical archeology, Egyptology or Mesoamerican archeology). Even though they may deal with different types of evidence (notably iconography and written documents), these disciplines provide the foundational methodologies used also in prehistoric archeology such as the establishment of a grid system to delimit an excavation area, methods of systematic artifact collection, data collection, stratigraphy rules, sampling of geological contexts, multidisciplinary analysis and dating of finds, restoration and conservation techniques and more).[2] In today's world, all types of archeological investigations have progressed into the computer age and are proficient in accumulating and processing vast collections of highly detailed data. Today, archeology *sensu largo* has moved from simple collecting and identifying to obtaining holistic reconstructions integrating a maximum of information available for each occurrence under study (artifact types, stratigraphy, interobject relationships, spatial distribution, etc.). That said, it is important that we remember that truly systematic fieldwork and the follow-up in the laboratory that it entails (cataloging, documenting, preserving, museography, displaying in public venues, etc.) were only seriously assumed in European archeology after the significant scientific and philosophical advances made during and after the Enlightenment transformed the emerging fields of science into maturity (paleontology, biology, geology and others). Prehistoric archeology developed somewhat differently from other schools of archeology, largely because of the deeply problematic philosophical connotations attached to human evolutionary theory in which primate lineages were proposed as biologically ancestral forms of humans,[44] thus gaining their place on one or another of the branches of the human family tree (the image of a tree with a single trunk has now fallen into disuse in favor of a more complex "bushy" evolutionary path). As systematic excavation methods became more commonly assumed within a recognized framework grounded in universally accepted laws conventionalized for the field as a whole, archeologists centered more on achieving holistic reconstructions of the past, improving the quality of their data and expanding on their hypotheses. All of this becomes very significant once we realize the responsibility borne by archeologists, whose results have a non-negligible impact on society, shaping the ways that we perceive, not only of ourselves and others, but also of our relationships to the natural and (now) constructed worlds.

It follows that modern improvements in the methods used to find, extract, interpret and conserve data from the archeological record are paramount to gaining a clearer understanding of humanity's evolutionary trajectory. Today, archeological research covers the entire time frame of human existence and is practiced in nearly all parts of the world. It focuses on human life in all of its forms – from the first phases of emergence in the furthest reaches of our prehistory in Africa, up to the present day. What we have learned so far is that humanity, although inexorably linked to the natural world from which it emerged, stands somehow apart from it. We shall see that this paradox is linked closely to the degree to which we humans have developed our reliance on the technologies we invent. From the first moments of stone tool manufacture more than 3 million years ago in Africa,[24] the growing complexity of human technological ingenuity has transformed the world and all living beings within it. In the case of humans, the plethora of material manifestations of this capacity to model and use objects from the environment constitutes the uniqueness of human "culture": the specifically human trait that has evolved through time into a myriad of modes of expression, both concrete and transient. The aim of prehistoric archeology is to discover and study specific manifestations of the distant past of human cultures, ultimately placing them within a timeline and, finally, establishing a coherent framework for the evolution of humanity throughout the globe. This chrono-cultural framework reflects a procedural, although not strictly lineal, evolutionary trajectory that is sometimes referred to as the hominization process.[3]

Over the years, specialists in the interrelated fields of archeological studies have worked toward the elaboration of globally accepted, regionally specific time frames within which to fit the cultural evidence (e.g. stone tools, pottery, cave paintings), largely based on the specific stylistic traits or fabrication modes of the finds and on the available chronological information. Prehistoric archeology (and its related fields of knowledge) further examines how biology and culture have combined through time to create the uniqueness of the human evolutionary process. As a possible outcome of this so-called hominization process, some now define another potential phase in the human evolutionary process referred to as *humanization*[45] in which we, as a species, might yet realize our full operational potential in more sustainable ways. According to this hypothesis, humanization can be reached only when (and if) our species finally learns to apply the knowledge accrued throughout the hominization process to build up more viable and durable structural entities and behaviors in harmony with the environment and innocuous to other life forms. In many ways, by developing our archeological consciousness, we are learning to value the past as a way to discover meaning in the modern human condition. Familiarizing ourselves with the scientific explanations of the long chains of cause and effect that have transformed the world over time helps us to learn about our origins and to rationalize our species' trajectory to the present day. Challenges affecting humankind today and the uncertainties of the future are consequently concerns especially close to prehistory as a science that brings us to reflect on the human condition: the past, of course, but also our present situation and the ways in which we might improve the future that now, so often, seems to have lost all rhyme and reason.

2

PREHISTORY
A Multidisciplinary Science

THE MULTIDISCIPLINARY APPROACH: ASSIMILATING KNOWLEDGE IN PREHISTORIC ARCHEOLOGY

Prehistoric archeology combines methodologies and data from numerous and distinct fields of knowledge that belong mainly – but not only – to the natural and social sciences. Each discipline contributes in its own ways to locating new finds, excavating archeological sites and interpreting the material evidence left behind by past human civilizations. In this "multidisciplinary" approach, each field of study contributes to the elaboration of workable scientific interpretations about how landscapes evolved during the Paleolithic, and how prehistoric animals and peoples acted and reacted (behaviorally and biologically) in each successive scenario. Specialized disciplines, such as geology and geochronology, provide environmental and chronological information for each period in which humans lived and evolved while others, such as stone tool analysis, contribute to the understanding of the development of human culture. A plethora of procedures and practices thus combines to draw up the most plausible chronological and cultural framework with which to understand the different phases of human evolution. Because of the changeable (and often unpredictable) nature of the archeological record, which remains in a constant state of flux in pace with new discoveries, this framework serves chiefly as a guideline to help us to understand the spatial-temporal agenda of the human odyssey. In this sense, I stress the flexibility of this framework, which must in no case be considered as a linear measure of "progress" because stylistic and technological developments vary significantly in different regions and time frames in accordance with external impact factors, such as climate change or resource type and availability,[46] among others. In order to better understand this phenomenon, I will reflect on how and when humanity consolidated a significantly high degree of technological prowess to actually strengthen technologies and knit them into the social fiber until they became an integral part of the human cultural agenda that we are keenly experiencing today. This will lead me to discuss how, through time, culture itself became profoundly shaped by social stimuli, engendering and exteriorizing humanity's deepest inner worlds of symbolic thought processes, transforming them finally into traditions, taboos, rituals and other regional-specific cultural heritage.

We strive to define and understand human cultural evolution by referencing scientifically grounded prehistoric reconstructions that are conceptually simplified by placing them within this constructed framework, which is constantly being revised. In the Darwinian sense, this background essentially reflects the specific strategies used by humans over time to adapt to their surroundings and to optimize their chances for survival. The changes that it records bear witness to an ongoing process of biocultural exchanges achieved through natural, social and technical selective processes and normalized to optimize group survival under specific conditions. Described in this way, we can draw some parallels between the mechanisms working as laws in anatomical evolution and those guiding change in cultural evolution. I will discuss this theme throughout the book, but as a starting point, let us consider the inner workings of natural selection and compare them to "technoselection." Both are contingent processes that achieve change through latent potential within an existing system: on the one hand, genetic mutation and, on the other hand, cultural anomalies or inventiveness. Both processes are triggered by external forces that will ultimately favor, in a new situation, the reproduction of the prototype until it becomes the morphological/technological norm. Concepts relating to biological evolution, such as mutation, selection and random drift, have long been used as metaphors to explain cultural evolution.[47] We must therefore acknowledge that both genetic and cultural factors have interacted in the complex cultural transmission processes that have occurred through time.[48]

While I will be explaining the process of technoselection further throughout this book, let us return now to the more functional aspects of how archeological data is collected and studied. Fieldwork is the first and foremost platform from which archeologists operate. After a significant discovery is made, the excavation strategies chosen will be tailored in accordance with the specificities of each context under analysis. Obviously, the methods that will be employed vary with each context. Yet some basic methodological notions unite all forms of archeological fieldwork, beginning with the need for meticulous recording of all excavation activities and the care taken to optimize preservation of both the artifact record and the site context. It is important to remember that archeological excavation is a destructive process; it involves the irreversible removal of artifacts from their original circumstances. Because of this, archeologists ideally collect sufficient information during fieldwork to be able to reconstruct the conditions of their archeological site in the laboratory as precisely as possible, using the information collected

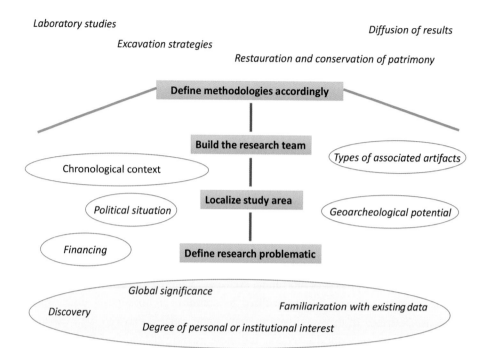

Figure 2.1
Different stages of archeological work and considerations for engaging in an archeological project

during the excavation process. In spite of this unifying doctrine, archeological methods are constantly evolving and highly flexible, and they must often be revised (sometimes creatively) to fit the specific (and often fragile) nature of each archeological site (see Figure 2.1). Today, modern technologies afford innovative answers to problems posed by each distinct archeological circumstance, providing ways to address the uniqueness of each situation. In addition, computerized systems have greatly improved the speed and accuracy of data collection and analysis, permitting the rapid synthesis of masses of information and facilitating the procurement of new types of evidence. Swift data accessing further simplifies inter- and intrasite comparisons, opening the way to new and sometimes unexpected hypotheses. Indirectly, this transformative modernization has also strengthened worldwide collaborations between specialists and their institutes, underlining once again the international character of research in human prehistory.

A BRIEF SYNTHESIS OF SOME METHODOLOGIES USED IN PREHISTORIC ARCHEOLOGY

The range of disciplines applied in prehistoric archeology today is rapidly changing the methods and theories currently radiating into the field of prehistory. While the list continues to grow on an almost daily level, I provide here a nonexhaustive summary of some of the fields of knowledge commonly associated with research into prehistory. First, evidence from disciplines relating to the fields of geology and geomorphology contributes invaluably to constructing a coherent record of global climatic trends through time. These fields of knowledge help us understand the natural forces at work in archeological site formation processes and in preserving (or not) specific types of artifacts inside a given depositional sequence. Information compiled from archeological survey and excavation is analyzed in laboratory conditions by scientists using specialized equipment in the aim of contextualizing and contrasting each archeological occurrence with what is known about regional and global environments and their evolution. Geological data is used to assess the effects of climate change over time and to evaluate its influences on the depositional and postdepositional conditions that affect the appearance, nature and preservation of the sites and the artifacts they contain. Archeological interpretations must be adjusted in relation to how these natural forces fit into the larger picture of climatic developments, such as the cyclical expansion and contraction of the polar ice caps, which have left traces on the landscape and affected the fossil record. Other natural phenomena relating to climate change and affecting landscape arrangements, such as tectonics, for example, altered continental alignments, in some cases bringing about earthquakes and volcanic eruptions, exposing or destroying landmasses and adjusting the natural equilibrium of the Earth's surface in relation to its coastlines. In archeology, volcanic events resulting in lava flows and ash layers provide one of the most reliable ways to obtain relatively precise age estimates using radiometric or radioisotopic dating methods.[49] Continental configurations undergo isostatic modifications, adjusting the lithosphere to the constant shifts of ice and water guided by climate change.[50] During glacial events, retreating sea levels exposed land bridges in some areas that allowed species (including humans) to migrate into new territories. During warmer interglacials, rising water levels shaped islands out of continental passageways, water-locking some species in and triggering allopatric speciation.[51]

Different erosive phenomena are known to occur on landmasses exposed to fluctuating climatic conditions (e.g. freeze and thaw), sometimes resulting in the displacement of huge masses of sediment or great bulks of rock, degrading and transforming terrains into different categories of sedimentary deposits (gravels, sands, blocks, etc.). Flowing water released during the more temperate climatic phases constitutes an extraordinarily powerful force capable of dramatically changing landscapes, both over time, like carving out caves or valleys, or suddenly, as in the case of catastrophic events such as mudslides or rapid flowing accumulations such as alluvial terraces. Wind is another powerful erosive force whose passage can be recorded in the Earth's soil record, rending, displacing and redepositing it in different ways. Aeolian transport of soil grains is a potent phenomenon that, in some cases, is observed over extensive geographical areas. For example, fine-grained wind-borne loess sediment can travel over thousands of kilometers, covering extensive landmasses and forming layers of dunes or bluffs that can be tens of meters thick. Driving geological phenomenon, such as plate tectonics or volcanic eruptions, weather conditions are largely responsible for shaping topographies and sometimes even dramatically transforming environments over time. Thus, geological research has revealed that even huge deserts, such as the African Sahara, were once rich tropical settings[52] and that vast areas of the northern steppe were covered in forested landscapes, as was the case in parts of western Eurasia throughout the Quaternary Period. These are the types of events discerned therefore by Earth scientists (geologists, geomorphologists, sedimentologists) working to discover the episodes affecting each site's depositional situation and to replace each recorded phenomenon into its proper place in an order of occurrence that will be read as so many pages of a book, ordering events into the layers composing a given stratigraphic context. Whenever possible, an age is attributed to each phase with as much precision as feasible. Stratigraphic reconstructions are absolutely essential in archeology as a way to understand individual site contexts, placing them within the larger scale of the global chrono-climatic framework. A range of physical, chemical and biological forces is constantly at work in the formation of archeological sites, regulating soil formation processes (pedogenesis)[53] and modeling specific types of soil layers, each accumulating or transforming under the dictates of specific climatic circumstances. Water often plays a key role, not only in dictating sedimentary accumulation processes but also in creating alternative postdepositional situations deeply affecting sedimentary formations and compositions over time. Sediment and gravels, sometimes accompanied by larger compositional elements (pebbles, cobbles, blocks), can be hydraulically deposited either in settings of long-term progressive water accumulation, as in lacustrine, palustrine or oceanic settings, or as rapid and sudden events driven by flooding or mudflow episodes. When sedimentary contexts enclose archeological materials exposed to water circulation, taphonomic alterations of their features (occurring postdepositionally) can reveal precious information about the climatic conditions and landscapes predominating after their deposit in a particular context.

Sedimentary samples from the full stratigraphic range of a given site or study area are required to obtain different types of information needed for understanding the climatic processes. Each strata must be replaced in its chronological order to understand the context under study. Sedimentary sampling procedures used in archeology are as varied as the types of analysis for which they are intended and the information they may (or may not) yield. In accordance with the type of geological information we look for, different types of sedimentary samples, each extracted using specific techniques, will be prepared and studied under controlled field and laboratory conditions. What archeologists are striving to achieve is the elaboration of a coherent stratigraphic log providing a schematic illustration that summarizes the different layers in a depositional sequence composing an archeological context. It synthesizes a site's formation processes into a schematic archeological section, providing easily interpretable contextual information about the depositional sequence. Stratigraphy is a central pillar of prehistoric archeology for it helps us to interpret the chronological order of the climatic events leading up to the superposition of rock/soil layers that enclose the archeological evidence: their composition and origins and the forces responsible for their successive accumulation. As a rule, the oldest layers are situated below the more recent ones; but this is not always the case, and it is up to the specialists to correctly interpret the succession of the events leading to each component of a depositional sequence. The thickness of each layer, for example in a cave context, can vary significantly, depending on the type and duration of the accumulative forces at play (natural or anthropic). Ideally, archeologists try to follow successive sedimentation events (layers, levels, beds) in conformity with the prominent features observed in the field (a sediment's color, texture, grain size and morphology, etc.). In situations where a sedimentary deposit does not present any clear features with which to individualize different layers, archeologists will excavate using a preestablished "artificial" stratigraphic subdivision of the layers, proceeding by successively removing a fixed thickness of sediment (e.g. around 4–6 inches or 10–15 cm). In such cases, excavations proceed horizontally while taking into account any superficial irregularities that the soil surfaces may present (slope, for example).

As excavations progress, each consecutive layer composing a stratigraphic sequence is named using a code, generally consisting of letters and numbers. This denomination will serve as a reference for any samples or artifacts coming from within the matrix. Obviously, it is preferable to sample layers prior to their removal by excavation to gain adequate understanding of their different components. Samples taken from different vertical and horizontal situations within a stratigraphic sequence serve to distinguish and confirm similarities or differences that will be indicated in the stratigraphic log. The main aim is to establish and characterize each of the different phases of an accumulation within a chrono-climatic framework in order finally to attribute a cultural agenda to the finds enclosed within. Preferably, a representative portion of a depositional sequence of an archeological site is preserved untouched so that it may serve in future as a source of data, assuming that forthcoming technologies could provide additional information. Schematic drawings of the stratigraphic sections exposed during the excavation process are generally elaborated on-site and then further revised in a laboratory setting. These drawings and their associated legends and field observations record all of the sedimentary information discerned by the successive removal of soil layers during an excavation. The sedimentary layers composing a depositional sequence of an archeological site must each be analyzed individually before being fitted into the larger picture of an archeological occurrence.

Among the methodologies, essential climatic and environmental information can be obtained from studying the grains, gravels and pebbles that compose the sedimentary matrix enclosing the artifacts (sedimentology). Within a site, sediment grain size and mineral composition can vary from one level to the next, translating change in ambient conditions. For example, in a limestone cave, clayey sediment containing tiny pebbles rolled by water circulating within the karst indicates an accumulation deposited during temperate and humid conditions with water percolating through the cave system. In this case, clays dissolved by water from the encasing limestone will form the sedimentary layers. Contrastingly, layers with a high sand content are revelatory of aeolian transport and generally convey cold, dry climatic conditions. By closely examining the surface features of individual grains of sediment, it is possible to determine not only the agent of transport (wind, water) but also the distance of the source of the sedimentary components. Grains that have traveled long distances by wind, for example, have rough (pockmarked), uneven surfaces; those that have been transported significant distances by water tend to display smooth, rounded profiles. Additional methods composing the branch of sedimentology are used to determine the mineral composition of sediment from a given archeological layer, helping us to learn about its formation processes and, by extension, its origin in the environment (geographical location). Micromorphology is a complementary branch of sedimentology that involves procedures to examine what happened after a layer of sediment has been deposited in a given context. It studies the "postdepositional" (or taphonomic) forces at play within a depositional sequence and their evolution through time. Different natural phenomena affecting depositional sequences are responsible for the variations we observe in a stratigraphy's present-day aspect, composition and integrity (roots, burrowing animals, geochemical events, faulting, etc.). As a rule, sedimentary sampling requires a high degree of rigor to avoid misinterpretations or incoherencies during the laboratory phase of analysis. Sampling from within a depositional sequence must be carried out under strictly controlled conditions for each type of analysis, recording the exact position in the stratigraphic sequence from which each sample has been taken because it would be meaningless unless it can be replaced within its original chrono-stratigraphical framework. Samples are taken from within the sections ensuring that modern pollutants that would falsify the results do not affect their composition.

Considering now to one of the more common types of finds documented within the sedimentary layers of a prehistoric archeological site, the fossilized bones of vertebrate fauna. Discovered in archeological contexts, animal fossils speak to us on numerous planes and are the focus of a number of applied disciplines in prehistoric archeology. Paleontology, one of the oldest disciplines, involves the identification of the different animal species, tracking their skeletal evolution over time. These disciplines examine the changes in animals' anatomical features over time, which we know to be largely affected by climatic forces and reflecting processes of natural selection, providing taxonomical classification and sometimes even allowing identification and description of new species. Paleontologists reconstruct the ancestral lineage for each species, looking at interrelationships to establish their evolutionary history and intraspecific affinities. Common ancestry is traced, for example, with cladistics, a biological classification method that organizes organisms (closer or more distant) in accordance with the ancestry of their shared common traits. Paleontology examines the measurable changes in the physical features observed from fossil bones, which designate both specific time frames and particular environmental contexts. Careful examination of the preservation of fossil bones, sometimes using microscopy, can also yield taphonomic information telling us about climate and other disturbances that affected the bones after their burial. Beyond their usefulness for understanding paleolandscape configurations (paleoecology), taxonomic determinations are also valuable for biochronology, a relative dating method that I will explain further in this chapter when I discuss how archeological sites are dated. Furthermore, trained archeozoologists are able to glean information about human hunting and butchery practices from fossil bones, which, in turn, designate varying degrees of behavioral complexity and modes of social organization. The types of anthropic activities sometimes discernible on fossils include intentional breakage (definable by systematic patterning) and cutting or crushing marks made with stone tools. The significance of the fossil animal register in an archeological site is thus invaluable for our understanding of prehistoric lifeways. Paleoanthropology englobes a range of associated disciplines, including biology, taphonomy, genetics and more. It is dedicated to studying fossil human remains to determine evolutionary variability and ancestral relationships within the human family.

Looking to the reconstruction of past landscapes, palynology (or archeobotany) studies microscopic vegetal remains, such as pollens and spores. Anthracology studies ancient charcoals found in archeological sites that can yield information about paleolandscapes and climate in prehistoric contexts. Determining the plant species subject to burning gives clues not only to paleoenvironments but also about human use of particular types of woods, seeds, fruits or tubers. Because vegetation is sensitive to variations in temperature and humidity, plant species' representation, or relative frequency, provides precious elements for reconstructing paleoclimatic conditions and are thus useful for checking data about the time frame of archeological sites. The pollen of every plant or tree presents a very distinct formal morphology that allows trained palynologists to identify species. However, depending on the sedimentary context, pollen will or will not be preserved. Contrasting data about the vegetation with that from other disciplines helps archeologists to corroborate their observations about climate and environment and thus to formulate viable hypotheses. As in sedimentological and other analyses, sampling methods used in palynology are performed following strict methodological guidelines to avoid modern contaminations. Once in the laboratory, the samples are processed using special procedures of chemical isolation that aid in extracting any pollens that might be preserved in the sedimentary matrix.

Dating an archeological site is evidently an important facet of prehistoric archeology. The age evaluation of an artifact-yielding site is indispensable for reconstructing paleohuman life and placing it within the reasoned, global evolutionary framework that I described in earlier sections. Indeed, a variety of different dating methods is available to archeologists today, each with its own range of constraints, advantages and disadvantages. Depending on the context, archeologists will choose which method or methods are best suited to the types of artifacts and their find context. Archeologists generally choose to apply more than one method to date a site in order to cross-check (calibrate) the age evaluations obtained from each one and give more coherency to the results. It is useful here to provide a brief, simplified description of some of the dating methods commonly applied in prehistoric archeology to determine the age of artifacts and of the artifact-bearing levels of an archeological site.[54] In archeology, age evaluations are obtained using absolute (or chronometric) dating, which involves radiometric (or radioisotope) methodologies, and relative dating, which establishes an age range dependent on comparative relationships. Absolute dating methods are based on the principles of known rates of decay or transformation ratios of some isotopes. For example, radiocarbon dating is used to provide age evaluations for carbon-based organic materials (i.e. charcoal, wood, bones, shells, pottery, pollen, coral, blood residue, resins, among others). Throughout their lifetime, plants and animals absorb and exchange Carbon-14 (^{14}C) present in the atmosphere or in the ocean (in the case of marine life). After the death of an organism, it ceases to acquire ^{14}C, which begins to decay into Carbon-12 (^{12}C) at a known and measurable rate. The carbon isotope's half-life, referring to the time it will take for one-half of the radioactive nuclei in a sample to decay, is 5,730 years. The oldest reliable radiocarbon dates do not exceed 50,000 years. However, other isotopes known to transform at higher rates allow measuring correspondingly longer time intervals. The radioactive isotope Potassium-40 (^{40}K), for example, converts into Argon-40 (^{40}Ar) at a known rate in some minerals that were recrystallized from a molten state (tephra). The time elapsed since recrystallization is measured by comparing the ratio of argon accumulated to the amount of potassium remaining in a sample. This makes it a suitable method for dating lava flows and metamorphic events. It can also be used to date sedimentary contexts containing evaporates, mica or clay minerals. Radiometric dating methods relying on the known decay rate of Uranium-234 (^{234}U) into Thorium-230 (^{230}Th) are used to date calcium carbonate materials (thorium-230 dating, uranium-series disequilibrium dating, uranium-series dating), such as speleothems, making them particularly useful for dating limestone karst cave sites.

Other methods, such as cosmogenic radionuclide dating, can be used to provide age estimates for sedimentary accumulations. In this case, cosmogenic isotopes present in surface rocks or soil are analyzed to determine the time of their exposition to the surface. As the name suggests, cosmogenic isotopes are formed when cosmic rays penetrate the atmosphere, showering the earth with extraterrestrial particles, which are actually isotopes originating from supernova explosions in outer space. When high-energy neutrons from the cosmic rays collide with the Earth's strata, they cause some elements to transform. The rate of transformation, translated into a ratio based on the known rate of radioactive decay of a given isotope, allows specialists to calculate the minimum exposition time of a surface. Thermoluminescence (TL) refers to a dating method used in archeology to assess age in prehistoric contexts. Thermoluminescence is one luminescence dating method used to determine how much time has expired since mineral grains were exposed for the last time to sunlight or heating (another is optically stimulated luminescence or OSL). It is applied to date the formation of inorganic materials of crystalline minerals that have been heated by fire (pottery, ceramics, burned flint tools, lava), or exposed to substantial sunlight (sediment). Electrons accumulate in microcrystalline structures at a measurable rate that is proportional to the radiation that the sample received from its environment (ambient radiation). Reheating the sample will free the ionized electrons trapped in microfissures of these materials, emitting energy that is measurable as a faint light signal (thermoluminescence). Its intensity is proportional to the dose of radiation absorbed by the sample since the formation of its crystalline structure.

Whenever possible, different dating methods will be contrasted with the chronological framework provided by periodic shifts in the Earth's paleomagnetic field obtained from the incidence of reversals in the Earth's magnetic polarity and other geomagnetic secular variations. These variations in the Earth's magnetic field are known to be caused by fluctuations occurring deep within the Earth's core. Periodic changes in the Earth's magnetic field have enabled scientists to elaborate a geomagnetic timescale of normal (or positive) events when the Earth's geographic North Pole coincides with the magnetic North and reversed (or negative) geomagnetic events when the Earth's polarity is opposite to the geographic North. The Earth's geomagnetic state is said to be "normal" when its magnetic polarity coincides with the present-day geographic North, and it is said to be "reversed" when its magnetic orientation points toward the South Pole. The mapping of these events through time has been achieved by documenting the orientation of iron-rich particles contained in deep sea (and other) core samples retrieved from drilling, which will have aligned with the electromagnetic force reigning at the time of deposit. In the archeological context, core samples obtained from within stratigraphic sequences are analyzed in the laboratory with a magnometer to determine the orientation (or to detect shifts in orientation) of particles that will indicate the position of the magnetic North at the time that the sediment was deposited. Establishing thus the age of the normal and reverse polarity events through time, an accumulation can then be accorded to one or another of these events. The results will be checked against other types of data, such as biochronology, geomorphology or artifact types. There are, of course, other time-relevant occurrences that can be measured to determine the age of an archeological context. Some of them use changes in the chemical composition of some molecules present in a sedimentary context to measure age. In layers containing volcanic ash, for example, specialists trained in tephrochronology can evaluate the timing of specific volcanic events. When a volcanic eruption discharges ash (tephra), its components have a distinct chemical signature that can be useful to elaborate a chronological framework based on the timing of discrete eruptive events. Chemical signatures recorded in distinct tephra layers can be compared regionally, for example, to determine if they belong to the same volcanic event. In some cases, data derived from biological sources can also yield reliable age evaluations. For example, dendrochronology is a science that uses growth ring patterns of trees or objects made from wood to determine age and to test the coherency of this information with existing climatic and environmental reconstructions.

Depending the geological context and type of artifacts, archeologists can verify their age evaluations by completing them with other types of relative dating methods. One frequently used method is biochronology, which specialists use to determine the age range of fossil finds within fauna-yielding archeological settings. Biochronology studies progressive changes in species' anatomy over time, attributing specific "morphotypes" (accepted formal variability within a group belonging to the same species) to their corresponding time frames. Different types of small and large animals (including amphibians and reptiles) are more or less useful markers for establishing an age range. As paleontologists chart species-type appearance/disappearance in different areas of the globe, they contribute to refining the regional-specific timeline of each animal's evolutionary trajectory. Similarly, paleoanthropologists chart the successive anatomical changes undergone by the human lineage over time. Thus, the evolutionary agendas drawn up by paleontologists and paleoanthropologists for each animal species are contingent on the principle that different anatomical expressions of their morphotypes appear and disappear in the fossil record at specific moments in time. Because anatomical change is particularly rapid among smaller-sized mammals, such as rodents, these animals are especially important for determining age in some archeological contexts where their tiny remains are preserved and collected. Their anatomical change through time, notably in shifting tooth morphologies, reflects the adaptations they have acquired, which, in turn, are linked to fluctuations in climate and environments. Identifying and describing different species of small mammals, therefore, generally involves the microscopic analysis of their tooth enamel relief patterns. Of course, this type of study precludes both favorable conservation within a site and very attentive excavating techniques. The use of microvertebrate remains to determine climate and environmental conditions helps to situate a given archeological layer within an established climato-chronological framework. Tiny bones and teeth from rabbits, rodents, amphibians, birds or lizards, for example, are hard to spot when excavating, and are usually recuperated after the sediment has been sieved, washed, dried and sorted.

INTERPRETING CULTURAL EVOLUTION FROM STONE ARTIFACTS

Because culture also evolves, artifacts left behind by humans, such as stone tools, may also give some indication of (relative) age, of an individual artifact or of an artifact-bearing level. Specialists study the features of cultural materials recuperated from archeological contexts, adapting their methodologies to the type of artifacts under analysis (stone tools, pottery, metal or glass, etc.). In lithic analysis, different methodologies are applied to study stylistic traits, technological or manufacturing features and functional aspects. Because stone tools constitute the main type of cultural relic from ancient prehistoric sites, it is key for understanding the evolutionary stages of ancient human material culture. Here, I focus especially on methodologies used in stone tool analysis not only because this is the science in which I trained but also because the study of the appearance and evolution of human technologies is central to discussions I will be developing throughout the latter chapters of this book. I stress once again that, from remote prehistoric times, stone tools are the only remnants of human cultural heritage, and this explains why it is so important to investigate their every detail. *Making silent stones speak*[55] is the work of "prehistorians." Overall, the Paleolithic artifact record has yielded an overrepresentation of stone-made artifacts simply because those items that may have been made from wood or other perishable materials (bones, wood, bamboo) are rarely preserved from the distant past. It is likely, in fact, that some of the stone tools we find were used to work with perishable materials, perhaps transforming them into other types of tools that we will never come to know. Analysis of the lithic record brings us particularly close to our human ancestors because it reveals bits of information that tell us about the thoughts and gestures used throughout the manufacture-use processes. The traits reflected in each individual tool help us to determine the cognitive capacities of our early human ancestors and to ascribe them a cultural designation. Stone tool kits are defined and compared across geographical and chronological ranges, contributing aspects of human behavior and culture into the global evolutionary framework.

Somewhat surprisingly, recognizable systems of production in stone knapping are discernible even in the oldest stone tool assemblages known to humankind. In very remote time frame, stone toolmaking can be seen as indicative of culture (*sensu largo*) because it reflects repeated chains of action whose systematic and sequential arrangements could have been transmitted from generation to generation only through learning. To study stone tool kits, we use a combination of different (nonexclusive) approaches. Initially, specialists sought to identify tool types using a method referred to as "typology," which is also used to classify other types of objects, including ceramics and bone tools among others. As one of the first methods developed to study stone tools, typology remains an important, although sometimes problematic, standard, often used to establish chronological, functional and cultural aspects relating to the tool kits. Typology came into its own as a methodology for the study of stone tools during the first half of the twentieth century, chiefly after the works of the famous French Prehistorian F. Bordes (1919–1981), who focused much of his research on developing specific definitions for tools found in Lower and Middle Paleolithic contexts.[56] His wife, D. de Sonneville-Bordes, likewise provided precise definitions of stone and bone tools dating to the Upper Paleolithic, thus contributing to the foundations for the cultural successions of this period.[57] Both of these influential specialists produced detailed manuals defining Paleolithic tool types and then relating them to specific cultural and temporal contexts. These handbooks are in fact classificatory lexicons, or rubrics, containing tool type denominations and their definitions, designating a very wide range of specific "morphotypes" discovered in Paleolithic contexts. But what are tools? In prehistoric archeology, "tools" are generally considered to be only those items that have been affected by some type of secondary modification to give them a predetermined form (by retouch or other stone shaping methods). Tools, as such, reflect the preconceived mental templates that served as models for their formal attributes that we find replicated in an assemblage. Because the know-how required to manufacture standardized and repeated morphologies on stone was, logically, passed on through social learning, it was rapidly equated with what we commonly call "culture." Accordingly, each morphotype constitutes a formal entity distinguishable by precise features that can be described using a predetermined set of observable and measurable traits. This type-related reasoning strategy was thus established quite early on in the development of the field of prehistoric archeology, largely based on tool assemblages from some key European (especially French) archeological sites.

It was in this context that archeologists emphasized that Paleolithic stone tools were not random forms but that they had recognizable features that could be defined in accordance with systematic formal traits. This can be illustrated empirically by taking an example from any of our modern tools. We can easily recognize a screwdriver, for instance, no matter its size or the material it is made from (wood, plastic, metal). A screwdriver cannot be confused, for example, with a hammer because each of these tools exists within its own specific range of variability; each tool encompasses a precise array of characteristics that define its "type." Although they have since been found to be insufficient or even misleading, typological classifications applied in archeology still often use the Bordian notion of *fossil-director*,[56] endorsing the idea that specific tool types can be linked not only to precise moments in time but also to specific cultural entities. From the appearance of the first true tool "types" (especially after the Acheulian cultural period), typological criteria have laid the foundations for the establishment of a so-called chrono-cultural framework defining successive Paleolithic cultures through time. Today, typology alone has proved insufficient to achieve this task and, while it is still used, it is completed in lithic studies by other analytical methods. An important drawback of the first typological studies was that they considered only what were (subjectively) considered to be the finest-made tools while simple knapping waste (always most numerous in an assemblage) was ignored or even discarded. Another major pitfall of a purely typological approach to lithic studies is that it does not consider the possibility that tool-type variability can be influenced not only by cultural factors but also by external impact factors, such as varying site functions, fluctuating climatic conditions, raw materials' type, availability and mechanical features, resource availability and so on. Seeking out effective approaches to catalog artifacts has been a concern addressed by prehistoric archeology since its inception. This task is particularly arduous in the case of the oldest tool kits (belonging to the Oldowan cultural complex, which I will discuss in some detail in subsequent chapters) whose manufacture by the human hand often needs validation by demonstrable systematic observations and whose components lack standardization. Although typology provides a methodology compatible with our brain's need to classify things in order to understand them, alternative approaches over time have been (and continue to be) developed and tested. Sometimes, theoretical perspectives guided by dominant social trends led to different ways of conceptualizing and studying lithic artifacts. For example, the methodology developed by G. Laplace in the 1950s[58] and its offshoots (the Logical Analytical System)[59] proposed coded language systems aimed at providing a scientifically more objective descriptive mode and to recreate gestural operative schemes.

Over time, progress has been made in lithic studies thanks in part to the growing number of discoveries that have sharpened the interests of numerous archeologists searching to understand how, why and under what circumstances specific types of stone tools (and their associated technologies) appeared. All of this has contributed to transforming the discipline of stone tool analysis, adding the idea of actually reconstructing the paleo thought patterns and gestures involved in their production. Today, typological investigation is generally supplemented by a "technological" analysis, incorporating different sets of concepts into stone tool analysis and giving emphasis to the manufacturing and use processes. Central to this method is the notion of *operative sequence* (Fr. *chaîne opératoire*) introduced by A. Leroi-Gourhan in 1943[60] (see Figure 2.2). This model proposes to consider the "life" of an artifact as so many links in a chain of procedural events leading from conception to manufacture, use, discard and (perhaps) reuse. It further proposes that each link in a given chain can be distinguished and characterized by the features of its coincident products, which, in turn, can be repositioned to find their place within the operative sequence. Bygone successions of thoughts and gestures leading to the elaboration of an artifact can thus be pieced together (reconstructed) as a chain of events, each of which may be understood thanks to the specificities of its by-products. An artifact's morphology thus reveals its place in an original sequencing of action–production, gaining significance for its role in recreating the story of its own making. Unlike typology that privileges only finished tools, the technological point of view incorporates the full range of artifacts composing an assemblage, attributing each one with intrinsic value as indicative of past conceptual and gestural stages. Furthermore, technological analysis seeks not only to reveal but also to experimentally reproduce manufacturing techniques used by prehistoric humans, providing a hands-on way to evaluate the difficulty and complexity of different production systems. Actually, replicating ancient technological know-how with stone provides a window through which we may examine the cognitive skills and mental processes of our ancestors. Properly contextualized within an inclusive time frame thanks to the cumulative knowledge obtained by multidisciplinary studies, stone artifacts are precious indicators contributing to gaining a fuller understanding of the emergence and development of the genus *Homo*.

At some point in the evolution of early *Homo*, or even of *Australopithecines*, the demands of survival-related thought-action processes intensified with the realization of the potential that object manipulation could provide for fulfilling their material needs.

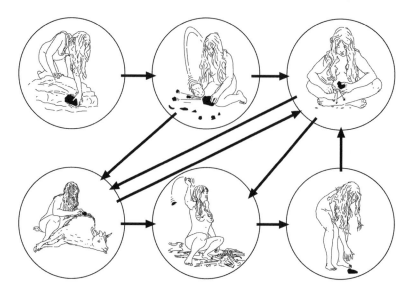

Figure 2.2
Operative chain after Leroi-Gourhan. Schematic illustration of the links in the chains of
action involved in making stone tools (operative chain drawing by Oriol Oms): gathering
stone raw materials, knapping and shaping, using, discarding and recycling. Specific kinds of
by-products or traces of use can be attributed to each phase in a technofunctional
operative chain. (Original drawing by Oriol Oms. Redrawn from José-Manuel Benito.
Credit: Locutus Borg via Wikimedia Commons.)

Hominins activated more complex behaviors that integrated extended thought processes
requiring planning, linking them to multilevel sequential actions involving object
transformation.[61] This involved the cerebral development of anticipative thought processes as individuals set about the material realization of specific "projects" involving
mediated resource acquisition and object transformation. To specialists in stone tool
technology, the first archeologically discernible gesture in a paleo chain of action
concerns the selection of a raw material appropriate to carry out the task at hand.
While at first glance this might appear simplistic, when considered more carefully, we
realize that many contemplative dynamics must in fact have been involved in such
decision-making processes. The archeology tells us that the first hominin toolmakers
carefully chose their lithic raw materials from local environmental sources, generally
selecting from the range of available rock types those with optimal mechanical features
for the goal they wished to accomplish.[62] These selective petrographic elections are
clearly evidenced even as early as the Oldowan, the oldest cultural complex known to
humankind.[63,64,65] From the dawn of technology, hominins were already predicting
stone breakage patterns and adapting them to produce tools for butchering or for
different types of percussive activities.[66] Moreover, Oldowan hominins made these
choices taking into account other geometrical and petrographical parameters and

conforming them to technofunctional requirements. Thus, they picked out rocks that fit specific qualitative needs and whose shapes provided natural angles for easy flake production without any need for additional actions to adjust the flake extraction platforms.[67] Like other behaviors, those linked to raw material selection patterns evolved over time in synchronicity with the ever-increasing spiral of technological mastery. Eventually, hominins came to explore areas further from their living spaces and so necessarily developed ways to transport the raw materials they wanted to bring with them. Over time, they increasingly freed themselves from the mechanical limitations posed by some rock types that are not well adapted for controlled knapping procedures (e.g. quartz), importing better quality materials from distant ranges. They also gradually overcame constraints posed by the shape of the rocks, developing new strategies to form and prepare flake extraction platforms, adding more links to their operative chains of action. Behavior related to the choice of raw materials is, in sum, one that changes through time, evolving in parallel with other evolutionary factors.

Sometimes the degree of technological know-how achieved by a given tool-producing group is deduced by identifying and then sequencing discrete stages in the manufacturing process. This is done by analyzing the morphological features of the material evidence beginning with the need to fulfill a plan and the collection of raw materials required to do so before moving through the different phases of production. Waste generated during each consecutive event accordingly becomes a precious indicator with which to establish each link in a chain of action: planning, obtaining materials, producing, using, discarding (reusing). Stone knapping processes (flake production) considered thus as phases of action, begin by the first blows given to a cobble whose flakes will be characterized by their cortical dorsal surfaces (cortex-smooth rolled or weathered surface of a rock). As knapping progresses, reaching into the volume of the cobble, the flakes that will be obtained will gradually display less cortex until, eventually, all of the outer surface of the cobble has been removed (see Figures 2.3 and 2.4). Each successive flake removal is discernible as a scar (or negative) left on the matrix (core) as evidence of preceding flake surfaces. The morphology of these scars provides information about directional changes in the blows delivered during knapping, allowing the identification of different strategies of stone reduction. These strategies, or techniques, have been shown to evolve over time, and some methods have been related to specific developmental phases or even particular types of hominins. Thus, along with typology, technology is a useful tool with which to understand the evolution of ancient human material culture and its associated cognitive processes.

Despite their significance for determining technological strategies, knapped stone cores are generally regarded as waste products (although they may sometimes have had a "second life," subsequently used as hammers, for example, to perform for other types of tasks). Alternatively, flakes were used, either without modification or after being retouched into different tool types. In this way, every element in an archeological assemblage has some intrinsic value as an indicator of a particular event composing a

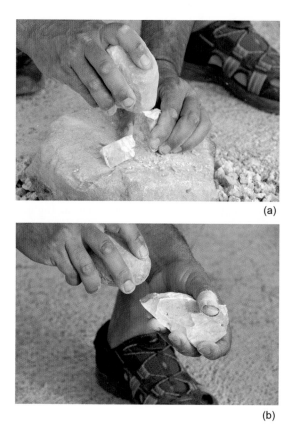

(a)

(b)

Figure 2.3
Experimental flint knapping. (a) The bipolar-on-anvil method. (b) The free-hand knapping method. (Jordi Mestre, courtesy of the IPHES-CERCA)

technological chain of action. Depending on the morphology of by-products and finished tools discovered in an archeological site, it is possible to ascertain from where and in what form the chosen raw materials were brought into that site. We can reconstruct the stone reduction sequences from the first blow applied to a cobble through the series of products (waste) and to the final formal object. When flakes were reknapped (retouched) to shape specific tools types (scrapers, borers), smaller flakes resulted. When these items are present within a site's deposits, we may assume that the tool retouching took place in situ. Systematic retouching and the first standardized tool "types" appear after the long period (nearly 2 million years) of nonsystematic brute flake production that typifies the Oldowan.[68] The standardization of retouched tools appeared during the Acheulian (see Chapter 4)[69] alongside other innovations, and such tools provide a useful criterion with which to evaluate the activities carried out by hominins. After the Acheulian, therefore, retouched tools are considered valuable

Figure 2.4
Experimental limestone core and flake. The impact point is clearly visible on both the core and the flake. The direction of the blow can be distinguished on both products by observing the direction and orientation of the striations. (Jordi Mestre, courtesy of the IPHES-CERCA)

indicators of regional cultural specificities and important elements for differentiating prehistoric cultures.

Traceology (also called *usewear* or *microwear analysis*), another branch of lithic studies, focuses on tool function helping to determine what prehistoric tools were used for. This discipline applies compound methodologies to explore this interesting subject with an emphasis on experimental archeology. The experimental phase of the work program involves reproducing items from a given archeological assemblage in the same raw materials and using them to perform different types of possible or probable activities in relation to site contexts. Experimental tools are used to work materials considered most likely to have been available during the prehistoric occupation of a site (e.g. meat, wood, skins). The activities and their effects on the worked materials are carefully monitored. Different types of gestures are carried out experimentally to work with stone, and these may leave characteristic microscopic traces (polish, striation marks) that can be identified under powerful magnification. First, the presence of traces on some pieces is identified using a binocular microscope before studying them more closely under higher magnification with the aid of an electron microscope. Such traces are telltale markings that can be compared with those observed on the experimental artifacts. Traceologists use this method to elaborate working hypotheses about the types of materials and gestures that might have been employed in the prehistoric context. Major obstacles, however, stand in the way of successful traceological analysis: It requires optimal artifact conservation. It remains very difficult to study, for example, softer lithic materials such as limestone or sandstone, which are more apt to have undergone severe alteration over time. Crystalline rock types like quartz and quartzite present other difficulties, such as high reflectivity under the microscope. Because of this, most traceological studies have so far been carried out on well-preserved flint items. Relating to artifact preservation, traceologists must consider the taphonomy of the sites (postdepositional disturbances that artifacts may have suffered), and it is often difficult to distinguish between anthropic traces and those due to natural causes, such as trampling (human or animal), water circulation or exposure to other natural elements. Finally, traceological assessments are difficult to establish in the context of assemblages containing very numerous pieces because it is feasible to study only a tiny fraction of them in a reasonable time frame using such painstaking analytical methods. However, progress is being made in this domain, which has indisputably come into its own in the last decades.

Other disciplines dealing with the development of the human brain and cognitive processes are also applied to the study of ancient human material culture. A humanly modified object is seen to reflect a certain degree of behavioral complexity and, as such, as representative of a particular stage in the evolutionary trajectory leading to ever-higher degrees of cognitive development that is inextricably linked to the evolution of the human brain. A common strategy is to analyze primate behavior using direct observation of living primates, our closest cousins, regarding them as a window through which we might glimpse past hominin behaviors. Chimpanzees and bonobos, for example, use a variety of materials as tools to obtain foods that are otherwise inaccessible to them.[70] Chimps have been observed using wooden sticks to catch ants and manipulating stone blocks to crack open nuts. Beyond primates, however, many other animals have been observed to make and use tools. For instance, crows modify branches and leaves, subsequently transporting them to be used as tools to poke food out from crevices, bottlenose dolphins have been observed transporting and using sea sponges to expose prey, sea otters use stones to remove shells stuck onto rocks and break them open for consumption.[71] But, in spite of all of this evidence from the animal kingdom, only humans have developed long and complex operative chains of production and a real reliance on toolmaking for survival. Furthermore, tool-using animals have not over time generated comparatively significant new competences from their manipulation of materials (innovation). The tool kits created by the earliest known hominins far surpass the capacities shown up to now by any other toolmaking species.

APPLYING MODERN METHODS TO ANCIENT EVIDENCE

Applying the use of modern technologies, archeology today is adapting rapidly to the changing schemes of human existence. In spite of the common methodological denominator of data collection, modern technologies are being used to locate and excavate archeological sites and to collect and process scientific data. This data is being communicated both within the scientific community and to the public through original and didactic venues. Archeological information considered for its value as shared cultural heritage is carefully stored and protected in museums, laboratories and research institutes. Excavation methods have been modernized to enable archeologists to interpret fossil contexts with minimal physical intervention and to recreate them into different types of usable imagery. New nonintrusive and nondestructive methodologies are now available for archeological survey involving aerial photography, drones and electromagnetic (magnetometer) surveys based on variable earth resistivity, ground penetration radar, electromagnetic methods analyzing conductivity, sedimentary magnetic susceptibility, sound navigation and ranging techniques and so on. Powerful microscopes are available for close-up observations of trace elements or other informative data that may be gleaned from the relics and their contexts. Computer tomography is used to generate precise three-dimensional digital images hidden within objects such as mummies, for example, or funerary urns, without having to disturb their original contexts. Geometric morphometric analyses are performed on artifacts reproduced in three dimensions allowing immediate and highly accurate results to be obtained that would require much more time-consuming work using traditional methods and enabling a completely new range of previously inaccessible objective data processing. These new technologies allow specialists to create exact three-dimensional reproductions of artifacts and even archeological site contexts. Computerized databases and data sharing allow specialists working in archeology to record, share and process gigantic amounts of information with a rapidity never before imagined, thus accelerating the interpretative processes. Exact copies of artifacts in three dimensions can be shared among researchers in data repositories or exhibited in museums without ever needing to expose the originals to the dangers posed by transport and handling. In addition, advancements made in restoration techniques are ensuring the longevity and conservation of all types of archeological contexts and individual objects for future generations.

Sequencing ancient DNA is another exciting research area recently brought to the fore by geneticists providing important advances, especially in paleontology and paleoanthropology. Today, genetic sequencing is providing new answers to old questions, especially in relation to human origins and ancient human migrations, among other issues. Results obtained from the sequencing of ancient genomes are being compared with those of modern populations, allowing the determination of their relatedness or genetic distancing and establishment of reliable cladistic reconstructions of species' ancestry. In the Paleolithic context, ancient DNA can be extracted from small samples of bone taken from hominin or animal fossil specimens while in more recent contexts, it can be obtained from strands of hair, fur and even blood. In 2017, researchers from the Max Planck Institute for Evolutionary Anthropology in Leipzig, Germany, in collaboration with a group of international specialists recovered and successfully analyzed DNA from Pleistocene sediment coming from a number of archeological sites (including the Denisova Cave site in Russia).[72] Their findings show that it is presently possible to find traces of mammalian — and even hominin — DNA in Late and Middle Pleistocene sediment, even in the absence of skeletal finds. Although still grappling with ethical issues and the need for larger samples, genetic studies and molecular biology today are providing a promising tool for better understanding the origins, migrations and mobility as well as inter- and intrapopulation mixing occurring among ancient populations of *Homo* throughout the world. In the future, this method will certainly continue to provide a powerful tool with which to (more reliably) construct the human family's evolutionary pathway.

All of these examples provide only a limited idea of the multidisciplinary nature of the science of prehistory for which, without written records, no one field of study is sufficient to reconstruct the past with an acceptable degree of accuracy. This scenario of expansive data exploitation from diverse fields of knowledge is effectively snowballing in today's world as modern prehistory embraces disciplines including genetics, neurosciences, nanotechnologies and many others. The vision we construct of prehistory thus evolves, not only to the rhythm of new archeological discoveries but also with all types of contemporary technological innovations. Our vision is further molded by dominant ethical and socially acceptable norms so that interpretations that appear factual today may be dramatically changed tomorrow. The chronological framework within which we strive to place each milestone of human ingenuity remains a reflection of this constant informational mutability. New technologies thus applied in prehistoric archeology are seemingly limitless, and novel methodologies are constantly being developed to improve the strategies used for finding, studying and preserving archeological sites and the artifacts they yield. Computerized systems have revolutionized the speed with which information is obtained and analyzed, facilitating the rapid synthesis of huge masses of data and enabling vast intra- and inter-site comparisons, opening the way to new and surprising conclusions. This limitless exploitation of new technologies explains the intellectual acceleration that prehistoric archeology has experienced over the last decades. Archeological methods are defined and adjusted in accordance with the nature of the finds, their geological context, the specific conditions of their preservation and even the political situation of the countries in which they are found. It is our responsibility as scientists working in the field to translate all of the accumulated data into accessible knowledge so that society can advance by modeling its behavior patterns in sustainable ways thanks to realistic, positive and lasting interpretations of our shared past. Through these processes, the studies of the distant past can provide a unique point of view to the ways that we see the world and perhaps even lead to the discovery of new means by which to meet the challenges we as a species face today and in the very near future.

3

BECOMING HUMAN

WHAT IT MEANS TO BE HUMAN

One of the characteristics defining humanity today is the existential need we often feel to understand our situation in the universe and to somehow attribute meaning to our existence. Our genus (*Homo*) appeared on the scene only some 3 million years ago – nothing in terms of the geological time scale – yet our organism and the ways in which we act and react have changed significantly throughout this time. We might describe the most apparent pattern of that developmental process as one of acceleration, especially in terms of the complexity of our social and communicative patterns as they are reflected by our material culture. Over time, radical environmental shifts have triggered genetic reactions latent in our DNA, leading us to adapt to new situations by undergoing changes to our physiognomy. Looking to our ancestral lineage, we observe that such changes over time are especially notable in terms of growth and complexity in the configuration of the human brain. This tendency is accompanied by a parallel evolutionary trend toward evermore multifaceted social behaviors facilitated in humans by strengthening technological innovation. The invention of technology has been groundbreaking in our evolutionary process because it has allowed our species to move beyond basic reactive physiological responses and into the realm of technological solutions that have successfully accelerated the normal adaptive process as defined by Darwinian natural selection. Looking to the deep past often gives the idea that human evolution occurred as a series of successive leaps from one to another major breakthrough (bipedalism, stone tools, fire, early communal settlements and urbanization, etc.).

However, it is important to keep in mind that the prehistoric archeological record is very partial; its fragmentary nature leaves us with this impression of change in terms of links in a chain of "remarkable" events, their sequencing seemingly occurring quite rapidly through time, even effacing any traces of transitional phases that might have existed between each achievement.

Toward the end of the Pliocene some 3 million years ago (Ma) and throughout the Quaternary Period after 2.5 Ma, significant changes in hominin physiognomy accompanied major technical innovations, allowing our species to successfully deal with associated environmental and social stresses. However, human evolutionary change was not only anatomical; it was also conceptual and behavioral. Of course, all of these processes are linked, and anatomical modifications in the hominin species over time must be put into perspective by relating them to particularly significant archeological indicators. Foremost for the present discourse is toolmaking, but there are certainly many more things that can be considered in relation to this – some visible in the archeological record, others only deduced or hypothesized from the evidence and still others (surely the large majority) – effaced forever by the effects of time. In the framework of this book, I will be looking at some of these signposts to learn more about some of the major evolutionary chapters composing the human story beginning with the first hominins to assume bipedal stature and gait, the development and evolution of stone toolmaking and the role it played in the emergence of language and symbolic thought. As we examine our ancestral heritage through the window of the archeological record, we observe that, for the earlier phases of hominin development, major achievements along our evolutionary pathway appear in broad association with anatomical changes affecting both skeletal and cerebral features, even sometimes to the point of giving way to new hominin species. Accordingly, different hominin species are associated with corresponding anatomical, behavioral and technological characteristics, which are made understandable by establishing them as species-specific hallmarks. Thus, *Homo habilis* is commonly lauded as the first toolmaker, *Homo erectus* as the species that migrated over large distances, *Homo neandertalensis* as the inventor of Levallois technology and so on. However, such species-behavior equivalences are often inaccurate and really reflect only how we ourselves have drawn up simplistic models that can easily be committed to memory. This interiorizing of past events helps us to conceptualize our own evolutionary process by transforming it into a seemingly logical chain of events, which we conveniently place within a theoretical anatomical-behavioral timeline, or evolutionary picture, sometimes referred to as the *hominization process*. However, we must be reminded that evolution involves appearances, mixture (hybridization) and disappearances of species that were not necessarily linked in a continuous chain and that these species created, shared and exchanged culture in uneven ways.

In my years as a professional archeologist and teacher of prehistory, I have often been asked why, in contrast to what we observe in the distant past, the very significant technological and behavioral changes undergone since the appearance of our species,

Homo sapiens, do not seem to be accompanied by any noteworthy changes in our anatomical or cerebral configurations. It is true that, even though subtle changes are constantly under way in our physiognomy,[73] no *really major* changes have occurred in our skeletal configuration since the first anatomically modern humans appeared thousands of years ago, in spite of the huge fluctuations in our life history. In fact, it seems that modern humans are responding to external pressures using an alternative strategy, one honed and perfected over thousands of generations since *Homo* first emerged in Africa: a technological strategy – diluted into culture – beyond the realm of natural selection. Indeed, more and more modern human actions/reactions call on nongenetic responses through a system of adaptation appropriately referred to as *cultural selection*.[74] Since its inception more than 3 Ma,[24] technology, as an adaptive strategy, has been converted into a specifically human, nonbiological response mode applied to deal with all types of situations. Human material culture as derived from acquired and accumulated knowledge has gradually become an evolutionary force in itself, taking on a developmental characteristic for which humanity has become both creator and created. As I have said, contemporary technological achievements are no longer accompanied by significant physical changes that we observe to have occurred progressively in the past and that allowed hominins to adapt physically and mentally as they acquired technocognitive skills. In contrast to all other living beings, technology has largely liberated us from biological constraints that impeded us from moving beyond the limits imposed by Nature. Today, technology continues to develop ever more rapidly and seems to be leading our species in an unpredictable and spiraling progression toward an evermore uncertain future. Without a doubt, the advance of systematized technologies initially recognized to have been made from stone has revolutionized the human evolutionary process, offering new and innovative solutions to the ways in which we adapt to changing situations in relation to the environment and to each other. We are increasingly aware that because we are no longer conditioned by Nature, our technology-based adaptive responses are now breaching Nature's delicate and universal equilibrium. No longer governed by Nature, human technological solutions to situations facing modern society present the danger of destroying organic harmony established over millennia, even at times positioning us in conflict with positive survival strategies for ourselves and, indeed, for all other species with which we share the planet. I propose a look into prehistory to provide a particular standpoint from which to try to understand the mechanisms through which our distancing from Nature occurred in the first place. There is no doubt that this situation of alienation from Nature is intimately related to the exponential development of human technologies that now confers on our lives such depth, potential, intricacy and even – for many – angst. I propose to make this long-term vision accessible to you by looking to the past and into our shared prehistory as an opportunity to reconsider our present situation, seeing it from a global viewpoint, not only of how we have become what we are today but also of what we may become tomorrow.

BIPEDALISM AND TOOLMAKING: MILESTONES ALONG THE HUMAN PATHWAY

Throughout prehistory, different criteria traditionally provide referents to define what it actually means to be human. Of course, it is impossible to specify an exact point in time in which hominins became humans if we do not begin by defining what being human means. How do humans differ from other primate species that existed during and after the Late Pliocene? Key events are brought to the fore for the crucial role they are believed to have played in human evolution. These evolutionary events are conceptualized as so many stages through which we as *Homo sapiens*, the last representatives of our genus, have passed. From this simplified (linear) viewpoint, each evolutionary stage is seen to have contributed in one way or another to our current state of being. The fossil record demonstrates very concretely that the adoption of an upright bipedal stature and locomotion was a highly significant landmark in our evolutionary process as stated by Sockol and colleagues:[75]

> As predicted by Darwin... bipedalism is the defining feature of earliest hominins... and marks a critical divergence of the human lineage from the other apes.[75]

Today, the reasons for this important anatomical shift in early hominins are still unclear, and different (but not necessarily self-exclusive) hypotheses of physiological (biomechanical) and behavioral nature are put forward as explanations. To make sense from the evolutionary standpoint, research has focused on finding explanations grounded in the evolutionary advantages they could have provided to hominins relative to their quadrupedal ape counterparts. Climatic and environmental changes are often put forward as the driving forces that were causal to the anatomic modifications observed in hominins, such as those incurred by the adoption of bipedal locomotion. Compared with quadrupedal mammals, bipedalism – as practiced by members of the human lineage up to modern humans – required the complete reorganization of the skeleton and associated musculature.[76] The fossil record is patchy, however, and the finds of bipedal-relevant skeletal remains are partially preserved and often misshapen by their sedimentary contexts. Hominins underwent radical anatomical changes affecting pretty much their entire skeletal arrangement, while the musculature was likewise readjusted to accommodate the need to hold the torso in equilibrium and significant charges in weight were concentrated on the two legs and feet (alternately, during walking or running). The vertebral column developed curves and the positioning of its insertion into the skull shifted downward, the legs bones became longer and the size and position of the knees was modified, the distribution of the foot bones was readjusted and the pelvis changed orientation and became shorter and broader. It is difficult to reconstruct the processes involved in the adoption of bipedal stature and locomotion by early hominins, however:

> A bipedal primate is something revolutionary and does not represent just a slight variation from other types of hominoids. It must be ruled out that the entire skeleton

was drastically modified at once and, on the other hand, it is not easy to imagine how you can go from a quadruped to a biped little by little. An interesting hypothesis is that the initial modification that made possible a principle of bipedal locomotion affected the orientation of the iliac wing. A simple change in this, which would move to looking more laterally, would provide a certain abduction capacity, which is one of the bases for standing. If walking on two legs increased the chances of survival and reproduction, new modifications would be selected later until they would affect the entire skeleton.[76]

A well-known paleoecological model initially referred to by A. Kortlandt[77] as the Rift Valley Theory describes this phenomenon. The idea was widely diffused after it was renamed the East Side Story (in 1983) by the famous French paleoanthropologist Y. Coppens.[78] At the time, the archeological record suggested that the emergence of bipedal hominins, such as Australopithecines and early Homo, coincided more or less with the important climatic shift to warmer and dryer climate conditions at the onset of the Quaternary Period. The theory draws a link between the climatic trends and the appearance of bipedal hominins, citing climatic isolation of territories situated to the east and to the west of the East African Rift Valley System (EARS) (see Figure 3.1). The tectonic processes responsible for the formation of the EARS, initiated some 25 Ma, would have maintained distinct environmental contexts on either side of the rift with dry conditions giving way to the spread of savannah-type landscapes on the east side while to the west, semitropical, wooded settings were maintained by more humid conditions. From this, the theory postulates that two distinct hominin lineages emerged from a common ancestor: arboreal apes west of the rift and bipedal hominins (Australopithecines) to the east. The story goes that bipedalism evolved through the process of natural selection as a more advantageous gait for hominins moving through the high savannah grasses, enabling them to more easily spot prey over large distances. It was further suggested that adopting bipedal stature presented the additional advantage of liberating the upper limbs from locomotor tasks, thus allowing them to more easily transport, use and throw stones or wield wooden implements to capture prey in the tall savannah grasses (see Figure 3.2). It was also postulated that this posture would have facilitated carrying foodstuffs and even young children as the hominins moved through the landscape. Nevertheless, this paleoecological model eventually fell into disuse, notably following discoveries of some far more ancient bipedal hominins living on the western side of the rift valley.

Other theories relate to heat dissipation capacities (or thermoregulation),[79,80,81] hypothesizing that an upright posture would have enabled hominins to better regulate body heat because standing bodies receive less solar radiation (especially when the Sun is at its zenith). Additionally, an upright posture would mean less exposure to heat stored in the ground. At the same time, it allows a body to more fully benefit from refreshing breezes. From this perspective, it would have been easier for hominins to cover large distances in open landscapes even during the hottest hours of the day. Even if

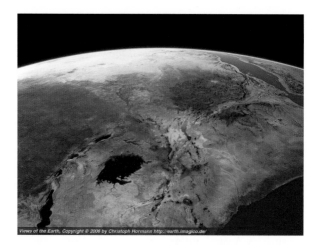

Views of the Earth, Copyright © 2006 by Christoph Hormann http://earth.imagico.de/

Figure 3.1
Views of the Earth Satellite image showing the East African Rift System (EARS), a disjointed tectonic and volcanic fault line some 6,000 kilometers long that extends from today's Mozambique in southeastern Africa to the Ethiopian Afar Triangle. A contiguous rifting system (once considered related to the EARS) extends to the northwest up into the Middle East. Continental rifting is a complex geological phenomenon, displacing plates of the Earth's crust and resulting in the formation of a more or less adjoining system of geologic fault lines (rifts). The rifts composing the EARS range from 3 to 100 kilometers wide and can reach up to several hundred meters deep. Seafloor spreading and plate tectonics led the Saudi Arabian Peninsula to separate from Africa as it pulled away from the Somalian and Nubian plates. This activity generated volcanic activity, further opening faulted areas that eventually created river systems and lake-filled areas. (Copyright ©2006 Christoph Hormann http://earth .imagico.de/)

Figure 3.2
Open savannah landscape in the Fejej region of Ethiopia (Lake Turkana-Omo basin) in the East African Rift Valley. (Photo by Deborah Barsky)

the first bipedal hominins evolved in mosaic environments, they may still have needed to cross through open areas of patchy vegetation.[76] Looking to thermoregulatory considerations, P. E. Wheeler established a connection between bipedalism, the loss of functional body hair and the development of an operative sweating mechanism,[80,82] proposing that sweating on naked skin benefits the body by optimizing airflow to standing bodies.[83] At the same time, increased locomotor efficiency and lowered heat stress advanced for bipedal hominins compared to quadrupedals[84,85] would have had the additional benefit of reducing food and water requirements. However, subsequent research shows that bipedalism would not have significantly increased foraging time for hominins and that it is unlikely that they would carry out lengthy displacements in the landscape during the hottest times of the day. Furthermore, most of the finds indicate that hominins lived in water-rich environments with abundant resources (both meat and vegetation). So while thermoregulation remains an important consideration for the advantages it afforded to hominins in dealing with heat (especially in open landscapes), it may not in itself provide satisfactory reasoning to explain why hominins adopted bipedal stature.[85]

Applying a biomechanical approach, research has also compared the energy cost efficiency of different locomotor strategies, advancing the theory that bipedalism could have been favored in the early human lineage because it was less "costly" than quadrupedal walking. Comparative analyses found that human walking expends 75 percent less energy than both quadrupedal and bipedal walking in chimpanzees (both of equal expenditure for these primates).[75] While anatomical dissimilarities (especially the pelvis and hind limb morphologies) and kinematics (muscle activation required in movement) certainly played an important role in favoring bipedalism in early humans, more fossils are still needed to demonstrate energy efficiency as a fundamental factor in the emergence of bipedal hominins.[75] In relation to body temperature regulation, it appears important to consider that the reorganization of the skeletal architecture provided new configurations for cerebral blood circulation, allowing the brain to cool more effectively, perhaps favoring (or enabling) its expansion (long after the emergence of bipedalism) in early Homo some 2.8 Ma.

> Expansion in cranial capacity developed along with a new pattern of cerebral blood circulation. Gravitational forces on blood draining from the brain differ in quadrupedal animals versus bipedal animals; therefore, when humans stand bipedally, most blood drains into veins at the back of the neck, which form a complex system around the spinal column. Savanna-dwelling hominins with this network of veins had a way to cool a bigger brain, allowing for an increased brain size, and further contributing to hominin flexibility in moving into and being active in new habitats with wide-ranging conditions.[86]

Interestingly, this period also coincided with genetic changes affecting the brain in relation to improved capacity to use oxygen[87] that are appreciated in terms of benefits provided for endurance-related tasks (such as long-distance running). If we consider that toolmaking hominins were probably gaining free time as they became more efficient in accessing resources, we may also contemplate the role of socialization in supporting bipedal stature and comportments. In this view, the bipedal proxy was advantageous to hominins as they organized themselves into more complex social group configurations, perhaps even practicing longer-distance food expeditions (that could have included hunting, although there is no direct evidence in the early fossil record of this behavior). Therefore, while bipedalism is widely recognized as one of the most (if not *the* most) important early events in the human story, the reasons for its emergence in early hominins remain to be fully understood. In any case, it is certain that contingency ruled the selective evolutionary processes that we know to be multifaceted and closely linked with climate, landscapes and wildlife interactions.

Let us turn now to the contexts in which these events took place and some of the most significant fossil finds that have allowed specialists to formulate their ideas about our ancestral heritage (this overview is based on data from the Smithsonian National Museum of Natural History and a range of published works). See Figure 3.3. To date, the African continent has yielded the earliest hominin species, and it is also the only continent that records the primate *Homo* transition. Over thousands of years, the waterways of the EARS have provided ideal environments for all species of life. Huge sections of the rift's thick formations of fluvial-lacustrine sediments are exposed along the fault lines of this system, providing an exceptionally rich fossil and archeological record within a well-defined stratigraphic context. Thanks to the intermittent accumulation of beds of volcanic ash or layers of effusive lava, the age of the sedimentary sequences bearing the paleontological and archeological materials can be evaluated using chronometric dating methods based (as we saw in Chapter 2) on the measurable deterioration or transformation of certain isotopes they contain. This particular geological context has resulted in an ideal environment for the preservation and accessibility of fossils and artifacts made by previously existing hominins. The discoveries made within this "readable" succession of geological strata are most conveniently contextualized by radiometric dating of the volcanic elements they contain. For this reason, some areas of the EARS, such as the Omo River and Lake Turkana Basin in Ethiopia and Kenya, the Awash and Hadar regions of northern Ethiopia and Olduvai Gorge in Tanzania, have been favored for intensive explorations by archeologists since as early as the 1950s. Still today, archeological surveys and excavations in these regions provide the foremost source of human and animal fossils in association with cultural artifacts ascribed to all periods of human prehistory and beyond.

Among the different species of hominins known to have roamed these African landscapes, gracile Australopithecines (*Australopithecus afarensis*) present both ape and humanlike features. Different forms of Australopithecines survived in mixed environments through periods of shifting climatic conditions for hundreds of thousands of years. The Afar region in Ethiopia whose name is derived from local tribespeople is a

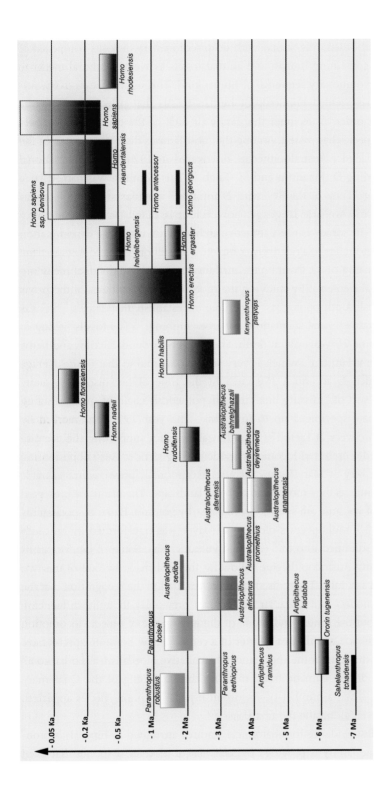

Figure 3.3

Chronology for known hominin species (as of the year 2021). The taxonomical links of oldest hominins (in black) to the human lineage are still unclear. The robust Australopithecines (*Paranthropus*, in green) were contemporary with gracile Australopithecines (in red) and the first members of the genus *Homo*. The genus *Homo* (in blue) to which our own species belongs (*Homo sapiens*) has recently been enlarged by the addition of a number of new species. (Modified by Deborah Barsky after *La nouvelle histoire de nos origines*. Science & Vie Hors Série 285, December 2018, p. 11) sunken triangular landmass (the Afar Triangle) formed by the triple rift junction. It is a graben (a depression bordered by faults) with deep sedimentary deposits composed of silt, clays and sands containing human and animal fossils as well as cultural evidence covering the entire evolutionary sequence of humankind. Throughout years of investigation, the region has yielded hundreds of human fossils that paleoanthropologists continue to study in order to decipher the nature of each of the evolutionary phases through which our species has passed. Among the most famous discoveries made in the Hadar region is the slender Australopithecine discovered in 1974 by an international research group including D. Johanson and M. Taieb.[88] This hominin was named Lucy after the Beatles song "Lucy in the Sky with Diamonds," popular at the time it was discovered. In the local Amharic language, however, it is called Dinknesh, meaning "you are marvelous." Its somewhat less attractive archeological catalogue denomination is AL 288-1.[89] This find refers to a relatively complete 3.2-million-year-old *Australopithecus afarensis* skeleton consisting of 52 fossil bones attributed to a single individual including cranial and postcranial elements. By studying the morphological attributes of the pelvis and femur bones, paleoanthropologists were able to establish that Lucy's gait was bipedal while she retained some adaptations for tree climbing.[90] The fossils belong to a female who was some 20 years old at death. She weighed around 25 kilos and had a cranial capacity of only 500 cm^3, which is very small compared to that of the average modern human, which is around 1,350 cm^3. At the time of her discovery, many considered Lucy as a sort of "missing link" in a (hypothetical) chain of species leading from the older primate specimens up to first *Homo*. The year 1976 was marked by another important discovery at Laetoli[91,92] in Tanzania, again supporting the premise that bipedalism was the preferred locomotor mode among slender Australopithecines. This remarkable discovery by Mary Leakey includes exceptionally preserved tracks made by animals and hominins as they moved through the landscape. The prints are preserved in a hardened layer of volcanic ash spewed from a nearby volcano. Dated by potassium-argon to be around 3.7 million years old, the ash layer was transformed by rain into mud that eventually solidified into tuff (lithified volcanic ash). Some of the footprints were made by a young Australopithecine following the trail made by one of the two individuals identified as adults. These discoveries contributed to the recognition that the shift to bipedal locomotion took place far earlier than previously thought, influencing what was known about the timing and mode of the emergence of bipedal locomotion among African hominins. Over the last quarter of a century, new hominin species have been found, pushing the date for the appearance of facultative bipedalism as far back as 7 Ma, well before the drying climatic trend marking the beginning of the Quaternary Period. After around 4 Ma, a number of coexistent bipedal hominin species appeared, some of them later even alongside the first *Homo*.[93]

Currently, the oldest evidence for anatomical features attributed to bipedal locomotion in the Homininae family is provided by *Sahelanthropus tchadensis*, a species that lived some 7 Ma (during the Upper Miocene) in a mixed grassland and forested environment west of the East African Rift Valley.[4,94] Informally referred to as Toumaï (meaning *life's hope* in the local Dazaga language), this genus and species was discovered in 2001 in the Tchadian Djourab desert by a Franco-Chadian team led by the French paleontologist M. Brunet. The specimen exhibits both modern and derived anatomical traits and while it is a candidate for one of the last ancestors common to both chimpanzees and humans, its link to the human lineage remains to be elucidated. With a cranial capacity comparable to that of modern chimpanzees (350 cm^3), it presents a rather elongated skull and prominent brow ridges, yet some of its other features, such as the relatively small canine teeth, appear to indicate some affiliation with later hominins. The occipital orifice (*foramen magnum*, where the spinal cord exits the cranium) positioned beneath the skull indicates a bipedal gait.[95] Toumaï's discovery and additional finds made west of the East African Rift Valley have progressively led scientists to change their hypotheses supporting an exclusively eastern origin for the first bipedal hominins. Earlier in 1995 in Koro Toro (Chad), M. Brunet and his team reported hominin finds now known as *Australopithecus bahrelghazali* (or *Abel*) with an age evaluated around 3.5–3 Ma.[96] Discovered before Toumaï, this hominin was the first to be identified west of the EARS and was described from only a few fossils, including a jaw fragment with several teeth. This hominin lived in a mixed environment close to water (lakeside, forest with open grassy areas).[97]

In 2001, a new species of Homininae dating to some 6 Ma was recognized by a Franco-Kenyan team directed by B. Senut and M. Pickford after finds (a series of teeth, a femur and phalanges) made in the Tugen Hills in Kenya.[98] Like Toumaï, this hominin (named *Orrorin tugenensis*, or *Millenium ancestor*) lived in open forest landscapes, and some of its anatomical features (for example, the femur) indicate bipedal stature[99,100] while some other characteristics (such as the length and shape of the first phalange) suggest tree climbing. Moving up through time and filling out the gaps, we encounter another ancestor some 5.8–5.6 million years old, discovered in 1997 in the Middle Awash Valley (Ethiopia) by Y. Haile-Selassie. More remains found some years later enabled specialists to determine that this hominin lived in mixed forest and grasslands settings. It was finally named *Ardipithecus kadabba* (by Y. Haile-Selassie, G. Suwa, and T. White), meaning *basal family ancestor* in the Afar language.[101] Among the postcranial fossils, toe and pelvis bone morphologies suggest that it maintained an upright stature, buttressing still further the hypothesis of an early emergence for bipedal locomotion. *Ardipithecus ramidus* (commonly referred to as *Ardi*) is a more recent hominin from Middle Awash and Gona in Ethiopia that presents features of bipedal gait some 4.4 Ma (in the Afar language, *Ardi* means *ground* and *ramid* signifies *root* while *pithecus* denotes *ape* in Latin). Importantly, its short pelvis with laterally oriented ilia is very similar to our own.[102] Ardi was first described in 1994 by T. White, G. Suwa and B. Asfaw, who later reported more numerous fossils.[103] Living in a wooded environment, Ardi's extraordinarily long arms indicate a tree-climbing adaptation, and this hominin preserves features reminiscent of both apes and Australopithecines.

Somewhat more recent *Australopithecus* specimens named *Australopithecus anamensis* (*anam* means *lake* in the local Turkana language), dating from 4.2 to 3.8 Ma, are now well documented from the Lake Turkana Basin (Kenya) and Middle Awash (Ethiopia). Represented at first by only a partial tibia discovered at Kanapoi (Turkana, Kenya) in 1965 by an American team led by B. Patterson, this hominin remained in debate until further finds were uncovered after new excavations at the site nearly thirty years later under the direction of Meave Leakey. This hominin has also been shown to have lived in mixed landscapes of open floodplain, gallery forest and dry shrub lands in other parts of the Lake Turkana Basin and elsewhere in Ethiopia.[93,104,105,106] Although some of its arm and wrist bones indicate sustained tree climbing, the morphology of the tibia evokes a bipedal gait. A more recent discovery of a nearly complete skull indicates that it may have rubbed shoulders with another Australopithecine, *Australopithecus afarensis*.[107] This renowned hominin described in detail, as we have seen from the famous finds of Lucy at Hadar (Ethiopia) in 1978, is relatively well known[89] because it existed for at least 1 million years (from 3.85 to 2.95 Ma)! Numerous remains of these gracile Australopithecines are reported from a number of East African sites (Ethiopia, Kenya, Tanzania). With a small brain size of around 500 cm^3, these hominins were effective bipeds that also maintained some arboreal adaptations. Analogous Australopithecine forms are documented from South Africa under the name *Australopithecus africanus* (3.3–2.1 Ma). The latter hominin was named and described very early by R. Dart (its name means *southern ape of Africa*) and is known from a few sites in South Africa (Taung, Sterkfontein, Makapansgat).[108,109,110] Dart's discovery in 1924 of the famous skull known as the *Taung child* was in fact one of the earliest hominin discoveries ever made. With a cranial capacity of only around 450 cm^3, these Australopithecines thrived in savannah landscapes and were attracted to more humid, water-rich settings, such as river or lake edges and flood plains, certainly for the resources offered by these locations.

Another, very different hominin, this time from West Turkana (Kenya), is described from a quasi-complete skull of *Kenyanthropus platyops* (3.5 Ma) discovered in 1999 by a research team led by Meave Leakey and colleagues from the Kenya National Museum.[111] Also bipedal and living in mixed grassland and forested environments, its name (literally *flat-faced man of Kenya*) designates a separate genus whose features differentiate it from both Australopithecines and early *Homo*. Adding to this ever-increasing list of early hominin species are numerous finds attributed to more robust forms of Australopithecines known as *Paranthropus*. These hominins shared the landscape with early forms of our own genus (*Homo*) over a long period of time. The earliest known *Homo* appeared in Africa some 2.8 Ma[23] (*Homo habilis*, a name meaning *handyman* because this hominin was long thought to be the first to make stone tools) and lived in the same savannah environments with *Paranthropus* (meaning *beside Man, Paranthropus boisei* in East Africa and *Paranthropus robustus* in South Africa) for a period spanning from around 2.7 Ma to as recently as 1.2 Ma. (see Figure 3.4). The *Paranthropus* were powerfully built and had a cranial capacity between 410–530 cm^3. Their curious skull features include very marked crests and arches

Figure 3.4

Paranthropus boisei skull (KNM ER 406) from Koobi Fora (Kenya) discovered by R. Leakey and H. Mutua in 1969. This robust hominin cranium has a projecting wide face with brow ridges. Its strongly marked facial features, crests and arches were designed to support the musculature, and the massive teeth needed for chewing the plant fibers in its diet. (Bjørn Christian Tørrissen at the Nairobi National Museum, creativecommons.org)

designed to support the heavy facial musculature they developed for grinding fibrous plant matter (nuts, seeds, hard fruit). Their faces were wide and prognathic and their molars and premolars were substantially large. Finds of *Paranthropus robustus* (1.8–1.2 Ma) from South Africa were first discovered at Kromraai in 1938 by R. Broom.[112] The *Paranthropus boisei* type specimen, *Zinjanthropus* (archeological catalogue name: OH-5), was discovered by Mary Leakey at Olduvai Gorge (Tanzania) in 1959;[113] it lived from 2.3 to 1.2 Ma. The *Paranthropus aethiopicus* (2.7–2.3 Ma) from the Lake Turkana–Omo River region in northern Kenya and southern Ethiopia was first described by C. Arambourg and Y. Coppens in 1968.[114] In 1985, A. Walker and R. Leakey found the famous Black Skull at West Turkana, contributing to the description of these robust hominins. Completing the early hominin family, *Australopithecus garhi* (2.5 Ma), whose cranial and postcranial remains were found in the 1990s at Bouri in the Middle Awash (Ethiopia) by B. Asfaw and T. White, also lived in the same area and has a chronological range overlapping with early *Homo*.[115]

In this context of branching hominin evolution, it is evidently impossible to establish a precise moment in time for the acquisition of bipedal locomotion among some ancient hominin species. However, we can surmise that there was not one single and unique missing link in the move to upright stature and bipedal locomotion. Rather, a series of forms presenting a range of evolutionary adaptations did eventually lead some hominins to favor this particular trait. What we can infer is that the tendency to adopt bipedal locomotion began perhaps as early as 7 Ma among some African hominins thriving in mixed environments. While the shift to habitual bipedal locomotion was thought to have been achieved in the framework of the climate and landscape changes from forest to savannah, marking the onset of the Quaternary Period, in fact, the earliest evidence indicates that bipedal hominins thrived in different types of environments, including settings with ample tree cover. This implies that ecological information is important − but not necessarily determinant − for understanding the emergence of a given trait or behavior. In addition, given the (growing) complexity of the hominin evolutionary framework, it seems plausible to propose that bipedal locomotion could have emerged more than once. Daniel E. Lieberman proposes three stages in the adoption of bipedal gait along the human ancestral lineage. The first stage concerns the earliest "facultative" bipedal hominins with anatomic features also indicating habitual tree climbing (*Sahelanthropus tchadensis*, *Orrorin tugenensis* and *Ardipithecus kadabba* and *Ardipithecus ramidus*). The second stage includes the *Australopithecus* who, while also retaining adaptations for tree climbing, were *effective, habitual bipeds*. The third and final stage corresponds to the appearance of the genus *Homo* with species who *walked and ran like living humans*.[90,91] Questions remain about the timing and conditions under which bipedalism emerged in some primate species. Whatever the scenario, the fossil record shows us that a range of environmental and social conditions favored bipedalism through processes of natural selection until it was fully adopted and perfected by early members of the human ancestry. The consequences of this adaptive choice included physical and behavioral changes that largely affected the human evolutionary trajectory.

4

THE EMERGENCE OF LOWER
PALEOLITHIC CULTURES

TOOLMAKING AND THE EMERGENCE OF CULTURE

Following the emergence of recognizable stone tools in Africa more than 3 million years ago (Ma) (the so-called Lomekwian industries),[24] the human evolutionary story continued to undergo countless transitions whose nature we endeavor to grasp from the sparse evidence left behind in the archeological record. We now perceive the evolution of early human populations as having occurred both diachronically and procedurally within the framework of the ongoing hominization process. As noted in Chapter 3, facultative bipedal locomotion is documented among some hominins living in Africa as early as 7–6 Ma and is considered an important evolutionary stage preceding intentional stone toolmaking. In this chapter, I explore the implications of this latter development in seeking to understand the significance of the role played by first technologies as a trigger force, leading humans to develop evermore complex systems of socialization needed to pass on technical know-how from generation to generation. In this diachronic process, humans increased their reliance on abstract thought processes that became multifaceted and even, through time, symbolic. Because learning to make complex tools requires at least some form of basic language,[61] it must ultimately be considered a behavior that guided our species toward modernity. Today, this unique evolutionary trajectory is at an apex point that is defined – now more than ever – by our heavy reliance on technology and its associated communication networks (see Chapter 8). By taking this step, we have increasingly distanced ourselves from Nature (even while remaining inexorably linked to Her), bringing our species to face new challenges as we embark on an entirely new (r)evolutionary process that some have called *humanization*.[45] It just may be that, in the next phases of human development, survival will depend on our successful assimilation of lessons from the past should we decide to act on the new courses of action they now imply. We, as a species, appear ready to exceed biological reliance, at least to some extent, gaining an advantage over natural selection by transforming technology into culture and creating very different realities from the ones we have experienced in the past. Nevertheless, we may concede that the warning signs are telling us that the next stages of our evolutionary pathway will be accomplished only if we conscientiously register, accept and appropriately act on the myriad of technical and social acquisitions gained throughout the earlier phases of our development.

Remnants of human material culture discovered in prehistoric archeological contexts reflect a world of unseen human behavioral traits that are the gist of archeological research. Archeologists develop scientific hypotheses based on plausible evaluations of empirical evidence while avoiding speculation and religious interpretations. In this dialectical process of knowledge through discovery, we have come to learn that Paleolithic cultures often evolved following surprisingly similar pathways even in widely distant areas of the world. That is to say, some of the major technological milestones appear in the same order along this route – although often within very different time frames – almost as though each achievement precluded the next in a type of structural continuity. In this sense, prehistoric cultural evolution frequently maintains an overall sequencing in spite of its diachronic representations. But how and where did all this begin? The oldest evidence of human material culture – the so-called Oldowan[65] technocomplex – appears in Africa, but we know that it also spread into Eurasia at a relatively early date. By studying ancient Oldowan stone tool kits, archeologists have concluded that hominins very early were capable of producing sharp-edged flakes by way of organized stone-knapping schemes with surprising dexterity. Nascent stone tool manufacture brought into play important cognitive constituents, which distinguish human-made from animal-made tools, such as memory, tradition and, progressively, the capacity to reproduce sequential actions based on predefined mental templates. In a broad sense, the first hominin-made tools may fit into our notion of *culture* since the methods used to make them were acquired through systems of social learning repeated and perfected over generations.

Toolmaking on a significantly large scale is considered a major breakthrough in the human evolutionary process. There is no doubt that freeing the forelimbs enabled by bipedal stature would have allowed hominins to more efficiently carry and wield stones and other objects available to them in the environment. In some situations, such behaviors could have presented survival-related advantages, thus transforming this conduct into a sustainable adaptive response to environmental and/or social pressures. Unquestionably, toolmaking deepened human polymorphism, allowing for adaptive flexibility in resource acquisition strategies and helping hominins to confront and deal with different situations. By bringing into play nongenetic and nonbiological response modes, humans began to act and react by modifying matter and, by extension, altered the organization of their own cognitive processes. Since its emergence, toolmaking has developed exponentially through time into an indispensable strategy of human survival. Today, we as a species rely entirely on our capacity to make, use, employ and understand a huge set of technosocial codes stored within our cerebral databank.

A Brief Summary of the Oldowan Technocomplex

The Oldowan cultural period is temporally and geographically very extensive, spanning a cumulative time of around 2 million years in Africa and Eurasia. Despite its relative stability as a technocomplex, the Oldowan is marked by incremental technological improvements in which hominins progressed in their ability to manipulate and shape stone. Throughout the Oldowan, we distinguish only subtle innovations in tool kits (e.g., the creation of new morphologies and stone-knapping methods). Sometimes, this variability depends on the types of lithic raw materials available to the hominins because each reacted differently to intentional stone breakage. As time went on, the morphotechnical potential within Oldowan formal variability would eventually lead to innovations and more elaborate technical capabilities until the emergence of the subsequent technocomplex called the Acheulian.

Although many specialists continue to attribute the first stone tools only to early *Homo* (*Homo habilis*), data shows that the first recognizable stone tools predate this hominin's appearance. This means that other hominins present in the African landscape at the end of the Pliocene and into the Early Pleistocene (Australopithecines and *Paranthropus*) could also have been making and using stone tools. Outside of Africa, in Eurasia, we know little about the ancestry of the first Oldowan hominins.

Main characteristics of the Oldowan follow:

- The Oldowan cultural complex is attributed mainly to early *Homo* while other hominins, such as Australopithecines and *Paranthropus*, may also have been toolmakers.
- It represents the early stages of systematic stone tool manufacture.
- According to data available today, the chronogeographical framework for the Oldowan ranges from 2.6 to 1.75 Ma in Africa, 2 to 0.9 Ma in Asia and 1.4 to 1 Ma in Europe.
- The Oldowan onset coincides with an augmentation in hominin brain size that is sometimes attributed to higher meat intake noted in hominin diets.
- Relative to subsequent phases of human cultural evolution, the Oldowan is represented by few sites with low artifact density.
- Oldowan stone tool kits are composed mainly of small cores and flakes associated with large or very large-sized pounding tools, generally made on cobbles.
- The tools are generally nonstandardized without premeditated forms.
- None of the tools appears to have been clearly designed for hunting.
- Oldowan sites often yield fossil bones of large to medium-sized herbivores, sometimes displaying butchery marks made with stone tools.
- Raw material procurement reflects low hominin mobility and exploitation of local resources.
- There is no clear evidence for controlled use of fire.
- The sites are almost always in open-air contexts and do not show any clear structures.

The question is often raised as to whether we can really consider toolmaking as a specifically human trait when so many other animal species are also documented to make and use tools. Primates (i.e. chimpanzees, bonobos) are leading examples because they make and use tools both in controlled laboratory experiments and (sometimes) in the wild.[116] Traditionally, primate tool use has provided real-life models used to compare the "emergence phase" of stone toolmaking in our own species. But we ought to keep in mind that many different animals are known to make and use tools including birds, dolphins, elephants and sea otters.[117] Yet because of their physical and even genetic proximity to humans, primates are most often brought to mind when considering toolmaking among species other than humans. Without entering too deeply into this polemic, I think that we can focus on what seems to be the key question here: How and why did prehumans choose to develop such a high degree of reliance on toolmaking? Presently, the partial nature of the archeological record makes it very hard to determine whether the capacity to systematically knap stone into flakes and cobble tools occurred abruptly or progressively. Let us consider the alternative scenarios. Stone knapping is not a random activity; expertise and dexterity are required to deliver blows with adequate force and precision to enable flake extraction. The knapping of stone matrices (called *cores*) must be worked by delivering blows to areas presenting angles that are suitable for successfully removing stone chips (flakes). Accordingly, we may suppose that some hominins inadvertently (or haphazardly) learned the mechanical gestures required to successfully knap stone, in time noticing which systems are useful to produce sharp-edged flakes effectively from cores. Then this technical achievement could have been adopted (and even rapidly integrated through imitation/learning) into hominin socio-behavioral patterning. It is observed that the flake production strategies that characterize the Oldowan technocomplex are comparable to what a novice stone knapper would (intuitively) produce.

Archaic stone toolmaking and tool use emerged in Africa sometime between 4 and 3 Ma, a period for which there is little material evidence. The oldest tool kits are characterized by mainly unifacial and unidirectional stone management strategies,[118] recognized as simple but organized systems. These techniques are already attested, for example, in the oldest stone tool kits known to humankind (3.3 Ma in Kenya, in Lomekwi 3 and 2.6 Ma in Ethiopia at Bokol Dora 1 in the Ledi Geraru research project area and Ounda Gona and Kada Gona localities in the Gona research project area [24,25,26,119,120,121]). But how did the techniques evolve? We might suppose that prehumans carrying, brandishing and pounding stone over millennia began *progressively* and *intentionally* to modify it into tools. It is plausible that, after having observed the features of stone fragments broken off accidentally during the earliest phases of stone use, hominins found these pieces useful for performing sustenance-related tasks. There would then have been a willingness (or readiness) to reproduce similar products *intentionally*, thus leading hominins (of different genuses and species) to invent the simple yet systematic stone-reduction methods known in the Oldowan. The presumption of a (probably very long) period of tool using (perhaps comparable to primate tool use) preceding intentional and sequential production of stone flakes from cores is sometimes referred to as "Mode 0" (or "homogeneity").[118] This is proposed as a period of tool use that (if it existed) is "invisible" in the archeological record because we cannot recognize human intervention on stone unless it displays at least some type of distinguishable system. Obviously, we cannot identify human action on erratically fragmented stones in the landscape because the breakage is entirely random. Nevertheless, archeologists working on this issue recently have been focusing their attention on stone-related percussive activities (such as throwing, pounding and hammering), similar to those observed among some primates (for example, in nut cracking), in an effort to develop new ways to recognize patterned traces of human pounding activities on stone.[66,122,123,124,125] Given this situation, we may expect to find evidence for the use-manufacture of stone even older than 3.3 Ma in the future. In any case, the fact that tool-using primates have never developed complex operative schemes close to those of the Oldowan suggests an evolutionary scheme wherein a "deviation" must have occurred, triggering the important shift from an initial phase of lithic tool use – shared by primates and early hominins – to a new level of systematic lithic tool production. This shift most certainly happened in early *Homo* but may also have occurred (at least to some extent) with Australopithecines and *Paranthropus*.

THE OLDOWAN TECHNOCOMPLEX AND THE BIRTH OF HUMAN TECHNOLOGIES

Evidently, what we broadly term the "Oldowan cultural complex" presently encompasses an enormous chronological and geographical framework.[126] The term *Oldowan* coined by L. Leakey in the 1960s derives from the eponymous Olduvai Gorge sites in Tanzania[113,127] (see Figure 4.1). Designated a UNESCO World Heritage Site in 1979, Olduvai Gorge constitutes a steep, branching ravine some 50 km long and up to 90 m deep that encloses abundant archeopaleontological localities within distinct archeostratigraphic layers (or Beds). Over the years, these sites have yielded some of the most important fossil and cultural records known today. The depositional sequence is composed of layers of fluvial-lacustrine sediment intercalated with layers of volcanic tuff covering a cumulative age range of nearly 2 million years. The archeological potential of Olduvai Gorge was first discovered in 1911 after which time (from 1931) the area was continuously excavated by members of the Leakey family who discovered, researched and amply published a large body of finds. Among the numerous interdisciplinary publications, the monographical work on the stone tools written by Mary Leakey and published in 1971[65] still stands out today as a reference for defining and classifying Oldowan and Acheulian tools. Currently, ongoing excavations at Olduvai Gorge by

Figure 4.1
General view of the thick depositional sequence at Olduvai Gorge (Tanzania) with its successive archeopaleontological layers that record nearly 2 million years of human and animal evolution in a controlled chronological and climatic context. (Photo by Deborah Barsky)

teams of international experts are employing modern technologies revealing significant new information about environmental and human evolutionary processes that occurred there over the last 2 million years.[128] To date, the Olduvai Gorge sequence has provided more than 60 fossil hominins and an exceptionally complete record of faunal and cultural materials, offering a quasicontinuous record of human evolution throughout most of the Quaternary Period. Its abundant artifact record has made it a long-standing reference for comparative research in archeology, paleontology, biochronology, paleo-ecology and more.

Oldowan tool kits are mostly characterized by small-sized cores and flakes (stone-knapping waste) that are generally associated with a range of larger-sized tools used for percussion, sometimes called "cobble tools." The assemblages are qualified as poorly standardized because they include few (or no) intentionally shaped tools – that is, to say, recurring tool "types" that were clearly manufactured according to a template – that could reflect some type of formal planning. Nevertheless, the ability to make and use small, sharp-edged stone flakes is thought to have provided early *Homo* with the advantage of more rapidly and effectively accessing a wide range of resources from their environments. Studies of African Oldowan tool kits older than those from the Olduvai Gorge (Bed I) have revealed that the tools reflect a remarkably high degree of technical know-how, proving that these artisans were capable of systematically executing operative stone-knapping methods for producing small sharp-edged flakes and pounding tools. Beyond Olduvai Gorge, a number of discoveries of stone tool kits significantly older than the oldest layers of the eponymous Olduvai Gorge site –

especially since the 1990s – have been made in Africa, extending the basal age of the Oldowan from around 1.8 Ma to more than 3 million years old. Among these, discoveries from Ethiopia have had an enormous impact, significantly changing our ideas about the first hominin toolmakers and their cognitive capacities including those from the Afar region of Ethiopia at East Gona (sites EG 10 and EG 12) and Ounda Gona (sites OGS 6 and OGS 7)[25,119,120,121] and the Bokol Dora 1 site (Lower Awash Valley, near Ledi Geraru where the oldest known *Homo* is documented).[23,26]

These and other discoveries are slowly changing the (anthropocentric) hypothesis that the ability to make tools systematically was the exclusive domain of our own genus *Homo*. In spite of the tenacity of this postulate, which is common in many textbooks about prehistory, the idea that hominin species other than *Homo* could be responsible for making and using stone tools is not new. In fact, as early as the 1970s, pre-*Homo* hominins were postulated as possible or probable candidates for having made stone tools and/or cut-marked bones found in ancient contexts, attesting to the use of stone for butchery purposes. As we have seen, a range of small-brained, bipedal Australopithecines (including *Paranthropus*) presenting a mosaic of primitive and derived traits, roamed the landscapes prior to, during and after the emergence of first *Homo* some 2.8 Ma. At the 3.3-million-year-old old Lomekwi 3 site in West Turkana (Kenya), for example, the stone artifacts are in spatiotemporal association with *Australopithecus* and *Kenyanthropus platyops* (a contemporary specimen found nearby).[24] Also, the *Paranthropus boisei* (Zinjanthropus, the so-called Nutcracker Man) type specimen OH-5 from Olduvai Gorge (Bed I) was discovered in 1959 in broad association with primitive stone tools.[127] In 1987, *Paranthropus aethiopicus* and *Paranthropus boisei* were claimed to be associated with stone tools found in the Omo-Turkana basin (Ethiopia).[129] Concerning the ancient finds from Gona, it is noteworthy that *Australopithecus garhi* fossils are found in broad territorial and chronological association with the Gona archeological sites (from Bouri, Hata Formation, Middle Awash Valley, Ethiopia).[115] In South Africa, stone tools have been associated with *Paranthropus* fossils in Member 5 of the Sterkfontein site (South Africa) with an age of between 2 and 1.7 million years old.[130]

It is important to consider, therefore, that early *Homo* shared the African savannah environments with a variety of other hominins over thousands of years: the gracile Australopithecines (from ca. 4 Ma to 2.5 Ma) and remarkably, the *Paranthropus* (from ca. 2.8 Ma up to 1.2 Ma). Consequently, *Paranthropus* species actually coexisted alongside *Homo* not only during the unfolding of the Oldowan but even after the onset of the more advanced technocomplex, known as the Acheulian that followed it. Surprising as this may appear and as we shall see throughout this book, our genus has in fact coexisted with other hominin species throughout most of its existence! While some researchers link the appearance of systematic toolmaking behaviors to external driving agents, such as changing climates and landscapes (environmental determinism), others claim higher variability both in the triggering forces causing adaptive pressures and in the range of responses by which the hominins were capable of dealing with them.[131] With technology, both biological *and* cultural factors contributed to cumulative adaptive flexibility in hominins, increasing the range of responses they were capable of providing as they faced different types of selective pressures. The paleoanthropological data signals changes in some hominin diets from around 3 Ma, especially a significant increase in meat intake. This is thought to have led to anatomical changes, most notably in the masticatory apparatus and overall skull morphologies but also in the unprecedented brain development noted after the appearance of early *Homo*. The coetaneous relationship that exists between anatomy and technology is accompanied thus by this shift to a protein-enriched diet, which was, very probably, facilitated by the innovation and widespread use of stone tool technologies.[132] The unprecedented expansion of the hominin brain transformed it into an *energetically expensive organ* whose requirements could be met by meat-enriched diets, which in turn, were made more feasible thanks to technological innovation. The archeological record confirms the coevolution of these phenomena in which stone tools enabled hominins to carve out their own niche relative to other large carnivores, even gaining primary access to the most choice portions of large herbivore carcasses they were scavenging or, as some postulate, capturing (for example by ambush predation).[133,134]

With all of the changes in hominin anatomical features, other signals from the archeological record gleaned from the animal fossils, for example, highlight the increasing importance of toolmaking in behaviors relating to the acquisition and processing of animal carcasses. In addition to the fossil bones displaying traces of butchery attributed to stone tools, the faunal spectrum in some cases is limited enough to suggest selectivity in the choice of animals consumed.[135] By around 2 Ma, the high protein levels offered by increased meat intake enabled hominins to reach their necessary daily caloric quota far more rapidly and efficiently than a dietary strategy strongly dominated by plant foraging. The choice to develop technologies to access resources had other repercussions on human cerebral features, which

> gained in complexity in synchronicity with the evolution of technological systemics. In relation to other animals, expansion of the neocortex permitted by cerebral asymmetry and laterality in the human brain, and the ensuing elevated degree of cephalization, is indeed often attributed to human reliance upon tool-making as a survival strategy.[118]

Furthermore,

> Cognition (or mental processing) demonstrated in object manipulation clearly involves problem solving that goes beyond reactive instincts or uncontrolled emotional responses. Recently, links between language and manual praxis have received support from cognitive neuroscience, with findings demonstrating that the brain's linguistic areas (Broca and Wernicke) also play a role in many non-linguistic behaviors including tool use... As toolmaking evolved through time, so did the need for longer and more complex demonstrative – and probably also linguistic – explanations, achieved through teaching. ....[118]

Table 4.1
Global temporal range of the Oldowan technocomplex (modified after Barsky[126])

		Combined duration	
Africa	2.6–1.75 Ma		
Europe	1.4–1.0 Ma	$\rightarrow$	1.7 million years
Asia	2.0–0.9 Ma		

Through this process, hominins would have gained more free time compared to those species following strictly plant-based dietary strategies. As the increase in relative abundance of stone tools in the archeological record shows us, it is evident that hominins were consecrating more time to expanding their nascent technological creativity and communicating it to their offspring. Less than a quarter of a century or so since the landmark Oldowan discoveries at the Gona research area,[25] interest in the origins of human technologies has since grown exponentially. Passionate inquiry into the origins of human technologies continues to be fueled by spectacular new discoveries and (as we saw in Chapter 2) by studies applying innovative methodologies to process data obtained from both new and previously known archeological occurrences.

FIRST MIGRATIONS: THE OLDOWAN EXPANSION

Oldowan archeological sites are currently known from several regions of Eurasia where data now extends the upper temporal boundary of this cultural complex to around 1 Ma, making for a global time frame of nearly 2 million years in duration (calculated from the first appearance of the Acheulian in each region). See Table 4.1.

Oldowan sites in Eurasia have an age range of around 2–1 Ma. In Western Europe, the oldest of these sites, which are (mainly) situated around the Mediterranean basin, date to around 1.6–1.2 Ma.[136,137,138,139,140] Very ancient dates are also being reported from China where Oldowan sites are attributed an age close to 2 Ma.[141] It is important to recognize how greatly these discoveries, most of which have been made only very recently, have changed our ideas about the first peopling of Eurasia. When I began to study prehistory in the early 1990s as a master's degree student in France, few prehistorians sustained the premise that hominins could have settled outside of Africa earlier than around 500 (Ka). A popular theory published in 1994 proposed a "short chronology,"[142] arguing that solid evidence for human settlement in Europe becomes evident only after this period. In spite of this, a persistent few continued to argue that hominins could in fact have maintained a lasting presence in Europe – perhaps even as early as 1 Ma. This hypothesis was supported by the numerous collections of archaic

Figure 4.2
Medieval cathedral at the Dmanisi site in the Georgian Republic. Located southwest of Tbilisi, the medieval city of Dmanisi was built in the ninth and tenth centuries on a basalt hill at the confluence of two rivers. The Lower Pleistocene formations (1.81–1.7 Ma) situated beneath its foundations have yielded a rich collection of fossil hominins in association with large mammals and Oldowan stone tools. (Photo by Deborah Barsky)

stone tools amassed over the years from high-altitude alluvial terraces of river systems all over Europe and whose age, generally estimated (at the time) based on geomorphological criteria, was thought to be in excess of around 1 Ma. In addition to difficulties in obtaining reliable dates for tools found in such open-air contexts, the integrity of the river terrace collections is often adversely affected by modern-day agricultural or urban activities. Today, however, such obstacles are being significantly reduced thanks to improved dating technologies and more efficient artifact collection and conservation strategies.[143] In the 1980s, one European cave site, the Vallonnet Cave situated in the south of France near the Italian border (Menton, Alpes-de-Haute-Provence), claimed a controlled Oldowan occupation around 1 million years old (the site has since been redated more precisely to 1.2 Ma).[140,144] In the 1980s, especially from the 1990s, a series of unprecedented discoveries shook the world of prehistory, completely changing what we know about the first hominin migrations out of Africa.

In 1983, excavations of grain storage silos in the medieval buildings and structures at the Dmanisi site (Republic of Georgia in the Caucasus) yielded teeth from an extinct form of rhinoceros identified by the Georgian paleontologist A. Vekua (see Figure 4.2). This site, situated on a promontory bordered by two rivers, had long been the source of important finds dating from the Bronze Age and up to medieval and even more recent historical times. In 1984, primitive stone tools associated with extinct animal fossils at an age of around 1.8 Ma were finally confirmed as ancient Paleolithic discoveries.[145,146,147,148] Thereafter, between 1991 and 2005 under the direction of

D. Lordkipanitze (general director of the Georgian National Museum), well-preserved hominin fossils were unearthed in unprecedented abundance (for this time frame) and integrity. These hominin finds show such a variety of anatomical features that precise species identification is very complex. Initially attributed to Homo ergaster, the Dmanisi hominins have also been claimed to show features bringing them taxonomically closer to the older and smaller-brained Homo habilis. Their cranial capacity, ranging from 700 to 800 cm³) as well as their sexual dimorphism and the variability of their anatomical characteristics finally led paleoanthropologists to agree on the creation of new species: Homo georgicus.[149] Whether the hominins present at Dmanisi could be descendants of Homo habilis and ancestors to Asian Homo erectus is debated. The abundant stone tools found with these 1.8 million-year-old hominins fit clearly within the Oldowan technocomplex and are similar to their older African counterparts.[150] Finally, and perhaps most importantly, Dmanisi provided indisputable evidence to prove that hominins were indeed present outside of Africa even far earlier than 1 Ma. Moreover, contrary to all expectations, the hominins discovered at Dmanisi did not resemble the supposed candidate for the first out of Africa Homo erectus, a hominin (generally associated with the Acheulian technocomplex) that was only just appearing in Africa[151] and Southeast Asia[152] in this time range (1.9–1.8 Ma).

Around the same time, additional discoveries from Spain were contributing greatly to the reconfiguration of the mindset concerning the first hominin occupations of Europe. In the early 1990s, highly significant finds including clearly human-made stone tools were reported, for example, from the Fuente Nueva 3 and Barranco León sites situated only a few kilometers from the town of Orce (Andalusia). These finds signaled the beginning of years of systematic excavations at these two sites that continue today.[153] The sites are located in the once lake-filled Baza sector of the Guadix-Baza Basin, a depression explored by paleontologists since the 1970s for its fertile record of large and small mammal fossils. The area provides a thick archeostratigraphic record dating from the later Miocene up to the late Middle Pleistocene (7–0.3 Ma). The age of these two Oldowan archeological sites has been assessed using biochronology of large and small mammals correlated with magnetostratigraphy.[154,155,156,157,158] Concerning the latter, reverse polarity obtained from both depositional sequences allows specialists to allot them to the Matuyama chron. By refining this information with data from biochronology, paleontology and U-series and ESR dating, their respective ages are now fixed at 1.2 and 1.4 Ma.[159,160] A hominin deciduous tooth fragment from Barranco León was published in 2013 and presently constitutes the oldest hominin remain in Europe.[136] These two sites have also yielded exceptionally rich large and small mammal assemblages and very significant Oldowan stone tool assemblages. The lithic assemblages comprise small-sized flakes and cores knapped from flint nodules and larger-sized pounding tools made from limestone cobbles and blocks.[161,162]

Also during the 1990s, the team working at the Sierra de Atapuerca (near Burgos, Castilla y León, Spain) announced startling new discoveries of a new species of hominin associated with fauna and stone artifacts from level TD6 (the "Aurora stratum") at the Gran Dolina site with an age exceeding 0.78 Ma[163,164] (this age has since been further refined to between 772–949 Ka).[165] This hominin coined a new species called *Homo antecessor* for its mosaic of anatomical traits. This hominin is believed to be the closest common ancestor to Neandertals and *Homo sapiens*.[166] Later, in 2007, the Atapuerca team reported even older hominin (*Homo* sp.) finds from the Sima del Elefante site (level TE9) dating to 1.3 Ma and associated with stone tools and faunal remains.[138] In light of the controversies raised by these highly important discoveries, an international congress was held in 1995 in the town of Orce under the coordination of J. Gibert. During the congress, finds from the Orce Oldowan sites and other ancient Eurasian occurrences were presented to members of the scientific community.[167] The antiquity of the human exodus from Africa and into Eurasia was discussed heatedly long into the night with some scientists still refuting the increasing body of data coming out of these occurrences. Today, evermore numerous archeological sites bear witness to the long chronological framework for the first human occupation of Europe. Although little is known about the first representatives of the human clade responsible for these occurrences outside of Africa, it seems likely that they were sharpening their social skills as they reaped the advantages from their technologies, successfully carving out their own ecosocial niches in relation to other large carnivores and benefiting from prime access to a wide range of animal resources. In any case, from the early phases of the Middle Pleistocene, increased human demography in the Old World demonstrates that exponential population growth was being achieved and this in response to the social and cultural investments being made in developing technological behaviors as a successful adaptive response to environmental pressures. In the face of cyclical climatic change, when populations might have dwindled or expired locally, the archeological record shows us that, at least in western Eurasia, there was a sufficient core population to maintain and establish occupation more than 1 million years ago (see Figure 4.3 and Table 4.2). Throughout this very long cultural period we call the Oldowan, therefore, hominins continued to make their tools using stones from nearby sources, reflecting low mobility patterns overall at least in terms of in lithic resource acquisition. The Oldowan tool kits encountered up to now do not include implements that can be clearly attributable to hunting activities, nor is there any clear evidence of controlled use of fire. Most Oldowan sites are situated in open-air contexts and, so far, there does not seem to be any evidence suggesting that individual sites were organized into recognizable spatial units that we could relate to task-specific criteria. While it is sometimes seen as a very long period of technological stability (or cultural stasis), manifestations of Oldowan cultural materials are, in fact, punctuated by subtle, incremental technological advances (while not progressive, innovation is demonstrated), showing that the hominins were steadily

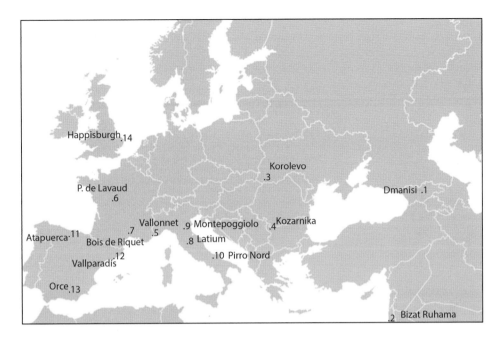

Figure 4.3
Map of key Western European Oldowan sites. 1. Dmanisi (Georgian Republic, 1.81 Ma); 2. Bizat Ruhama (Israel, 1.6–1.2 Ma); 3. Korolevo VII (Ukraine, 1.95 Ma); 4. Kozarnika (Bulgaria, 1.6–1.4 Ma); 5. Vallonnet Cave (France, 1.2 Ma) ; 6. Pont-de-Lavaud (France, > 1 Ma); 7. Bois-de-Riquet US2 (France, 1–0.9 Ma); 8. Arce, Colle Marino, Fontana Liri (Italy, > 0.78 Ma); 9. Ca' Belvedere di Montepoggiolo (Italy, 1 Ma); 10. Pirro Nord (Italy, 1.6–1.3 Ma); 11. Sierra de Atapuerca, Sima del Elefante level TE9 and Gran Dolina level TD6 (Spain, 1.3 Ma and 0.9 Ma, respectively); 12. Vallparadís (Spain, 1.2–0.6 Ma); 13 Barranco León and Fuente Nueva 3 at Orce (Spain, 1.4–1.2 Ma, respectively); 14. Happisburgh (England, 0.95–0.7 Ma). (After Barsky et al., 2015a)

improving their capacity to manipulate and shape stone (see Figures 4.4 and 4.5). As these achievements accrued, so were some changes introduced into the tool kits whose morphotechnical variability perhaps unknowingly provided a source of new developments.[168] Oldowan technological expertise was acquired and transmitted thanks to timeless learning strategies, expanding into traditions and moving humanity beyond innate, reactive behavioral responses into the realm of what we call *culture*. Evolving in synchronicity with the complex development of the human brain – and even the evolution of language itself – first technologies must be appreciated for their importance as a foundation for truly human social phenomenon.[169] In Oldowan tool manufacture, we can appreciate the complex technosocial thresholds that were being attained at first in Africa by early *Homo* (and perhaps also *Australopithecus* and *Paranthropus*). They are the spring out of which inventiveness would be impelled to grow into the fantastic story of endless human creativity.

Table 4.2
Discoveries leading to interpretation of the timing and modalities of the first peopling of Eurasia

Dmanisi (Georgia) 1.81 Ma	1983 Discovery of extinct rhino teeth
	1984 Discovery of primitive stone tools
	1991 Discovery of hominin mandible
Orce (Spain) 1.4-1.3 Ma	1991 Discovery of lithics at Fuente Nueva 3
	1994 Discovery of lithics at Barranco León
	2013 Publication of hominin tooth from Barranco León
Sierra de Atapuerca (Spain) Gran Dolina TD6 0.9 Ma	1994 Discovery of hominin remains with stone tools and fauna in the Aurora Stratum
Sierra de Atapuerca (Spain) Sima del Elefante 1.3 Ma	2007 Discovery of hominin remains with stone tools and fauna

(a) (b)

(c) (d)

Figure 4.4
Orce Oldowan sites (Andalusia, Spain) (a) and (b) Barranco León (1.4 million years old) and (c) and (d) Fuente Nueva 3 (1.2 million years old) have presently yielded the oldest hominin remain in Western Europe as well as exceptionally rich Oldowan stone tool assemblages associated with large and small mammals. (Deborah Barsky, courtesy of Consejería de Cultura de la Junta de Andalucía)

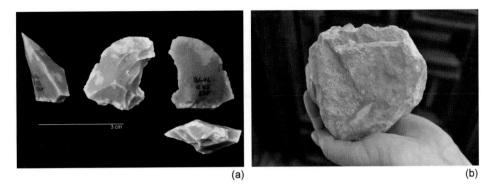

(a)   (b)

Figure 4.5
Oldowan tools from Orce. (a) Several views of small flint flake from Barranco León. (b)
Limestone chopper tool from Fuente Nueva 3, dating to 1.4 and 1.2 million years ago,
respectively. (Stefania Titton, courtesy of Consejería de Cultura de la Junta de Andalucía)

THE ACHEULIAN TECHNOCOMPLEX: THE FIRST CULTURAL REVOLUTION

Increasingly, environmental and social triggers produced renewed technological potential within the formal variability of the Oldowan[168] that was utilized and transformed to
create more elaborate objects, finally incurring the significant fundamental changes that
designate the emergence of a new technocomplex, the Acheulian. This can arguably be
seen as the first major human revolution in which technological capabilities underwent
substantial transitions, not only in the in the types of tools that were produced but also
in the behaviors that these objects are thought to reflect. The oldest evidence for this
important cultural change is from East Africa and dates to 1.75 Ma.[170] However
revolutionary it may appear today, this cultural transition – from the Oldowan to the
Acheulian – likely did not occur abruptly, but evidence is still lacking to understand the
modalities of change in these very ancient times. In any case, its development more or
less corresponded to the appearance of relatively larger-brained hominins Homo erectus
and Homo ergaster (an African form of Homo erectus) with anatomical features very different
from earlier forms of Homo. As early as 1891, the first Homo erectus specimen was
discovered in Indonesia by a Dutch surgeon named E. Dubois, who coined it
Pithecanthropus erectus, meaning "erect ape-man" (the genus name Pithecanthropus was later
replaced by Homo).[171] Homo erectus existed in Africa from around 1.9 Ma to 140 Ka and is
taxonomically related to the Middle Pleistocene Eurasian Homo. The denomination Homo
ergaster derives from the ancient Greek word for workman in reference to the advanced
toolmaking abilities of these Acheulian-producing hominins. In Western Europe, the
Acheulian evidence appears after around 1 Ma[172] and is generally attributed to another
hominin known as Homo heidelbergensis, an eponymous denomination derived from a
Middle Pleistocene hominin mandible found at Mauer (Germany) by O. Schoetensack
from the University of Heidelberg.[173] This hominin displays anatomical features linking

Table 4.3

Global temporal range of the Acheulian technocomplex

	Combined duration		
Africa	1.75 - 0.35 Ma		
Europe	1.0 Ma - 0.35 Ma	→	**1.4 million years**
Asia	0.9 Ma- 0.35 Ma		

it to *Homo erectus* but also evoking some traits of *Homo neandertalensis*. While *Homo erectus* is still often cited as the first to have migrated out of Africa, as we have seen, recent discoveries seem to be pointing to a very different scenario for the first colonization of Eurasia (see Table 4.3).

Despite the uneven global temporal scales for the arrival/presence of Oldowan-producing hominins, this technocomplex was replaced in most areas by the Acheulian. Thus, thousands of years after its first appearance in Africa (at 1.75 Ma),[170,177] the Acheulian is recognized in Europe only after 1 Ma.[172] Meanwhile, Acheulian evidence is identified in South Asia as early as around 1.5 Ma[174] and is manifest in East Asia from 0.9 Ma.[175] Compared to the Oldowan whose combined duration was of some 2 million years, the Acheulian is estimated to have lasted some 1.4 million years (global duration of the Acheulian technocomplex: 1.75–0.35 Ma). Interestingly, the Acheulian seems to have emerged from expansive foyers, perhaps developing out of preexisting Oldowan cultures that had already been occupying these same regions over thousands of generations. Because of population increase, the situation subsequently gave way to more intense dispersion and cultural transmission through social networkings because different groups would (logically) have more frequently come into contact.[176] Looking to the chronological context for the emergence of the Acheulian, a fascinating pattern appears. As we have seen, the first Acheulian tool kits appeared in East Africa some 1.75 Ma[170,177] while, in relatively "close" chronologies, the Acheulian is documented around 1.6 Ma in both South Africa[178] and thousands of kilometers away in Israel.[179] It also appears in a similar time frame in distant southeast India from 1.5 Ma.[174] It seems from the growing density of sites after this time that these Acheulian "hotbeds" diffused (evermore rapidly), growing into a widespread phenomenon of ever-increasing thickness until around 1–0.8 Ma by which time Acheulian peoples had spread throughout much of Africa and Eurasia.[172,175,180]

The evidence from this very long period of relative cultural stability, tells us that Acheulian hominins were successful in confronting changing climatic conditions of the Middle Pleistocene and ensuring demographic continuity throughout the vast regions in which they thrived. Changes in the quality of the stone tools and higher complexity in

Figure 4.6
Example of the Victoria West cleaver production method (large flake Acheulian phase): (a) Different views of fitment of Victoria West core from the Canteen Koppie site with cleaver from Pniel 6 site. (b) Core from Canteen Koppie site and (c) Cleaver from Pniel 6 site. Note the highly standardized volumetric concept of these stone tools that fit together even if coming from different sites. (Courtesy of Gonen Sharon after Sharon and Beaumont 2006)

the techniques with which they were manufactured are hallmarks of the Acheulian. They reflect superior cognitive capacities of the hominin groups thriving after the Oldowan and indicate a comparatively wider range of activities and behaviors. Following the Early Acheulian in some areas, tool kits became characterized by the production of large-sized flakes (>10 cm) knapped using advanced prepared core technologies,[181,182] a feature that is not observed in Oldowan assemblages. Acheulian peoples invented very intricate stone-knapping strategies involving the hierarchical removal of flakes, shaping cores in accordance to specific and preconceived volumetric patterns enabling large flake production (see Figure 4.6). The formal features of Acheulian large flakes made them suitable for simple shaping into a variety of representative Acheulian cutting tools: bifaces (or hand axes), cleavers and picks (see Figure 4.7). Also, Acheulian hominins made a wide range of standardized retouched tool "types," contrasting sharply with the previous Oldowan assemblages. These flake tools display edges modified intentionally by small removals (retouch) that enabled hominins to model them into specific (standardized) shapes that we recognize as tool types (scrapers, burins, points, awls). In the Konso region of Ethiopia, where the oldest Acheulian has been situated, a series of localities excavated by Y. Beyene and colleagues dating to different periods of the

Figure 4.7
Early Acheulian stone tools from the Barranc de la Boella site (El Forn and Pit 1 localities, La Canonja, Tarragona, Spain). The open-air alluvial site context currently excavated under the direction of P. Saladié and J. Vallverdú (IPHES-CERCA, Tarragona) has yielded a rich archeopaleontological record that includes the oldest Western European evidence for Acheulian large cutting tools (1 million years old). (a) Cleaverlike tool made of schist from level 2 of the El Forn locality in the Early Acheulian site of Barranc de la Boella. (b) Pick made of schist from level 2 of the Pit 1 locality in the Early Acheulian site of Barranc de la Boella. (Andreu Ollé, courtesy of the IPHES-CERCA)

Acheulian reveals how the emergence and evolution of the Acheulian phenomena occurred through time in a single regional context punctuated by typo-technological changes.[170]

While they continued to exploit locally available lithic resources, Acheulian stone knappers also brought raw materials from sources distant from their dwellings, underlining their high mobility compared with that of the Oldowan peoples. Along with the evidence for wider-ranging lifestyles, the relative abundance of Acheulian sites denotes significant increases in overall population densities. In addition, Acheulian sites yield a far greater abundance of artifacts than the previous Oldowan ones, suggesting that the groups were composed of a higher number of individuals than previously. Successive layer sites, rare during the Oldowan, become common, attesting to a certain "regionalization" of Acheulian groups who were evidently returning to the same places over generations. Acheulian hominins often occupied caves (geographical context permitting), alternating with other large cave-dwelling carnivores such as bears, lions and saber-toothed cats. Sometimes the taxonomic analyses of the fauna discovered in association with Acheulian tool kits reveals a specific species' representation indicative of selective and organized hunting[183,184] (even if tools specifically designed for this purpose are still not clearly identifiable in most assemblages). With hunting assuming a strategic role in food accessing, more complex behavioral strategies emerged, perhaps eventually requiring hunter-gatherer groups to organize into hierarchical units, suggesting the early stages of social status beginning to take form. Because of the relatively high intellectual investment it entailed, hunting offered hominin groups open-ended potential for socially complex developments while providing a high yield relative to the time invested (obtaining the necessary caloric intake from gathering, digging and collecting vegetal foodstuffs is comparably much more time consuming than a diet comprising meat).

Additionally, controlled use of fire becomes quite widely documented during the Acheulian at first sparsely and then more systematically through time. By the later Acheulian, archeological sites denote habitats – or even home bases – that reflect complex spatial organization, often relating to the situation of a hearth (or several hearths) or even sometimes mega-hearth structures (fires kindled in the same location within a site over long periods of time[185]). We cannot understate the significant role played by fire as a transformative technological milestone achieved by early humans during the Acheulian.[186] In order to situate this important accomplishment in the evolutionary process, some specialists differentiate between passive and active uses of fire. The Acheulian strata of the Wonderwerk Cave site in South Africa presently provides evidence for intentional burning in an archeologically controlled context dating to some 1 Ma.[187] While there is older evidence for fire in a few African open-air sites,[188,189,190,191] these might be ascribed to passive fire use in which brazes could have been gathered from naturally ignited contexts (from lightning, original pyrogenic situations or other forms of spontaneous combustion).[192] Still, solid evidence for active fire production as reflected by organized combustion structures remains to be clearly established in archeological sites predating around 1 Ma. Outside of Africa, the *ability to set fire at will*[193] at first sporadically documented (for example, at the 0.78 Ma Large Flake Acheulian site of Gesher Benot Ya'akov in Israel)[194] becomes more commonly associated with the Late Acheulian peoples of Europe by around 40–300 Ka (for example, at Beeches Pit in Great Britain, Terra Amata and Menez Dregan in France and Gruta da Aroeira in Portugal)[195,196,197,198] as well as in the Near East (at Tabun and Qesem caves)[199,200] and other areas occupied during this time frame.[186] In Asia, the famous Chinese multilayer Acheulian site of Zhoukoutian has reported *in situ* burning in levels dating to 0.8–0.6 Ma.[201] Toward the end of the Middle Pleistocene in Africa and Eurasia, hearths become a prominent feature in multilayer sites as, for example, in the Spanish site of Cueva del Ángel.[185] At the threshold of the Lower to Middle Paleolithic transition, hearths played a major structural role within the new economic system of repeatedly inhabited provisioned base camps as hominin groups were identifying more closely with defined regional areas and sharpening their social skills.[192,202,203,204,205,206] During the Acheulian, the controlled use of fire contributed (increasingly prominently) not only to the survival and reproductive success of human groups but also to the mounting complexity of their social conditioning. While fire does not appear prerequisite to migratory expansions throughout Eurasia in the earlier phases of the Acheulian, there is no doubt that fire equipped human groups formidably as they penetrated into northerly situated territories, confronting harsh climatic conditions and exploiting the advantages offered by virgin lands. So, while the ability to make fire seems a likely explanation for the impressive migration patterns observed during the Acheulian, in particular the settling of the more northerly latitudes of Eurasia, findings of fireless sites predating the accepted age proposed for active fire-making capabilities seems to suggest it was not an essential prerequisite (Marine isotope stage [MIS] 12-11).[205]

Hominins experimenting with fire discovered its numerous advantages, for example, in cooking their food, softening it and improving its quality with the added benefits of reducing risks posed by parasites. Furthermore, fire allowed hominins to improve some aspects of their toolmaking such as hardening wooden spear points. Through time (especially after the Neolithic and into the Metal Ages), humanity discovered new ways to manipulate fire that included the transformation of organic matter into new combinations. By controlling fire, hominins came to possess a formidable weapon for hunting and trapping game while affording protection from predators. Although anachronistic, we can easily envision how fire would have become the center of community life with glowing embers of the hearths lengthening potentially active hours into the night, allowing humans to reflect on and share the day's events. While the extent to which Acheulian hominins mastered complex language is still under debate,[206] we can infer a scenario wherein the emergence of story telling and even the creation of myths and traditions could have emerged around fireplaces, which had become a hub of community life within the base camps. Ultimately, the mastery of fire would through time have contributed in so many ways to intensifying life experiences and cultural identities within human groups, linking them to newly developing symbolic sensitivities as social lives became more carefully structured.

All of the benefits offered by fire-making skills finally fostered the burgeoning human pioneering spirit. Today, fire remains an essential element of our lives, conserving within its mysterious aura the very essence of our shared collective consciousness and deeply underlining our separation from the animal realm through its generous offering of superior means of control. And so it was during the Acheulian that cultural processes strengthened by the controlled use of fire, organized hunting, standardized tool manufacture and the consolidation of language capacities fostered abstract, intergroup divergences: *differences between peoples that were founded in cultural habits or traditions*. Hominins could more effectively face the pressures of periodic fluctuations in temperature and humidity, enabling them to thrive even within constrained geographic regions to become tied – as it were – both physically and culturally to a specific geographical area. This more stable residence of groups of peoples within a relatively constrained regional context (as attested by multilayer sites) eventually led hominins to establish (abstract) land-linked identities. As successive generations lived and died in a more specific, delimited area, so their technologies and tool morphologies came to be linked to that space, strengthening their identity with the land. I am proposing that during the Late Acheulian, especially after around 450,000 years ago, noticeable cultural idiosyncrasies observed in the archeology of specific regions bear witness to the emergence of a new form of separation within human groups, one that was both cultural and geographical. This is the departure point for culture-based identity recognition that led our hominin ancestors to make sharper definitions between "us" and "them": this was the birth of what was to become the human abstract conceptualization of borders. Henceforth, as Acheulian hominins prospered from their newfound technological successes, so did they reap the advantages from their ever-increasing thirst for discovery. As their technological capacities progressed, this know-how was transmitted through learning and intersocietal contacts, spreading and developing the new technoforms that emerged with novel behaviors that are the building blocks of culture.

So-called handaxes (or bifaces) are often referred to as the most representative among the Acheulian tools. Because these tear-shaped tools exhibit bilateral and bifacial symmetry, they are believed to indicate the capacity for hominins to transfer mental templates sourced from abstract thought into material creations. This, in turn, is thought to reflect a newfound sensitivity to *nonfunctional* and even esthetic concerns that are not recognized in the more random lithic forms produced during the Oldowan. Yet I argue that Acheulian innovation goes beyond the manufacture of these singular tools, including in its material repertory other highly complex and standardized technological developments, incorporating many types of tools and regional-specific prepared core and flake production methods. From its appearance in the archeological record some 1.75 Ma, the Acheulian spread evermore rapidly throughout the Old World, assuming exponential growth in pace with each achievement, a feature that is now recognized to be a trademark of the human species.

SOCIAL NETWORKING IN THE LATE ACHEULIAN

Observing with retrospect the hugely important space and time ranges occupied by the Acheulian phenomena serves to further underline the significance of the formidable adaptive strategy that toolmaking had become by this time nearly 2 million years after its invention. As time progressed, ever-increasing technical achievement attesting to already well-anchored cultural traditions and even regional variability signaled the founding of compartmentalized cultural identities. This process becomes more clearly visible, for example, when we consider the numerous appellations referring to the lithic assemblages of this period, dividing it, both culturally and spatially, into distinct entities – all affiliated somehow with the Acheulian technocomplex.[207,208] The strengthening of cultural traditions spreading and transforming over generations of population migrations and intricate social networking gradually converted earlier traditions into new subsistence strategies as hominins confidently interacted with their environments by way of their own material realizations. This networking (expansion) phase was strengthened during the Late Acheulian and documents regional cultural multiplicity.[176] As I have shown, this phenomenon is underpinned by the plethora of cultural denominations (many of which emanate from eponymous sites) recognized by prehistorians as representative of one or another cultural variant of the Acheulian. Still, this denominative complexity does serve to demonstrate the evolution of our understanding of the Acheulian as a complex cultural unit with multiple facets of expression in the artifacts found in different parts of the world in different chronologies. These artifacts also remind us to bear in mind the dangers of creating classificatory systems based on single-site features. These terminologies become problematic when displaced from their original region to other geographical contexts where they provide only very broad definitions that generally diverge from their original connotations. While one may argue that a lithic series with original technological or typological characteristics justifies a specific denomination within the Acheulian, it may be that the same features are recognized elsewhere or that they are attributed to functional – rather than cultural – reasons. Diversity between tool kits can occur even within a single temporal and regional context due to different factors, such as raw material variability, for example (a flint tool kit will appear very different from a quartz tool kit), or divergences in site function.

What we do see rather clearly, however, is that, from the Acheulian onward, this multifaceted aspect of the lithic assemblages provided hominins with a working foundation, a sort of technological and morphological database from which they would continue to develop their ever-widening range of tools that facilitated (improved) their ability to adapt to specific situations. In other words, by the end of the Acheulian, hominins were equipped to confront a very extensive assortment of survival pressures. Ultimately, the immense wealth of the Acheulian archeological record superbly reflects the exponential increase in human reliance on technological responses for survival. Our own need for multiple terminologies to describe Late Acheulian cultural entities only exposes the richness of the regional differences of its expressions. If one admits that a purpose of the work we are doing on stone tool assemblages is to insert them into a chrono-cultural framework, then it seems important that we apply an open-ended system of classification that takes into account these multiple expressions of culture as they developed throughout the Middle Pleistocene. In studying the Acheulian techno-complex, therefore, we observe finally how differences expressed as culture are related first to external forces (climate fluctuations, type of hunting, diversity of exploited rocks and their sources) and second to various developmental stages in the spiral of human technosocial evolution. The immense chronological duration occupied by the Acheulian phenomena, unthinkable only a few years ago, shrouds the existence of traditions and emphasizes our own tendency to simplify the archeological record by homogenizing the data. The terms we use today are thus hardly satisfactory because they are simply too general to consider the intricacy of such multilayered cultural aspects. As I explained previously, most of the terms still employed today by lithic analysts have lost their original meaning or been deliberately modified to adapt to new discoveries. However, we preserve them in prehistory because they do still provide a means of communication between researchers, helping to compare between assemblages and even simply to understand one another. Despite some discordance, it is generally accepted that progressive stages were reached during the Acheulian and that their empirical realities are related to the appearance of specific attributes that materialized diachronically in the tool kits on a global scale, forming our current perception of this important phase of early human cultural evolution.

5

THE ASCENT OF PALEOLITHIC CULTURES

EXPANSION AND TRANSFORMATION AFTER THE ACHEULIAN

Variability, diversity and multiplicity have been used as keywords for describing the progression of human technologies through time[168] – from the Oldowan into the Acheulian and beyond. As we have seen, both the Oldowan and the Acheulian technocomplexes were of very long duration, and these denominations really serve as umbrella terms to refer to (relatively coherent) sets of technological and behavioral characteristics. These concepts remind us that cultural denominations are not meant to refer to stagnant phases of cultural development but rather to stages of growth within the human evolutionary technospecific systemic which, at least at first, are represented by only very subtle changes through time. In this view, each development within a technosystem is seen as stemming from those preceding, thus engendering a branching evolutionary structure based on the concept of cumulative culture. Therefore, we observe over time evermore profuse culturally transmitted processes that were (initially) only passively experienced. In turn, each technological advancement was(is) inexorably linked to a social process, prompting new behaviors linked to survival strategies. When a given technical activity is consciously or subconsciously found useful (adaptively advantageous), it is established into a normalized behavior through socialization processes. Therefore, as the tree grows to have more branches, so do human socialization processes become more diverse. In human societies, an expanding degree of knowledge is required for individuals to function within technological systems grounded in accumulative progress. Over time, we humans have chosen to deal with this problematic by investing evermore time into administering teaching with learning as prerequisite to mastering not only the new technologies but also their associated symbolic behavioral repertory. Thus, I argue that, from the Acheulian onward, developments in technologies triggered the need to adopt newly invented socialization processes, which, in turn, acted as catalysts for grafting new cultural traits. This explains why socialization processes themselves have also become so intensively complex through time. The evolution toward evermore complex technologies and behaviors in methods of stone tool production and use begun so long ago provides the advantages that allowed our species to continue to invent ways to overcome subsistence-related pressures and, eventually, to gain free time to dedicate to inventiveness. In what is sometimes referred to as the "technoselection" process (as an analogy to Darwin's natural selection), the most advantageous technological systems are those that will be favored, learned and adopted. These systems then spread within specific human groups or are generalized through (evolving) social systems until full accomplishment of their potential.

While each new cultural expression contains within itself all of the know-how accumulated during preceding stages of unconscious and conscious development, novel forms can and do occur, heralding a technological revelation and signaling cultural change within the complexes. Although such "revelations" are perceived in archeology as transformative stages within an evolutionary process, they are not necessarily entirely new because they have been built up from elements of preexisting know-how latent within a foregoing formative phase. Such latent (transformative) technologies serve therefore as a source of evolutionary change within human techno-systems, once again in a way analogous to those functioning within a genetic system. That is to say, technological innovations are the realization of potential already existing in each stage of human cultural development, generally in the form of subtle and discrete structural anomalies, which offer evolutionary promise. As for the biological (genetic) process of natural selection, latent "potential" will develop when prompted by specific circumstances occurring within the process of technoselection. Subsequent to the selection of a novel technological behavior, a new spiral of development occurs, provoking the exploration of the full range of possibilities offered by this new adaptation. What generally follows is the exhaustion of the system at which time it will be changed or replaced by something new, and the process begins anew. Because each successive phase of technosocial development integrates knowledge from the previous one, each phase along the evolutionary trajectory tends to be more multifaceted and of shorter duration. The lack of direction of the technoevolutionary processes can also be likened to the biological genetic processes. Contrastingly, technological evolutionary processes differ from natural ones especially by virtue of the fact that they are detached from natural limiting forces, such as those guiding genetic selection, and, therefore, the technological choices we humans make are not always favorable to the successful reproduction of our own (and other) species. Today, more often than not, these processes even upset universal states of equilibrium because they tend to be disconnected so completely from the natural world.

In the shift from the Oldowan to the Acheulian, bifacial stone knapping was one means through which groundbreaking technologies were achieved. In some of the oldest Oldowan sites, for example, at Gona or Dmanisi, bifacial stone-knapping methods were occasionally tested. Nevertheless, it was only later during the Acheulian that they came to be far more intensively developed, even becoming a hallmark of this latter technocomplex. Following this logic and citing another example from the archeological record, I have suggested that a similar process could also have led to the systematic production of small tools on flakes – another trademark of the Acheulian.[68] By reknapping flakes or using them as cores, an activity observed in the Oldowan, small notches were formed by the negatives left by the tiny extractions. Detaching small-sized flakes from larger ones, hominins would have inadvertently produced serrated edges on them. Why not assume that over time these edges could have been found useful, inspiring hominins to reproduce them deliberately in accordance to new mental templates engendered by observing their features over hundreds or even thousands of years. This could explain why the first tool types that appear in the oldest Acheulian tool kits are generally of denticulate form. The invention of retouch as a way to modify the form of a blank later diversified to include other modalities, ultimately leading to the invention of the types of small tools that proliferated markedly from the Acheulian onward.

THE NEANDERTAL WORLD

Toward the end of the Middle Pleistocene, the Acheulian was reaching its cultural apex, and the archeological record bears witness to an exponential increase in its multiplicity and regionalism – especially after 450 thousand years ago (Ka). In the Eurasian Middle Paleolithic, major changes once again materialized from the existing foundations of human culture, exploding into the world and expressed in synchronicity with important transformations in hominin anatomy and cerebral features. *Homo neandertalensis* appeared and prospered in Siberia, Western and central Asia, the Near East and Western Europe, emerging some time after around 400 Ka (after studies from the Atapuerca Sima de los Huesos hominin site)[209] up to around 30 Ka (evidence that these hominins might have lived in other regions of Eurasia is lacking, but this could point to a lack of Paleolithic research in these areas rather than true absence). This timing is important because recent discoveries from Greece (Apidima Cave), for example, may push back the date for the arrival of an early form of *Homo sapiens* in Europe to as early as 210 Ka,[210] indicating a complex scenario in which Neandertals and modern humans cohabited in the context of a mosaic of biological, cultural and behavioral settings. The novel and extremely diverse material culture of the Neandertal peoples (commonly referred to in Europe as Mousterian) replaced the Acheulian in most regions (except Siberia where there is to date no evidence of preexisting Acheulian populations). Transitional tendencies in cultural materials are observed, however, at some European end-Acheulian sites from as early as 0.4 million years ago (Ma), perhaps suggesting that a gradual shift to the Mousterian was a change that occurred in a mixed way.[208] Moreover, Mousterian-type stone tool assemblages (European holotype) are documented in the Near East in association with both Neandertals and anatomically modern humans (or archaic *Homo sapiens*). In North Africa, another cultural complex referred to as Middle Stone Age is attributed to modern humans. In other words, Neandertals were not the only hominins manufacturing the plethora of lithic tool types using very advanced technological modes of production that characterize this time frame.

The most recent evidence for the Neandertals (dated to 28 Ka) is recorded from the extreme south of the Iberian Peninsula at sites including Gorham's Cave (Gibraltar), which some consider a refuge area for the last Neandertals.[211] While much of Europe was covered in ice sheets at this time, this coastal region maintained an open-wooded landscape that may have been more favorable to the survival of the Neandertals. Some argue that this area might have acted as a sort of "geographical dead end" into which the last Neadertals were driven after failing to compete successfully with the rapidly expanding anatomically modern humans (AMH) populations. We should remember, however, that alternative hypotheses are also being considered. Neandertals are the closest extinct relatives to modern humans; they lived during part of the Middle and into the Upper Pleistocene in varying climatic and environmental settings. They occupied the caves and rock shelters in a vast territory and flourished in open-air contexts as nomads, hunting large and small game and foraging plants. Neandertals controlled the use of fire. The spatial distribution within Neandertal archeological sites reveals structured habitats often divided into butchering and stone-knapping areas centered around one or several hearths. Neandertal sites are abundant relative to the earlier Oldowan or Acheulian ones and generally yield very numerous artifacts.

To date, no Neandertal fossils have been found in Africa where at this time (the African Middle Stone Age) cultural evidence is attributed by some specialists to hominins from *Homo erectus* to archaic *Homo sapiens* engaged in an alternative evolutionary process of replacement.[212] The artifacts belonging to the chrono-cultural phase of the Middle Paleolithic (Mousterian) or (in Africa) to the Middle Stone Age were subsequently supplanted by those of the *Upper Paleolithic* or African *Late Stone Age* with a more complex series of new technocomplexes attributed to modern humans. Neandertals are not the only hominin that does not appear to have originated in Africa. Others include *Homo antecessor* from level TD6 of the Gran Dolina at Atapuerca (Spain) that, as we have seen, is considered ancestral to *Homo sapiens*, *Homo neandertalensis* and the Denisova hominin.[163,166,213] *Homo sapiens* ssp. Denisova was identified in 2010 at Denisova Cave (in the Altai Mountains of Siberia). Denisovans are the first hominins to be recognized from DNA studies and have yet to be formally taxonomically defined).[214] This hominin differs genetically from *Homo neandertalensis* and *Homo sapiens*, both of which are also said to be present at the Denisova site. Sequencing of the mitochondrial DNA from a finger

Table 5.1

Global temporal range of the Middle Paleolithic technocomplexes

	Combined Duration		
Africa	0.35–0.07 Ma		
Europe	0.35–0.04 Ma	→	310 thousand years
Asia	0.35–0.04 Ma		

bone discovered in the cave has led to the suggestion of cohabitation between these *Homo* groups (although there is no direct evidence for contemporaneity) while genetic information suggests a shared common ancestor around 1 Ma.[215,216] *Homo floresiensis* is an extinct species of the genus *Homo* that was discovered in 2003 in the Lian Bua Cave on the island of Flores (Indonesia) by M. Morwood (Auckland University, Australia). This hominin was also found with faunal remains and stone tools and dates from 100 to 50 Ka[217,218] (see Table 5.1).

The name *Neandertal* is an eponymous denomination deriving from the Neander Valley in Germany where human fossils were fortuitously discovered in a cave during mining operations in 1856.[219,220] The name originates from a Greek translation of the family name of a local seventeenth-century pastor named Neuman, meaning "new man." The first Neandertal fossils were discovered in the early nineteenth century: in 1829 at Engis 2 in Belgium (formalized only much later in 1936), and in 1848 at Forbes' Quarry in Gibraltar.[221] Physically, Neandertals were very stocky and had thick, heavy-set bones and very developed musculature. Their posture and locomotion were fully bipedal, their arms and legs were relatively short, and their torso was wide and heavy. Although their cranial capacity actually exceeded that of modern humans, their brain was organized very differently (average Neandertal brain size was ~1.500 cm^3 versus average modern European brain size of [~1.350 cm^3). The most significant anatomical differences between modern *Homo* and Neandertals concern the cranial features. Most notably, Neandertals retained the receding forehead (reduced frontal lobe) that is also present in earlier hominin species such as *Homo erectus*. Neandertal skulls bulge in the occipital zone and lack prominent, protruding chins like our own. Some believe that Neandertals had red hair and fair skin like some of today's Nordic peoples.[222] Female Neandertals were considerably smaller than males (a feature formally referred to as "sexual dimorphism"). Despite these important differences, Neandertals are sometimes classified as a subspecies of *Homo sapiens* (*Homo sapiens neandertalensis*). The issue of the origins of Neandertals persists unresolved: it is unclear whether they emerged from locally existing populations (*Homo heidelbergensis*?) or from elsewhere (Asia?) before spreading over vast areas of Eurasia (see Figure 5.1). Although their physical features designate adaptations to cold, harsh climates, it is true that Neandertals also lived through more temperate, interglacial climatic episodes.[223]

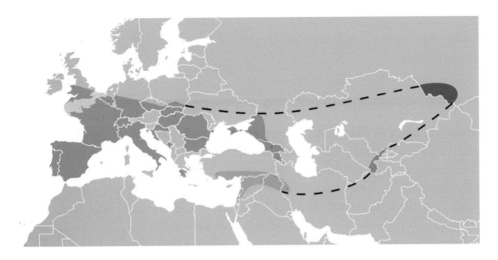

Figure 5.1
Geographic range of Neandertals based on finds of skeletal remains only: (blue) Europe; (orange) Southwestern Asia; (green) Uzbekistan and (purple) Altai mountains. (Nicolas Perrault III via Wikimedia Commons)

As work progresses in the many fields linked to archeology, we are constantly expanding our knowledge about the lifeways and culture of the Neandertals. Presently, paleoanthropological data seems to suggest that they could have descended from the Eurasian populations of the late Lower Pleistocene. European Homo erectus (Homo heidelbergensis)[224,225] displays "transitional" anatomic features, recalling those of Homo erectus while presaging (as it were) other traits typically found in Homo neandertalensis. Over the last two decades, paleogenetic studies have been making headway in resolving the enigma of the origins of the Neandertals, suggesting, for instance, that Eurasian Homo erectus and Neandertals might have shared a common ancestor around 1 Ma.[166] Meanwhile, "the particular combination of skeletal and dental characteristics observed in the hominins of TD6.2... suggests that Homo antecessor is phylogenetically close to the divergence between Neandertals and modern humans."[213] Some 28 Ka, more than 180,000 years after the arrival of modern human forms in Europe and nearly 150,000 years in the Levant,[210,226] the last Neandertal populations documented in the Iberian Peninsula disappeared from the planet. Whatever the cause(s) of their extinction may be, a growing body of evidence now shows that Neandertals had attained a highly advanced degree of technological and artistic achievements[227] and that their level of socialization, especially in terms of symbolic cultural transmission,[228] was far more developed than previously believed. Like modern-day hunter-gatherer societies (such as the Inuit), Neandertals apparently exploited all parts of the large and small animal carcasses they hunted (fat, skin, bone, antler, blood, meat). Their selective hunting strategies and probable right-handedness (a modern pattern of brain dominance) indicate complex social and linguistic skills.[229]

Hierarchical role-playing (in the sense of established social hierarchies) arguably existed within each group, and populations were surely organized, perhaps even into regional tribes.

THE MYSTERIOUS DEMISE OF THE NEANDERTAL

The world of the Neandertal as we perceive of it today captures our imagination and far exceeds the closed-minded vision of these populations when they were first discovered. Indeed, after the early discoveries of Neandertal fossils were made at the beginning of the nineteenth century, these hominins were often depicted as primitive and even beastly life forms, just barely humanoid. Today, we have cast off the fetters of these early biased interpretations as we explore the Neandertals from the vantage point of new discoveries and gradually overcome our own socially generated ignorance through science, learning through archeology all that can be offered of their complex world. It is fascinating to consider that our species existed over thousands of years in Eurasia alongside other species of the genus *Homo*: the Neandertals but also the small-bodied *Homo luzonensis* from the Philippines (Callao Cave, 50 Ka),[230] *Homo florensiensis* from the Island of Flores in Indonesia[217,218] and even *Homo sapiens ssp. Denisova*.[214,221,222] The oldest *Homo sapiens* is now documented from North Africa at the Moroccan site of Jebel Irhoud dating to some 300 Ka.[22] While other ancient modern human sites are complicating the picture of how and when our species dispersed into different parts of the world (in South African sites from 100 Ka,[231] in the Near East around 180 Ka[226] and in Western Europe human groups with primitive and modern features appearing more than 200 Ka[210]). These discoveries suggest an earlier age for the arrival of AMHs than previously thought, considerably lengthening their coexistence with the Neandertals.

It is common to seek out cause-effect relationships connecting AMHs and Neandertals that could ultimately explain the demise of the Neandertals. While we have only partial data with which to reconstruct the circumstances and settings of the extinction of the Neandertals, the hypothesis of their coexistence with modern humans is now largely acknowledged. In fact, many believe that Neandertal populations could have lived for some time in the same geographical regions as AMHs (and Denisovans). We can only postulate about how possible encounters between these different species of *Homo* might have been. Did they interbreed? Or did they react in fear, choosing to eliminate one another through violent conflicts? Did they demonstrate simple curiosity for each other's physical features, culture and traditions? Was there any cultural exchange between them? Looking at the current level of human intolerance and xenophobia even among our own single species, it is both fascinating and disturbing to consider what an encounter between more than one *different* human species might have been like. To be sure, today's social predispositions seem to draw a desolate scenario for such paleoen-counters. But can we attribute the disappearance of the Neandertals to a genocide on behalf of AMHs? Solid evidence for violent encounters between these two species is lacking from the archeological record, and such hypotheses are principally based on extrapolations or analogies from modern contexts (one example is tribal warfare behaviors observed among existing hunter-gatherer societies). In feeding this supposition, it is often underlined that in comparison to the Neandertals, AMH likely possessed more advanced and finely tuned (blade-based) weaponry, eventually including such innovations as the bow and arrow and atlatls (spear-throwers) that would certainly have afforded them a considerable edge over the Neandertals (at least for long-distance track and kill hunting). Concerning cultural transmission, there is (so far) no clear evidence, at least in Western Europe, that the cultural transition from the Middle Paleolithic to the Upper Paleolithic technocomplexes was gradual; that is to say, in sites where this transition is registered, there does not seem to be intermixing of the cultural evidence. Curiously, this lack of amalgamation is also observed in other major cultural complexes discussed in this book (as in the transition from the Oldowan to the Acheulian). As always in prehistory, things are not so clear cut. Take for example the case of the so-called *Chatelperronian*, a cultural entity defined by H. Breuil in 1906 (Périgord, France), sometimes considered to represent a transitional phase between the Middle and Upper Paleolithic in Western Europe.[232] The Chatelperronian cultural complex is distinguished by a specific tool type (the Chatelperron point) as well as an increase in the presence of thin, elongated stone flakes (blades). However, Chatelperronian assemblages are not systematically present where they might be expected in multilevel archeological sites with stratigraphic sequences recording the Middle to Upper Paleolithic transition. In the majority of these cases, the Upper Paleolithic sequences appear directly above the Mousterian generally with the first phase of the Upper Paleolithic cultural succession, the Aurignacian technocomplex.

After their emergence in Africa some 300 Ka, AMHs settled in different areas of the globe and their populations experienced exponential demographic success. Their migrations are often visualized as successive events or "waves." In any case, it is clear that the increase in the density of AMH populations in Eurasia took place far more rapidly compared to the spread of other extinct hominin species. In addition to their basic foundational abundance, other reasons for this are proposed. Some suggest that their success was due to their "more advanced" tool kits while others argue that they had higher cognitive capacities or that they had a more fully integrated and extensive set of technosocial competences throughout the hominization process. Up to now, it was believed that Neandertal populations disappeared shortly after the arrival of AMHs in Europe (previously thought to have occurred around 40 Ka) where they had reigned for more than 100 thousand years (Kyrs). It now seems that their disappearance, although seemingly abrupt on the biogeological timescale, probably occurred fragmentally – even over a period of thousands of years. Climate change is among the most common reasons cited to explain the disappearance of the Neandertals, especially in relation to other hypotheses, such as physical specialization and geographic variables.[233] Indeed, Neandertal body proportions reflect adaptation to cold climatic conditions (large and wide noses, stout bodies). Yet as we have seen, Neandertals survived over a significantly long period as to have faced a wide array of climatic conditions. Some scientists argue that the Neandertal extinction can be explained by low intraspecific variability because it would have limited their capacity to adapt and reproduce quickly enough in the face of rapid environmental change. Evidence also shows that Neandertal groups may have found themselves isolated in restricted numbers, making them more vulnerable to adaptive challenges in the face of climate forcing.

Of course, an important question is what the chances are that encounters between these different species of Homo could have led to interbreeding. Paleogenetic studies are useful to determine the degree of kinship between existing and extinct species and now indicate that the Neandertal genome differs little from that of non-African modern humans.[234] A German fossil specimen serves as a holotype for the first Neandertal mitochondrial DNA sequence to be published (in 1997)[235] and was followed with the full sequencing of the Neandertal genome (published in 2008).[236] But empirical evidence is still lacking in the fossil record to support the theory of interbreeding between Neandertals and AMH. One example is from Abrigo do Lagar Velho (Portugal) where remains of a modern human child dating to 24 Ka are documented as showing both Neandertal and AMH traits.[237] New studies of ancient DNA appear key to resolving questions about interbreeding between the Neandertals and modern humans. Comparisons between samples of nuclear and mitochondrial DNA extracted from Neandertal and modern human bones have shown Neandertal DNA to be present (in 1 to 4 percent) of non-African modern humans.[234] The age for the last exchange of genetic material flowing from Neandertals to modern humans is likely to have been between 65,000 and 47,000 years ago.[238] However, there is also evidence of ancient gene flow from modern humans to Neandertals as early as 100 Ka.[239]

The prehistoric and evolutionary conduits of disease have also been explored to examine epidemiologic transmission as a possible explanation for the disappearance of Neandertal peoples.[240] According to this hypothesis, the demise of the Neandertals might be attributed to the spread of infectious diseases carried by AMHs arriving from Africa. Ultimately, the Neandertals would not have been able to sustain their populations because they lacked the time required to build up antibodies to protect themselves. Becoming increasingly isolated into small groups, they eventually would have died out. Of course, this hypothesis takes on special meaning in the present situation in which I write this book as the world is facing the (new) global pandemic of COVID-19. Indeed, throughout recorded history, widespread contagion of infectious diseases (pandemics) have occurred regularly, and such events are known even in the more recent phases of prehistory (examples include a 5,000-year-old case of a deadly viral epidemic at the Hamin Mangha Neolithic site in Inner Mongolia and the first recorded spread of smallpox some 3,000 years ago).[241] Examples from historical times underpin this periodicity.[242] Among the numerous recorded massive infectious events that have affected humanity through recorded time, smallpox killed millions of people around the world, the Bubonic plague (or Black Death) killed some 200 million people in fourteenth-century Eurasia and North Africa, and nearly 4 million people died during the so-called Great Plagues of the seventeenth and eighteenth centuries. More recently, infectious diseases continue to cause episodes of mass death, killing a combined tally of more than 14 million people in the nineteenth century alone (cholera, yellow fever, bubonic plague, Russian flu). Just after World War I, the "Spanish flu" (originating in the United States) infected some 500 million people, resulting in 50 million deaths while Asian flu and Hong Kong flu killed more than 2 million people. Today, HIV/AIDS continues to affect large numbers of people worldwide, bringing the total number of known deaths to some 35 million. The Ebola virus disease (EVD) is spreading in some West African countries where medics are struggling to prevent it from transforming into another global pandemic. Only one year after the disease was declared a pandemic (in March 2020), the World Health Organization (WHO) reported a global death toll due to the flu virus COVID-19 of nearly 2.6 million people with nearly 120 million cases confirmed in 219 countries and territories worldwide.[243]

Toward the end of the Middle Paleolithic and into the Upper Paleolithic, therefore, it seems likely to assume that as humanity expanded demographically, so too did the likelihood of contagion of different strains of deadly diseases. We know only too well, for example, how entire populations of indigenous peoples of the Americas were decimated after contracting diseases brought by colonizing Europeans during and after the fifteenth century. The victims were peoples who had been living in these areas over thousands of years but simply were not protected from the diseases carried by the new arrivals since they did not have the time to adapt by developing the necessary antibodies to protect themselves. So, might we consider their encounters with modern humans originating from Africa a viable explanation for the disappearance of the Neandertals? For the moment, this hypothesis – while remaining a viable explanation *comparatively* – has not yet been backed by conclusive evidence. It should also be underlined that disease transmission can occur in multiple directions. Citing pathogens and diseases as *"the most important selective forces experienced by humans during their evolutionary history,"* a recent genetic study provides evidence that Neandertal DNA contributed to the modern human immune system in response to bacteria, fungi and parasites.[244] In this scenario, modern humans dispersing out of Africa into Eurasia were also subjected to different types of pathogens for which they did not have the protective antibodies. Encountering (and interbreeding) with Neandertals (and perhaps Denisovans) living in these regions over thousands of years, the new arrivals inherited some of the protective genetic material by introgression (interspecific exchange of genetic material). Finally, even if we assume that Neandertals closely rivaled the AMHs in intellect and cultural advancement, some still maintain that the Neandertals were just *too specialized* (physically and culturally) to face the challenges that rapidly prevailed after the spread of AMH throughout Eurasia because the Neandertals also experienced pressures from climate instability recorded during Marine isotope stage (MIS) 3 (60–27 Ka). We may most prudently consider all of these explanations as factors contributing to the ultimate fragmentation of Neandertal populations leading finally to their decimation. We must remember that the different hypotheses discussed are not self-exclusive and it just may be that more than one (or even all) of these premises serves to explain how and why the Neandertals disappeared only some 28 Ka.

THE TECHNICAL SKILLS OF NEANDERTAL PEOPLES

In the Neandertal world, fire continued to play an increasingly important role in shaping lifeways and occupational norms of these peoples. Hearths and evidence of by-products produced from burning, sporadically reported in the European Lower Paleolithic (see Chapter 4), become truly pervasive in the Middle Paleolithic record (especially after 200 Ka).[198,204] Structured combustion features (hearths) played an important role in Neandertal lifeways and are documented in both open-air and cave contexts (for example, in the Israeli sites of Nesher Ramla and Kebara).[245,246] Combustion by-products found associated with the hearths in Neandertal sites include charcoal and burned bones and stones (as well as rubified sediment), all attesting to the various manifestations of fire (different degrees of heating, different objects and structures reflecting different usages for fire). Archeologists have also signaled a range of uses for fire recognizable from the spatial patterning and activity areas within some sites. One example is from the Abric Romaní site (see Figure 5.2), a deeply in- filled rock shelter at Capellades in Catalonia, Spain (discovered by Amador Romaní in 1909). After a first period of excavations by E. Ripoll in the 1950s and 1960s, ongoing excavations since 1983 have been conducted at this site under the direction of E. Carbonell, M. G. Chacón and P. Saladié (IPHES-CERCA and URV),[247] underlining the important role played by fire in the organization of life within the habitats.[192] Fire afforded warmth and light, but it was also instrumental in preserving and cooking foods and providing ways to limit alimentary toxins, bacteria and parasites. Its uses were extended to altering materials or hafting and fashioning resistant tools.[248,249,250] Fire-making humans were provided formidable protection from inclement weather and could easily ward off dangerous animals. As we saw in Chapter 4, the impact of fire-making went beyond the utilitarian, expanding human socialization processes and associated symbolic expression that cannot be accurately measured in the archeological record but are reflected in the expanding range of new behaviors perceptible from the Middle Paleolithic onward.[204]

The special features of the Mousterian technocomplex were recognized soon after its discovery in late nineteenth century France, in particular thanks to archeological work in multistratified sites such as Le Moustier (Dordogne, France). These sequences allowed specialists to compare the artifacts coming from different levels and to observe their evolution within single-site contexts (intrasite) and to compare different sites (inter-site). Neandertal toolmakers were talented artisans who demonstrated a clear predilection for flint, a smooth-grained rock type that is well suited for realizing the complex hierarchical stone-knapping strategies they practiced with operative schemes that

(a)

(b)

Figure 5.2
Abric Romaní Middle Paleolithic rock shelter (Capellades, Spain) discovered in 1909 by Amador Romaní is the object of an excavation and research project started in 1983 under the direction of E. Carbonell, M. G. Chacón and P. Saladié and with the collaboration of numerous researchers from the IPHES-CERCA (Tarragona, Spain). The site has yielded an extraordinarily rich succession of Neandertal occupations (115–40 Ka) with Mousterian stone tools, faunal remains and imprints of wooden elements as well as more than 400 hearths and evidence for spatial organization and habitat structuring. The faunal assemblages include mainly horse and deer as well as rhinos, aurochs and a range of other herbivorous and carnivorous species. (a) General view of a series of exposed hearths on the surface of level Q (58 Ka) of the Middle Paleolithic site of Abric Romaní (Palmira Saladié, courtesy of the IPHES-CERCA). (b) Detail of a hearth and stratigraphic section of the one of the hearths in the same level with microcharcoal layer (ashes are not conserved) and rubified sediment (reddish color resulting from heating). (Palmira Saladié, courtesy of the IPHES-CERCA)

demanded high levels of dexterity and complex volumetric planning. During the Mousterian, stone-knapping methods followed a uniform set of mechanical rules reproduced throughout much of the territorial and temporal span of Neandertal existence. Mousterian cultural relics indicate their highly developed degree of cultural complexity and the presence of deeply anchored traditions. Neandertal hunter-gatherers often chose the location of their longer-term occupations in relation to their physical proximity to abundant flint resources. During their travels, they transported flint nodules or even ready-made tools or chose to exploit other types of lithic resources encountered along their way. The making of every-day objects for domestic purpose attests to the use of wood and bone tools. For example, in addition to the richly documented Middle Paleolithic faunal and lithic register, the multilayer Abric Romaní site has yielded wooden implements dating to more than 50 Ka mainly preserved as imprints in travertine deposits.[37] There is no doubt that the Neandertals possessed a high degree of technical skill and that they were capable of performing very intricate operative schemes aimed at obtaining sharp-edged tools (flakes, blades, points) and producing blanks with specific and predetermined morphological and dimensional features.

The Mousterian technocomplex is notably characterized by a special series of stone-knapping technologies called Levallois methods. These are aimed at producing sharp-edged flakes or points with carefully preplanned shapes and sizes. The name Levallois has been used to refer to these methods since the early twentieth century and derives from the eponymous Levallois-Perret archeological site (Paris) where they were first identified. Levallois stone knapping involved careful preparation of the cores by successive blows with a hard percussion instrument (often a fist-sized limestone or quartzite cobble). The first stages in Levallois core processing involved the modeling of two opposed knapping planes known as the preparation and extraction surfaces. These surfaces were typically separated by a sinuous equatorial edge, lending a disklike morphology to the Levallois core. The surfaces, separated by a sinuous edge, were carefully managed to provide both an adequate extraction volume and a perfectly prepared striking platform. Once this volumetric configuration was established, the knapper delivered the final blow in the procedure, producing the Levallois blank (flake, blade or point). For more precision, this final blow was often applied using a soft hammer (made of hard wood or antler). Different types of Levallois stone reduction methods were designed for the production of flakes, points and blades with predetermined morphologies. The Levallois method has been recognized in much older contexts, and it is even documented in Africa during the Acheulian.[181] Apart from the Levallois stone-knapping methods, Neandertal groups likewise maintained and developed many other technologies, taking advantage of know-how acquired and transmitted over the very long evolutionary period of stone knapping (discoid, centripetal, Quina, uni, bi and multidirectional methods) (see Figure 5.3).

While Neandertal peoples innovated stone-knapping methods and created new tool forms, they also continued to use cobble tools for hammering and pounding activities (choppers and other heavy-duty tools). Even handaxes, the emblematic tools of the

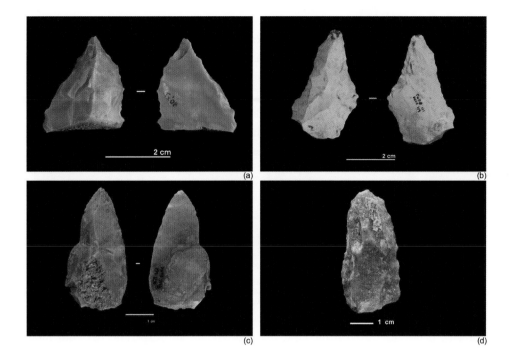

Figure 5.3
Middle Paleolithic tools from Teixoneres Cave near the town of Moià (Barcelona, Spain). (a), (b), and (c) Retouched points from level IIIb, (d) Retouched tool from level IIIb. Teixoneres is a small cavity with a stratigraphic sequence that covers much of the Middle Paleolithic (> 250 Ka at the bottom and 35 Ka at the top). The cave was regularly used by carnivores, mainly cave bears in winter and hyenas during the breeding period. Teixoneres was also a referent place for the human groups of the region. Generally of short duration, the human occupations were developed at the entrance of the cave and are characterized by the presence of hearths, lithic tools and small fragments of ungulate bones, mainly horses, red deer and aurochs. The IPHES-CERCA studies in this site show a clear organizational pattern, which consists in the development of domestic activities around the hearths: knapping tools, processing and consuming animals, sleeping, and so on. Lithic tools display an interesting dichotomy: while discoid reduction sequences were used to knap local raw materials (quartz), Levallois methods were applied to the rocks coming from farther away (>30 km). The most common tools at Teixoneres are points and side scrapers, which allow inferring the significant role played by this place for the hunting activities of the Neandertals of the region. (Text, Jordi Rosell, director of excavations at Teixoneres (IPHES-CERCA); photographs by Gerard Campeny and M. Gema Chacón courtesy of the IPHES-CERCA).

Acheulian, are present in some Mousterian tool kits (the so-called Mousterian of Acheulian tradition).[232,251] Often, blanks obtained from cores were shaped by small removals (retouch) into a range of light-duty tools, including a wide array of pointed tools that were sometimes hafted for use as projectiles. As with the previous techno-complexes we have seen, the European Mousterian did not in fact designate a single cultural entity but rather the entire range of Middle Paleolithic cultures defined for the most part by the features of the stone tool kits found in their different regions of representation.[56,232] For a long time, different cultural strains within the Mousterian were ascribed by "classifying" individual tool kits in accordance with their typological features (tool types) and the proportional representation of their components (tool types, Levallois products, etc.). As discussed in Chapter 2, the "typological" system based on the proportional representation of specific morphological criteria contributed largely to defining the Mousterian cultural denominations that are still in use today, notwithstanding the (more recent) recognition that other factors played a role in final tool kit morphology and composition (site-specific functional aspects, raw materials, regional tendencies, traditions, etc.).

THE NEW FACE OF THE NEANDERTAL

It is important to acknowledge the growing body of evidence showing that Neandertals were capable of realizing artistic undertakings, that they used body decoration (feathers, jewelry, ocher) and that they demonstrated altruistic sensibilities.[227,252,253,254,255] While the cultural practice of decorating the body with adornments (jewelry, tattoos, clothing and pigmentation) was initially believed to have originated only with modern humans, it has now been made clear that Neandertals also experimented with body ornamentation underpinning their symbolic behaviors (see Figure 5.4). This has important implications concerning the degree to which Neandertals practiced complex social and even spiritual behaviors in relation to symbolic and linguistic faculties, suggesting advanced cognitive competences. Recently, cut marks on bird bones of raptors and corvids found in Neandertal (Middle Paleolithic and Chaterlperronian) occupations have been interpreted as evidence for the ornamental use of feathers and bird claws for body decoration purposes.[253,256] Recent finds in the Chatelperronian levels of the Cova Foradada (Calafell, Spain) identify the probable use of imperial eagle phalanges for body ornamentation, underscoring similar finds of large raptor phalanges manipulated by humans in *at least 10 sites dated between* ~130 *and 42 ka*,[256] all suggesting a pattern of symbolic use of feathers as personal ornaments. At the Croatian Neandertal site of Krapina (130 Ka), no less than eight white-tailed eagle bones (talons, phalanxes) with traces of human intervention in some cases suggested that they were mounted to form a part of a jewelry assemblage.[257]

At the Spanish site of Cueva de los Aviones (120–115 Ka), perforated marine shells with ocher (red and yellow colorants) and other shells with pigment residues apparently used as containers support the hypothesis that Neandertals were carrying out symbolic behaviors (comparable to those attributed to modern humans recorded in the South African Middle Stone Age [MSA]).[227,231] The finders of these discoveries have argued that this evidence, together with data indicating that the Atapuerca Sima de los Huesos fossils (0.43 Ma) possessed the auditory structure required to produce and recognize the sounds emitted by modern human language, suggests that the capacity for modern language (emblematic of symbolic culture) could have evolved in a common ancestor existing prior to the divergence of the Neandertals lineage more than 0.5 Ma.[258,259] Meanwhile, an early emergence for art (with a progression from the Middle Paleolithic and Chatelperronian into the Upper Paleolithic) is now supported by evidence of cave art from three Neandertal sites (La Pasiega, Maltravieso and Doña Trinidad or Ardales) dating to around 65 Ka.[227] Indications of "modern" symbolic behavior by Neandertals strengthen the findings of natural pigments in Middle Paleolithic sites (such as red ochre, manganese and hematite), sometimes imported from considerable distances.[260] In the archeological contexts, symbolic use of these natural pigments for body decoration is inferred based on ethnographic indications while there were in fact many other uses for ocher such as preserving foodstuffs, tanning hides and making medicinal preparations, adhesives and even insect repellant.[261]

Going a step further, there is also evidence that Neandertals occasionally practiced symbolic burial of their dead. Natural phenomena or taphonomic reasons are sometimes evoked as causes provoking burial-like accumulations, causing them to be mistakenly interpreted as deliberate or symbolic mortuary practices. For example, outdated excavation methods or hasty interpretations might lead to misinterpretations of some archeological contexts. In spite of this, a number of sites have now yielded unequivocal evidence of this. One example is the Shanidar site in Iraq with deposits dated to around 50 Ka where an impressive number of Neandertal finds are attributed to intentional burial (eight adults and two children).[262] Pollen analysis was put forward as evidence that a child was buried on a bed of flowers, although this interpretation was contested after claims that the pollen could have been transported by rodents or other natural agents.[263] However, revisiting this site using new methodologies to analyze the archeological context has allowed confirmation of the intentional nature of the Shanidar burials, and, even more recently, a new skeleton attributed to a deliberate burial of an adult male has been documented.[264] Another example is from the La Chapelle-aux-Saints cave site (France) dating to around 60 Ka.[265] During the early excavations by the Bouyssonie brothers (who were Catholic priests) at the beginning of the twentieth century, archeologists discovered a Neandertal skeleton in anatomical connection in a depression that appeared to have been intentionally carved out of the encasing limestone. While the anthropic character of this depression has been questioned,[266] recent reevaluations support the original hypothesis of intentional inhumation.[267] Furthermore, skeletal remains from La Chapelle-aux-Saints are attributed to an elderly individual with physical handicaps and lacking most of his teeth, implying that the person would have needed constant care for feeding and mobility from other group members. This buttresses increasing evidence that European Neandertals practiced altruism even prior to their contact with AMHs (although this hypothesis is contested by some).[268] The Neandertal fossil record contains other examples of individuals that apparently survived a number of years in spite of severe physical impairments. That disabled individuals received care during the ancient Paleolithic is known from older evidence, too. For examples, one of the Dmanisi hominins dating to ca. 1.8 Ma survived

Figure 5.4
Display of a *Homo neandertalensis* bust in the Museum of Human Evolution in Burgos, Spain, with ornamentation, face paint and a feather headdress based on evidence from the Italian site of Fumane Cave by F. Fogliazza, Laboratory of Palaeontology at the Natural History Museum of Milan. (Photograph courtesy of Denis Dainat, Établissement public de coopération culturelle–Centre européen de recherches préhistoriques de Tautavel)

some years even after losing all but one of its teeth, certainly with aid from other group members[269] or "cranium 14" from Atapuerca Sima de los Huesos that revealed a rare brain deformity in a child who, in spite of this, survived for more than five years.[270]

The Neanderthals have intensely marked our perception of human evolution during the later phases of the Paleolithic. Theirs was a distinctive world that included unique forms of cultural expression on the threshold of modern humanity. How aware were the Neanderthals of their own origins and ancestry? Neanderthals are our closest extinct relatives, and their anatomical differences distinguish them from modern humans even though the evidence indicates that they possessed a high degree of intelligence and a capacity for artistic and altruistic behaviors. Neanderthals disappeared from the archeological record following the conquest of AMHs who migrated (from Africa and other lands) to occupy all areas of the globe. Although there are many hypotheses to explain the reasons for the extinction of Neandertals, in regard to modern human behavior, one may tend to agree with the postulate of a grim end for these last survivors in a world where humans still held to their natural links with the universe around them. With this vision in mind, we can establish links in taxonomy, behavior and culture to seek to understand the origins and evolution of our own cultural universe.

6

CONQUEST
The Final Phases of the Stone Age

THE FIRST ANATOMICALLY MODERN HUMANS

Our own species, the earliest members of which are referred to as *anatomically modern humans* (AMH), is described taxonomically as a subspecies of Homo called *Homo sapiens*. In 2003, American paleoanthropologist T. White (professor at the University of California, Berkeley) and his research team announced their discovery of a very ancient form of modern humans found in 1997 in Ethiopia (Upper Herto Member of the Bouri Formation in the Afar Triangle) ascribed an age of 160 thousand years (Ka).[271] Named *Homo sapiens idaltu*, the so-called Herto Man fossils constituted at the time the oldest remains attributed to an ancient member of the *Homo sapiens* lineage. Today, only a quarter of a century after White and his team revealed their discovery to the world, new finds from Morocco (at Jebel Irhoud) have pushed back the date for the emergence of our species in Africa to as early as 300 Ka, almost doubling their presumed antiquity.[22] Elsewhere in the world, AMHs appear in various chronological contexts, but as confirmed everywhere by the archeological record, the impacts of their incursion into new lands was never a trite affair. More recently, the unexpected finds published from the Mislya cave in Israel and the Apidima cave in Greece have greatly pushed back this date (to nearly 200 Ka), considerably increasing the age previously accepted for the arrival of modern humans (presumably) from Africa (and the presence of mixed hominin forms).[210,226,272]

This vitally important new information greatly changes what we know about our direct ancestors, their presence in Western Eurasia and their encounters with other (now extinct) forms of *Homo*. The implications for the overlapping of different hominin species with *Homo sapiens* is indeed among the most important consequences of this change in the timing for the arrival and spread of modern humans in Western Eurasia (and Siberia) because we know that the Neandertals (and Denisovans and the newly published Nesher Ramla Homo[273]) were thriving there in this time frame. Meanwhile, *Homo floresiensis* and *Homo luzonensis* were occupying territories as far away as Indonesia and the Philippines.[217,230] While the possibility for encounters between different species of *Homo* is still being archeologically explored, we are reminded that this is not the first time that the archeological record shows such overlapping of hominin species in different geographical areas throughout the past. Nevertheless, the fact remains that modern humans inexorably became the only hominin species to inhabit the planet. As we have seen, the demise of the Neandertals at least in Western Europe was generally thought to have quite closely followed the arrival of AMHs. Indeed, compared to other hominins, AMHs rapidly occupied lands even beyond the Old World, reaching North America perhaps some 20,000–15,000 years ago[274] (some have claimed a far earlier age of 130,000 years ago,[275] but this has been refuted) and Australia some 65,000 years ago.[276] While we tend to visualize this phenomenon as dispersion (or demographic trend), some experts have pointed out the possibility that AMHs could even have derived from preexisting forms of *Homo erectus* (North Africa),[212] *Homo antecessor*[163,166,213] or *Homo heidelbergensis* (Europe).[277]

Let us now examine more closely the form of archaic *Homo sapiens* that appeared in Western Europe and that is especially well documented from around 40 Ka under the name *Cro-Magnon*, a classification coined by L. Lartet in 1868 after the eponymous French site of the same name (Abri de Cro-Magnon) in Les Eyzies-de-Tayac. These modern humans were the craftspeople of the remarkable cultural technocomplexes of the Upper Paleolithic succession. Each phase of the Upper Paleolithic cultural sequence has been denominated and defined almost exclusively from the material evidence these populations left behind in the archeological record, notably tools made of stone, bone, antler and ivory as well as with different artistic expressions. Modern humans have an average brain size of about 1,350 cm^3 (with some differences between the sexes),[278] which is actually smaller than that of the Neandertals.[279] But, unlike the Neandertals (and their forebears), *Homo sapiens'* skulls boast a bulging frontal area resulting from the expansion of this cerebral region (or forebrain), known especially to be largely responsible for abstract and symbolic thought processes, planning, memory and social skills. Modern humans present other distinctive physical differences such as their relatively gracile skeletal features, especially when compared with those of Neandertals. Their legs are proportionately longer and their arms are shorter relative to body height. Modern human cranial features further differ from those of preceding hominins with, for example, the disappearance of brow ridges, the development of a prominent chin, a less robust masticatory region and smaller teeth. In addition to the anatomical changes evident in the AMH, their development occurred in synchronicity with very significant technobehavioral changes that would indelibly mark our evolutionary trajectory. Remarkably, these transformations have a tendency to become more pronounced throughout the evolutionary progression of AMHs, especially around 15,000 years ago by which time, in some areas of the world, populations had began to cultivate wild grains and domesticate livestock, gradually establishing the first semisedentary civilizations.[280]

The disappearance of Neandertals from the archeological record in most regions is often associated with (or attributed to) the appearance of AMHs (although new data is changing this scenario); their cultural trademark included novel tool kits with some implements recognized as effective weaponry. Throughout the Upper Paleolithic, modern human populations continued their rapid demographic expansion even as they widened their range of tool types and perfected their skills, (most notably) making expert use of blade-producing technologies. Their gear was manufactured with care and dexterity using techniques that economized on their preferred fine-quality raw material, flint. In some areas, for example, Africa, modern humans largely exploited obsidian, a glasslike rock favored in places where volcanic activity gave rise to its formation. The fine-grained matrix offered by these rocks presented clear advantages to the artisans.

After their African genesis, modern humans set out to write a series of new chapters in the story of their evolution, sharpening their cognitive development by increasing symbolic thought processes ever further. In the archeological register, this phenomenon is materialized by the ever-increasing rapidity with which technological advancements were invented and (ultimately) executed to perfection. During the Upper Paleolithic, unique and groundbreaking technologies boosted the range of cultural expression far beyond survival-related or purely functional aspects, often demonstrating a more pronounced concern for aesthetic quality than ever before.

At a comparatively early date, the South African Middle Stone Age (MSA) archeological record reveals some very significant and relatively ancient archeological sites that have yielded evidence for modern human activity in a rich archeological record dating up to some 100,000 years ago. This time frame corresponds with the African MSA and temporally overlaps with the bourgeoning Neandertal populations living in parts of Eurasia (European Middle Paleolithic). The South African evidence comes from abundant cave sites (for example, Blombos and Klasies River caves) situated mainly along the coastline and whose long stratigraphic sequences attest to the extraordinarily sophisticated material culture and complex behavioral patterning of these early human groups. The finds include hearths, remnants of marine and terrestrial faunal resources (fish, shells, eggshells, animal bones) and interesting uses of organic materials, including ochre.[231,281] Archeologically perceptible symbolic behaviors are especially noteworthy. The stone tools made by the Homo sapiens inhabiting these sites, such as the finely worked bifacial leaf points (Stillbay points), present remarkable technical and morphological analogies with the European Solutrean foliate points (ca. 20,000 years ago). They also bear resemblances to tools found in Siberia (ca. 14,000 years ago) and to

Figure 6.1
Member of the pastoral Hamar tribe from southwestern Ethiopia (Omo River valley) wearing shell and bead jewelry and entirely covered with a mixture of red ochre and animal fat. (Fabio Mondelli from Pixabay available at https://pixabay.com/photos/ethiopia-tribe-ethnicity-4089002/)

those made by the Clovis peoples of North America (ca. 11,500 years ago). This has led some researchers to claim that these technomorphological similarities extending over such wide geographical areas could indicate some type of cultural continuity or connection, perhaps telling of ancient human migrations (the Solutrean hypothesis) although this premise remains to be solidly demonstrated in the archeological register.[282]

The South African evidence reveals that early modern human groups mastered a complex set of subsistence strategies, which enabled them to very effectively exploit the different environmental niches available to them including marine settings. Their activities included not only scavenging, hunting, trapping and fishing but also artistic endeavors. The discovery of pieces of ocher engraved with geometrical designs at the MSA occupation of Blombos cave with levels dated to between 100–70 Ka, for example, shows that the sophistication of culture was derived from criteria beyond usefulness, founded in artistic design and reflecting even basic notions of geometry.[231,281,283] In addition, perforated shells that were likely used for personal adornment point toward complex codification, perhaps linked to social ranking and ritual. Furthermore, abalone shells that were used as containers for processing ochre suggest that these human groups even possessed rudimentary notions of chemistry.[281] Ochre, a mineral that has been linked to symbolic behaviors through time, was used at Blombos for a variety of functions, associated with representational, aesthetic and artistic endeavors. This multifunctional mineral, still used today in some tribal contexts for painting, makeup and other forms of decoration, also provides effective protection against harmful solar rays and insects when applied to the skin[284] (see Figure 6.1).

Toward the end of the twentieth century, these findings led to a paradigm shift in our understanding of the timing and geographical situation of the development of modern human behavior.[285] The South African evidence designates a seemingly rapid transformation toward advanced degrees of complex symbolic behavior attributed to *Homo sapiens* at least 100 thousand years ago (in relative synchronicity with the European Middle Paleolithic). According to this view, *Homo sapiens* was using complex (coded) language, developing spiritual consciousness and creating innovative artistic realizations whose relative sophistication is presumed to eventually and inexorably have usurped the Neandertals in Western Europe (and other hominins encountered along the way) at the beginning of the Upper Paleolithic. We saw (in Chapter 5) that it is probable that this "revolution," should it have occurred, must have happened on a very different footing than previously believed given what we now know about the relative complexity of Neandertal lifeways and culture and the fact that there was interspecific breeding. Perhaps most outstanding overall in this bushy evolutionary framework of the genus *Homo* is the tendency by which shared technological skills, knowledge and, especially, communication assumed an *increasingly symbolic character*. Reflecting on this link between material culture and complex human behaviors, we sense that there must be fundamental adaptive advantages that could explain why modern humans and their direct ancestors chose to develop symbolic behaviors so extensively. This massive implementation of symbolic behaviors and abstract communication modes was *an evolutionary choice* that was hemmed into the social fabric; it continues to be a key strategy guiding and strengthening human intra- and intergroup relationships within the framework of the ever-increasing trend toward population growth among our species. Symbolic communication networks established through time must therefore be seen as qualitative adaptive responses that provide(d) an abstract manifestation of the internal human universe. Their evolution occurred in synchronicity with the development of the human brain and the capacity to allocate (all types of) tasks to technological innovations. Symbolic behavior provides a road map that is shared on the deepest subconscious and conscious levels between those individuals who join together to commonly recognize symbolic representations as a set of meanings attributed to specifically developed abstract concepts.

Any given set of symbols shared within a human group has significance only to those who identify with that group and who agree on their meaning. In this way, physical or behavioral symbolic expressions provide individuals with a sense of belonging or membership to a given sociocultural entity, which is (as we saw in Chapters 4 and 5) generally linked to a specific regional context. Shared symbolic references thus allow peoples to identify with one another in specific group settings and, importantly, to contrast their own referents with those of other groups. In short, symbols and symbolic behaviors are the basic building blocks of identity linked thought patterning – contributing to the separation of humans into their regional entities of "us" and "them."[286] I suggest that, in the later phases of the Paleolithic, the abstract reactive process based on symbolic communication was amplified because it provided a useful way to regulate behavior within populations as their scale increased numerically. This abstract perception of belonging to a group (because understanding and sharing its symbolic manifestations) was beneficial on the individual level because it favored the integration of communal rules that were advantageous to the group as a whole, allowing it to best reap the fruits of its technosocial achievements. Furthermore, the socially generated need for symbolic communication directed humans to cultivate increasingly intricate ways to express self-awareness and mutual understanding through spoken language, of course, but also through art, music, ritual, body ornamentation, gestural and body language and so on. Sharing different forms of symbolic expression with their community, individuals were able to rapidly transmit meanings and emotions beyond the inner realm, and this "catharsis" was evidently favored as a sustainable conduct. Once given up for public scrutiny by way of symbolic representation, personal feelings and inner spirituality were exposed to community rigor and judgment, paving the way for the indoctrination of socially dictated rules of what was and what was not acceptable in a given social context. Thus, in the same way that new technologies emerged out of existing technovariability, so modern humans chose to massively develop the potential advantages posed by the use of symbolic communication, as we have seen, as a discrete proto-phenomenon as a uniquely human evolutionary strategy to favor the survival of ever-expanding social units. Seeking to develop a maintainable strategy to preserve the advantages of group living, symbolic expression progressed as humans favored abstract communication systems as a way to unite individuals into functional group entities. We shall discuss the impact of this choice further in upcoming chapters.

THE MATERIAL WORLD OF UPPER PALEOLITHIC HOMO SAPIENS

The global duration of the Upper Paleolithic (African Late Stone Age) varied according to the different regions but was certainly shorter compared with the nearly 300 thousand years of the Middle Paleolithic (and MSA), 1.4 million years for the Acheulian, and an immense 1.7 million years for the Oldowan. Beginning with the major cultural transitions observed occurring in relative synchronicity with the disappearance of the Neanderthals, the Upper Paleolithic duration is short, therefore, in retrospect, compared with the previous periods of the Paleolithic. The Upper Paleolithic was brief relative to the stretch of the Acheulian time span, measured here from its appearance in Africa 1.75 million years ago (Ma) up to around 350,000 years ago. Finally, it was exceedingly short compared to the Oldowan whose global cumulative duration is of 1.7 million years (restrained here from its appearance in Africa nearly 3 million years ago and up to the beginning of the Acheulian in Europe and Asia 1 million years ago). We shall see that this "acceleration" in the relative length of each succeeding cultural phase was, and continues to be, a characteristic trend in the human evolutionary trajectory. Once established, the cultural tendencies demonstrated by AMHs continued to develop throughout the Upper Paleolithic, even as human technological dexterity grew. As we can see, this cumulative process was expressed by distinct cultural traditions (defined from material cultural remains), *succeeding one another with increasing rapidity as we move through time.* Therefore, we are dealing here with something very different from the long phases of comparable cultural stability during the Acheulian and, especially, of the Oldowan.

The technoevolutionary force conveyed by modern human populations combined with demographic expansion and migration flows as they confronted new challenges with ever-greater feats of cultural innovation. Two prime examples are the bow and arrow and the atlatl, both formidable weapons that certainly made modern humans unparalleled in long-distance hunting. Of course, we can also consider the unprecedented proliferation of artistic expression as an outstandingly remarkable modern innovation during the Upper Paleolithic. Relative to previous time frames when artistic endeavors are considerably less commonly recognized in the archeological record,[227] the Upper Paleolithic abounds with of all types of artistic manifestations, seemingly indicating an explosion of creativity and communicative spirituality among modern human peoples. In the Paleolithic context, increased development of artistic expression can be interpreted as a means by which complex human thought processes were being exteriorized and shared on a communal level. When considered thus, prehistoric artistic creations represent a means by which the human inner realm was transposed into the material world. This exteriorization process was so sublimely achieved thanks to the developments in symbolic expression whose intrinsic meanings, by definition, could be understood only by individuals living within the same community and sharing the same network of meaning. Even though today we do recognize forms of artistic expression among the earlier Neandertal populations, or even spiritual tendencies expressed by pre-Neandertals,[287] the Upper Paleolithic archeological record shows us, comparatively, a period when these phenomena entered a highly culminated developmental phase. We may therefore consider "art" as a holistic phenomenon linked closely to modern humans (in Europe especially after around 40,000 years ago). Its rapid proliferation in relation to modern humans is explained by changes in their evolving social and technological worlds.

Despite what we know about the infancy of human artistic expression, therefore, there is still some tendency to perceive the emergence of Paleolithic artistic works as an abrupt and even somewhat synchronous phenomenon as though all of its forms of expression (painting, sculpture, engraving and ornamentation) appeared at once like an upsurge of human expressivity. But in reality, this type of "compression" of the archeological evidence is certainly very imprecise because we can rarely separate distinct chronological episodes so precisely in inter- and intrasite contexts. Anatomically modern humans consummated their artistic creations on different types of surfaces from cave walls to individual objects and, undoubtedly, their own bodies, as they sought the most appropriate canvases for the exteriorization of their aesthetic wonder. Body ornamentation and paintings on cave walls, sculptures and engravings abound relative to preceding

Figure 6.2
Chauvet cave gallery of the lions (Caverne du Pont d'Arc, Musée Caverne Du Pont d'Arc, Ardèche, France). Now a UNESCO World Heritage Site, the Chauvet cave discovered in 1994 constitutes one of the most impressive sets of Upper Paleolithic cave paintings ever identified. Attributed to the Aurignacian and Gravettian cultural complexes, it is also among the oldest. The richness and sophistication of the paintings have contributed to changing our ideas about the emergence of art in the prehistoric context. (HTO, Wikipedia)

cultural complexes as though initiation implied acquisition. Oddly enough, humans themselves are scarcely represented in these early art forms (generally only as abstract, partial, or shamanic forms) and there are few, if any, depictions of landscape or vegetation (trees, grasses or flowers). In contrast, geometrical images and other symbols whose meaning we may only conjecture, are frequent. Some artistic creations were undertaken in the darkest, most obscure areas deep within cave systems, apparently intended for limited sharing or perhaps even only for personal catharsis. We can evoke the play of firelight in appreciating these art works with the changing luminosity of torchlight intensifying their powerful symbolic force (see Figure 6.2).

Why, when and how symbolic communication was selected as a favorable agent among modern human populations remain largely unanswerable questions in archeology. However, numerous hypotheses can be collectively considered as potential factors contributing to the exponential development of this singular phenomenon, perhaps the most outstanding among early modern human populations. Some consider the array of geometric and other signs and symbols (including negative or positive impressions of handprints on cave walls) as a sort of social signaling born of the necessity for peoples to communicate with gestures, perhaps from a distance, for example, during hunting excursions. It should be recalled here that AMH groups were dealing with the expansion of their societies and that this required them to sharpen their social skills and to find ways to innovate operative inter- and intragroup cooperative behaviors. Ultimately, they would have been forced to choose those behaviors that were most favorable to the survival not only of the individual but also of the group. This fundamental concept in the Darwinian "survival of the fittest" doctrine (from individual to group consciousness) precluded the need for each individual to refine his/her ability to accurately evaluate and predict the behaviors of other members of the group, each playing an active role within the social unit. Consequently, the need to hone in on some type of "mental reading ability"[288] could have engendered a niche for gestural and other forms of symbolic language. Evidently, we may concede that the development of social skills was/is an adaptive strategy for survival within group contexts, and, furthermore, as our own modern societies attest, the larger the social group is, the more elaborate the network of communicative symbolic repertory will be. This evolutionary shift toward exceedingly complex thought patterning was achieved through cooperative symbolic representation, be it pictorial, gestural, verbal or other. The anatomical repercussions of these behavioral choices are indeed observable in the changes undergone through time within the human brain itself. The physical embodiment of these anatomical repercussions is notable in the remarkably high degree of cephalization in modern humans compared with all other animal species (the modern human brain reflects the exponential development of the neocortex – the so-called gray matter – and of the frontal region of the brain from which emanate high-level cognitive functions necessary for abstract thought patterning).

AN OVERVIEW OF THE SUCCESSIVE CULTURAL COMPLEXES FROM THE EUROPEAN UPPER PALEOLITHIC

The Upper Paleolithic refers to a chrono-cultural division in prehistory during which modern humans expanded over the globe, developing their cultural materializations to embrace largely blade-based technologies that would eventually evolve toward microlithic and often composite tools. Modern humans innovated highly standardized new tool types that were taken historically as indicators of cultural successions in the different regions. They frequently added bone, ivory and antler to their raw material repertoires, creating new types of tools as well as artistic objects. They produced art and used natural pigments and other items for ritual body ornamentation and decoration (shells, teeth). Archeological evidence shows that modern human populations ranged over very large distances, which would in later periods lead them to develop the first forms of trade. High mobility during the Upper Paleolithic on a regional level is also tangible as is demonstrated, for example, by the presence at some sites of exogenous flint collected from different areas around the sites or of objects (shells, fossils, odd stones or rare raw materials) alien to the immediate environment around the sites. In some cases, objects were transported over hundreds of kilometers:

However, most researchers agree that the observed cultural and technological traits, as well as the population increase during the Upper Paleolithic, were more rapid and had distinct global effects across Eurasia and Africa when compared with the slow pace of cultural changes during the Middle Paleolithic. Not the least of the human achievements of the Upper Paleolithic were the long-distance exchanges of raw materials and precious items, the occupation of the northern latitudes under periglacial conditions, the colonization of the Americas, and the first steps in coastal navigation and seafaring.[289]

To sketch out the major cultural achievements characterizing this time frame in Western Europe, I propose here only a brief description of cultural *facies* presently identified for the Upper Paleolithic based on a synthetic work by the French prehistorian A. Leroi-Gourhan.[232] This synthesis still represents the basic typological framework forming the original definitions from the major cultural complexes of the Upper Paleolithic established on the Western European (especially French) prototype[57] ("homeland of the discipline of prehistoric archaeology"[289]). Therefore, while mention in this chapter will be made of the expansion and variety of Upper Paleolithic (or end-Paleolithic) complexes on a wider geographic scale, the present discourse centers on the original French typo-cultural framework. That said, I urge you to keep in mind that each continent or geographic area had its own cultural succession with denominations fitting the particular contexts (often deriving from eponymous sites or relating to the geographical area in question). Indeed, at this point in the human evolutionary trajectory, material culture had diversified and spread such that its geographic complexity would be too wide ranging to describe in the framework of this book. In spite of the end-Paleolithic cultural diversification, common denominators do exist in most regions, at least in terms of the major tendencies such as the shift to blade technologies and (in some cases) microlithization. There was also more frequent use of bone and antler tools, increasingly widespread manifestations of art, diversification of the tool kits and behaviors, long-distance mobility and trade and so on (exceptions include, for example, southeast Asia's cultural complexes with flaked cobble tools). Of course, the scenario for the chrono-cultural successions described in different areas of the globe for this period also continues to evolve, as does their complexity, in pace with new discoveries and improved modern technologies applied to archeology. In fact, the complexity is such that very detailed cultural categorizations subdivide the general frameworks outlined here, varying per the different regional contexts. All of this simply reflects, once again, the tendencies I have defined in previous chapters: the exponential intensification of accumulated culture occurring through time due to increased intergroup networking and exchange of ideas, innovations and objects. Improved language and deepened symbolic communication further allowed the preservation and transmission of huge amounts of accumulated (and even very multifacetted) information with ever-increasing efficiency. As humans settled all over Eurasia and Africa, they grouped into new cultural units in relation to relatively constrained regional contexts, giving way to the plethora of cultural denominations existing today to describe their manifestations in each part of the world during and after the Upper Pleistocene.

However unsatisfying they are, the profiles of these cultural units conserve their characterizations from the range of tool types discovered in the different eponymous site contexts. I remark that the "typological" tradition used in prehistory remains, at least for the Upper Paleolithic, the dominant strategy for inter- and intracultural differentiation as perceived in the global chrono-cultural framework built by prehistorians. The European Upper Paleolithic cultural succession (from the oldest to the most recent) is categorized as *Chatelperronian*, *Aurignacian*, *Gravettian*, *Solutrean* and *Magdalenian*. Each of these cultural units is presented briefly here in accordance to its general features and its chronological and geographical representation (mainly) in Western Europe.[232] This is because this part of the world has been an important source of archeological data that served (early on) to define these cultures, and this is historically where the eponymous sites are situated. Therefore, I provide here a general description for each cultural unit, underlining salient features and historical context (further subdivisions and diverse representations exist for each of these Paleolithic technocomplexes that interested readers can find more amply described in other works).

The *Chatelperronian* cultural complex, first defined 1906 by H. Breuil, is believed to indicate a transitional phase from the Middle to the Upper Paleolithic in Western Europe and is commonly attributed to Neandertals, although this relationship is currently under debate.[290] First defined from *La grotte des fées*, a cave site situated in Châtelperron (France) and dating to around 45–40 Ka, Chatelperronian cultural assemblages (analogous to the Italian *Uluzzian*) are documented essentially from southwestern France, the Atlantic Pyrenees, Catalonia and northern Spain. Their main defining components include pointed tools denominated *Chatelperron* points, splintered flake pieces and retouched end scrapers and awls as well as truncated blades (that were hafted). Mousterian-type denticulate tools are also a hallmark. Bone tools such as bi-conic spear tips, bird-bone tubes and some sawed antler tools are also found in Chatelperronian assemblages. Bone-cut pendants and perforated teeth also form a part of the Chatelperronian cultural complex. Post holes identified in some sites provide evidence that Chatelperronian peoples lived in structured habitats with circular huts.

The *Aurignacian* is a relatively widespread cultural complex recorded in Western Europe from around 40 Ka (the Early Aurignacian and proto-Aurignacian real chronostratigraphic positions are still not clearly distinguished). This cultural facies was first defined by E. Lartet in 1860 at the eponymous Aurignac site (Haute-Garonne, France). Even though (in many cases) it is the first cultural entity recognized in the Upper Paleolithic, the Aurignacian presents a break with the preceding Mousterian technocomplex. However, it is not to be considered as a single cultural unit because although it has some unifying features, it presents typological and technological variability, often interpreted as successive evolutionary phases that have been diversely described by prehistorians over time. At the turn of the century, Breuil recognized three distinct phases (lower, middle and upper) within the Aurignacian, basing his observations on key sites situated in Belgium and France. Breuil's classification of the Aurignacian was further refined following D. Peyrony's observations of the industries from two major sites in southwestern France, La Ferrassie and Laugerie-Haute. Peyrony thus coined the "Perigordian" as a (regional) parallel cultural facies with its own sequential technotypological evolution. The complex vision of the Aurignacian was later refined by D. de Sonneville-Bordes and others and continues to evolve as new sites are being documented from a relatively wide geographic area. In agreement with the precepts of a typological approach, the defining factors within the Aurignacian have been based on the presence/absence of specific tool types (Fr. *fossile-directeur*, in the classical Bordian sense)[56,57] and/or relative tool frequencies (especially regarding bone tools). As specialists examined the tool kits, they also took into account their chrono-stratigraphic positions in the different sites. Because there was not always agreement on the chronological position of each of the defined typological entities within the Aurignacian, it was only with difficulty that the complex was finally organized into a more or less coherent succession of intracultural units. Different phases of the Aurignacian assemblages are generally characterized by large flint blades that sometimes have stepped retouch as well as by bone points with split bases and the so-called Dufour bladelets. Meanwhile, the more recent Aurignacian assemblages tend to include smaller-sized blades and bladelets. Aurignacian assemblages also comprise very finely crafted ornate objects made from bone and antler accompanied by a series of retouched flint tool types. Aurignacian cultural evidence spans beyond Western and central Europe into the Levant and southwestern Asia (Iran). Humans attributed to this phase of cultural evolution created remarkable cave paintings, such as the one brought to light in 1994 at Chauvet in Vallon-Pont-d'Arc (Ardèche, France).[291]

Bone and stone tool assemblages of the *Gravettian* cultural phase (32–26 Ka) follow the Aurignacian chrono-stratigraphically. This cultural unit was first defined at the eponymous site *La Gravette* in the Dordogne region (France) and is known to have spread throughout much of Western Europe. Its geographical range covers a vast area from the Russian plains through central Europe and northward from France into Belgium and Great Britain following the impulse of different phases of expansion. The Gravette point (a small, backed and straight-edged pointed blade tool likely to have been hafted and used for hunting) is one outstanding element defining the Gravettian tool kit. Again, the Gravettian phase of the Upper Paleolithic represents a period of great technosocial sophistication whose successive expressions vary on a regional scale. These variations are experienced in archeology as different units of material culture, but they must in fact be attributable to various causes such as shifting environmental conditions and local traditions. The Gravettian is also thought to be representative of the more recent phases of Peyrony's so-called Perigordian cultural complex (named after the French region of Périgord), especially in central Europe. Gravettian human groups were formidable hunters of large game, especially reindeer and mammoths. In Ukraine, Gravettian peoples built circular huts with mammoth bones and tusks.[292] Gravettian peoples carved

(a)

(b)

Figure 6.3
Typical Gravettian flint tools from SMA-Esterno Stratigraphic Unit 9 (SU9), Santa Maria di
Agnano cave (Ostuni, Brindisi, Italy). (a) End scraper on a blade retouched on both edges
(Ancient Gravettian, 25521–24549 cal. BC). (b) SMA-Esterno Stratigraphic Unit 10 (SU10),
Santa Maria di Agnano cave (Ostuni, Brindisi. Italy). Foliated point on blade (Ancient
Gravettian, 25521–24549 cal. BC). (Courtesy of Henry Baills and Donato Coppola)

"Venus" figurines that are thought to represent fertility goddesses and are among the
most outstanding artistic feats characterizing this cultural complex[293] (see Figure 6.3).

The Solutrean cultural phase recognized from sites situated mainly in France, Spain
and England, age-bracketed to around 26–20 Ka, is especially defined by an outstanding
series of finely crafted foliated tool types (generally made from flint). These tools
were shaped using very fine and flat retouch. The Solutrean was first defined in
1864 after excavations in Les Eyzies, France (by E. Lartet and H. Christy) yielded pointed
tools with affinities to those described at another site, *Cros du Charnier*, at the eponymous
Solutré. As I have mentioned, analogies in the morphology and techniques used
by Solutrean peoples to make their foliated points and tools discovered in Siberia
(20–14 Ka) and North America's Clovis culture (roughly 12 Ka) have been noted in
terms of a (still unconfirmed) migration link.[282] Solutrean peoples also made a wide
range of artistic creations such as cave paintings, sculptures, ornaments and jewelry.
They worked with different materials including ivory, bone, antler, ochre and other
natural pigments.

The final phases of the Western European Upper Paleolithic cultural sequence
are marked by the appearance of Magdalenian civilizations documented from around
20 to 12 Ka from Western Europe and into Poland. The name of this cultural unit was
coined in 1863 by E. Lartet and derives from the eponymous *La Madelaine* site situated in
Dordogne (France). Like the previous Upper Paleolithic cultural entities, the
Magdalenian was subdivided early on into six distinct phases (by Breuil) and identified

Figure 6.4
Typical Magdalenian flint tools from Les Conques cave (Vingrau, Pyrénées-Orientales, France). (a) Scalene bladelet (Final Magdalenian 13350 ±140 years BP) (b) Retouched blade (Final Magdalenian, 13350 ±140 years BP). (c) Straight dihedral chisel (Middle Magdalenian, 14320 ± 90 years BP). (Courtesy of Henry Baills)

by the presence/absence of specific types of tools and their relative representations in some key sites. Currently, however, these subdivisions have been largely replaced in favor of "ancient, middle and final." Magdalenian stone tools were generally made of flint, and they are characterized by small-sized backed blades and bladelets, retouched end scrapers, awls and chisels as well as a wide range of bone tools including harpoons for fishing and sewing needles. Magdalenian peoples also made remarkable artistic creations using different types of materials available to them. Their technologies and aesthetic creations attest to the fact that these peoples had attained a peak in the degree of sophistication and intensity of artistic sensibility and spirituality (see Figures 6.4 and 6.5). This phase of human culture is sometimes referred to as the "age of reindeer" because of the extensive hunting and carcass exploitation of this animal practiced by Magdalenian peoples.

In an analogous time frame to the European Upper Paleolithic, other parts of the world were experiencing similar cultural "revolutions" triggered by the sociotechnical advancements achieved by anatomically modern humans. The archeological registers from Africa, Asia, the Levant and even the Americas and Australia by the end of the European Paleolithic all bear witness to the same intensely accelerated advancement of modern human culture and the sheer density of the remnants of their civilizations as inventors and creators of a new world order. All of these unprecedented breakthroughs in technology and art occurred with ever-increasing rapidity in a snowball effect as

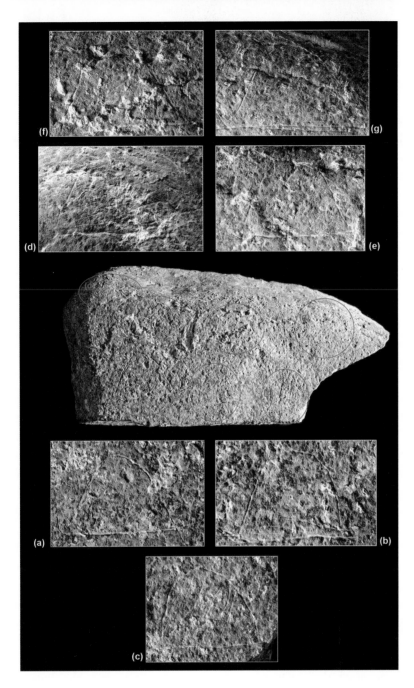

Figure 6.5

Engraving from Molí del Salt rock shelter (Conca de Barberà, Tarragona). This site contains Mesolithic and Late Upper Paleolithic (Late Magdalenian) layers. This engraving made on a schist slab was found in one of the Magdalenian layers and shows seven semicircular motifs that have been interpreted as huts. This would be the oldest representation of a hunter-gatherer campsite. A bone fragment located next to the slab has been dated to ca.13,700 years cal. BP (excavation directed by Manuel Vaquero and Susana Alonso, Universitat Rovira I Virgili and IPHES-CERCA in Tarragona, Spain. (Manuel Vaquero, courtesy of the IPHES-CERCA) different elements combined to favor the exponential development and perfection of Stone Age technologies. In spite of their heterogeneity, Upper Paleolithic cultures express the culmination of a fixed set of developmental tendencies that, as we have seen, were deeply rooted in the procedural evolution of technology from its inception through each successive landmark of its evolutionary trajectory. Still, we sense that the creators of these Upper Paleolithic technologies were still clinging to their foundations, maintaining survival-related advantages while transforming them into something more – greater and deeper – by way of aesthetic pleasures and inventiveness. And yet, at the twilight of the Stone Age, humanity was teetering on the verge of its divorce from the universal harmony of its animal-nature relationship – guided by controlled and reasoned action/reaction triggers – toward the more frenetic and chaotic spiral of modern technological development lacking in reasonable constraints. The Upper Paleolithic may thus be considered as a transformative juncture leading to the domination of the externalization of the satisfaction of basic human needs through material creations and, ultimately, to our complete dependency on them.

Presently, the human condition is even more strongly conditioned in this way, characterized by our ever-widening dependence on the now explosive rate of human technological innovation. Our voyage through the past has allowed us to distinguish the most fundamental evolutionary aspects of this technoselection process in spite of its multiple expressions. One that I would like to underline again here is the tendency for Paleolithic technologies to become more standardized through time and for this standardization to establish ever-stronger links to specific geographical regions in pace with demographic growth. As we will see in the upcoming chapters of this book, this tendency ultimately generated and strengthened what we call today "traditions," themselves transformed through time into the very essence of cultural "differentiation" among peoples. In sum, the evolution of technology through time clearly reflects complexity in the increased diversification of intentionally shaped objects and their intimate linking into especially designed social networking systems that they eventually came to represent. Ultimately, we have witnessed the objectification of human spiritualism through art, language and now even more abstract (digital and virtual) communication systems into something shared and transposed through time as a message linking all humans together: the materialization of (now global) symbols existing as collective consciousness.

The stage on which these transformations played out was set by the climatic oscillations of the last glacial age, which constantly presented new challenges to humans and that they effectively met by creating, increasing and refining novel technoadaptations that improved survival skills and favored their reproductive success. Climatic instability of the periodic glacial expansions experienced during the Upper Paleolithic caused temperatures to drop relatively rapidly, unleashing environmental changes marked by the development of massive polar ice sheets, the lowering of sea levels and fluctuating ecosystems. But these changes also offered new opportunities to modern humans as pathways were opened into new territories into which they moved to exploit the wealth of virgin areas and their resources. In the latter phases of the last glacial maximum (LGM) around 20 thousand years ago, humans reached the Americas, perhaps via the Bering Straits, a barren land mass that emerged after the sea levels had receded. Later, around 17–15 Ka, warmer temperature trends commencing in the northern hemisphere and spreading to the far reaches of the planet progressively reversed these glacial trends. Melting masses of polar ice caused sea levels to rise once again, inundating land bridges and islands exposed during the colder glacial events. Oblivious to the future impacts of their conquest, human beings, thriving in their mobility, strengthened their capacities to transport and transmit their objective universe, eventually developing trade, exhibiting their cultural identities and contrasting them with those of other existing civilizations. Technical innovation enabled populations to grow and prosper while more efficient survival strategies increased life spans and strengthened family ties, permitting younger individuals to benefit from the cumulated knowledge of their elders. While the earlier phases of technosocial development were marked by long periods of equilibrium, the Upper Paleolithic was punctuated by relatively rapid cultural upheavals in which emerging cultural entities attained short-lived cycles of stability before new innovations transformed them once again.

REPERCUSSIONS OF THE EXPANSION AND PLANETARY CONQUEST OF ANATOMICALLY MODERN HUMAN POPULATIONS

Beyond the marvels of human sociocultural development during the Upper Paleolithic and in the framework of the objectives of this work (to better understand the roots of the present human condition), it is important to provide here some additional observations regarding this phase of human development. While there is no evidence that the extinction of the Neandertals and other species of Homo resulted from genocidal acts by modern humans, we cannot but admit that certain aspects of our own behaviors could perhaps portent a destructive relationship between modern humans and other forms of life, let alone other forms of Homo. Keeping this in mind, the archeological record does hold some indications of such circumstances. One example is the notable disappearance of numerous species of megafauna (including large and very large herbivores such as mammoths, rhinoceros and hippopotamus as well as carnivores such as cave bears, hyenas and saber-toothed cats) in close temporal synchronicity with the arrival of modern humans into newly colonized areas. Extinction episodes are in fact documented in close chronological and spatial proximity with the arrivals of modern humans into new territories (North and South America, Australia and Madagascar, for example) while this tendency is not observed in other parts of the world where humans had been present over many millennia (India, Southeast Asia, Africa). It has been suggested[294] that in the case of animals and humans having shared space over very long time spans, the animals would have been aware of the potential dangers posed by

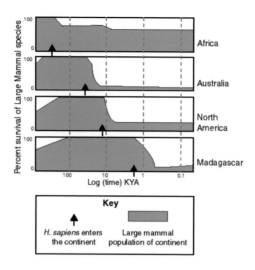

Figure 6.6
Timing of extinctions follows the march of man. (After Martin, 1989, Elin Whitney Smith at English Wikipedia via Wikimedia Commons)

humans and would therefore have developed (over time) the appropriate "flee and hide" strategies that would have allowed them to survive. On the other hand, in the case of arrivals of modern humans into new territories, those animals that did not have the experience of long-term encounters would not have demonstrated fear and would thus have easily succumbed to human hunters[294] (see Figure 6.6).

While different hypotheses have been put forward to explain these phenomenon (climate change, an extraterrestrial impact, epizootic diseases),[295,296] the exact causes for these extinction episodes and their possible links with *Homo sapiens* has not yet reached scientific consensus. Still, the fossil record indicates that many species did vanish during this peak human developmental phase of the Upper Paleolithic preceding the warming conditions marking the beginning of the Holocene. The humans living during this time frame had already proven their capacities to adapt and survive through very different climatic contexts, and their ancestors had long overcome the challenges caused by shifting climatic conditions (during previous glacial/interglacial periods). Concerning the hypothesis of devastating panzootic bacterial diseases that could have been carried and transmitted by the colonizing modern human groups, it is plausible that these diseases might have been contracted by some animals, especially considering the lack of time for them to develop the antibodies to combat them. This hypothesis therefore also provides a viable alternative explanation for the observed synchronization in the timing of the arrival of modern humans and the disappearance of multiple species in newly colonized areas of the world. It could also explain why other large-sized mammals, such as moose and caribou, that could have crossed the Bering land bridge into North America along with the first human colonizers did not suffer from the end-Pleistocene extinction events. In a similar vein to the cohabitation hypothesis, animals and humans developing immunities to potentially shared diseases over the long periods of coexistence in some regions could explain why extinction episodes were relatively less drastic in Africa and South Asia, for example. While the hypothesis of human violence toward other life forms to the point of causing extinctions may be difficult to verify in the prehistoric context, evidence for human violence toward other humans is not lacking in subsequent proto-historic iconography, nor later on, in the written documents of the first literate civilizations. If we look to the tendencies observed from the end of the Upper Paleolithic, we can identify that this constitutes an ominous pattern whose acceleration we are continuing to experience in today's world. What has changed, perhaps, is the fact that overhunting in the prehistoric context might have been attributed to a lack of retrospective or, to some extent, ignorance, as human groups selected the simplest of strategies in obtaining foodstuffs for survival. Arguably, prehistoric and even early proto-historic civilizations lacked the hindsight provided by accumulated experience and knowledge offered by written documents concerning, for example, the reproductive cycles of the different animals they were sampling and the ecosocial limits of their survival patterns. However, today, indeed, modern societies do possess the hindsight with which to make conscious and responsible choices in their killing practices.

Another point that we have considered here, albeit invisible in the prehistoric archeological record, is that of language and communication development. With increasing demography and evermore complex lifestyles, modern humans needed to invest in improving their communication systems, thus explaining, in part, the expansion of art. While still maintaining a nomadic existence, increasing survival rates augmented individual group sizes, thus precluding more intricate patterns of role-playing within each social unit and between different groups in their evermore numerous encounters in the landscape. Such meetings would likely have involved exchanges of different types, not only of objects but also of sexual partners, needed to maintain diversity within each gene pool. Concerning these encounters, strengthened group identities that had given way to regional traditions expressed as material culture could have been exchanged in a variety of ways through learning (cultural transmission) or through intrinsic value attribution for some objects. On the one hand, learning through cultural transmission would have contributed to accelerating the ability for human groups to innovate culture as they profited from knowledge accumulated by others, thus saving time and allowing them to move to new advances. On the other hand, value was "attributed" (as it is today) by investing specific objects with worth in some cases justified by evoking their scarcity (for example, inland dwellers valued shells from coastal areas). In the preliterate societies of the end-Paleolithic, this knowledge-exchange network was still in its primitive stages but was already recognized – and selected for – as an operable behavior with fabulous potential for advancing the conquest of the last human species on the planet, *Homo sapiens*.

7

THE NEW WORLD ORDER FOLLOWING THE PALEOLITHIC

THE EPIPALEOLITHIC PERIOD: A PROLOGUE TO NEW PATTERNS OF PRODUCTION

A warming climatic trend following the last major ice age (ending ca. 11,600 before the present [BP]) marks the transition from the Pleistocene to the Holocene – the temperate period in which we currently live). By this time, humanity had consolidated the numerous technosocial achievements developed throughout the Pleistocene into finely tuned cultural norms. Settled thus into a "transformative" existence (a state of constant transformation), humankind continued to cultivate innovative sets of intra- and extra-somatic psychosocial and technological aptitudes, activating increasingly intense repercussions. Each secured accomplishment served as a new source of inspiration feeding into spiraling human inventiveness. The sophistication, however, with which humanity wielded its technological advances at the end of the Pleistocene – just prior to the so-called *Neolithic Revolution*,[297] was already beginning to have effects of significant magnitude not only on human societies in general but also on other life forms on the planet. Unlike during the earlier evolutionary phases of the Paleolithic, the technosocial transformations observable from the end of the Pleistocene took place far more rapidly than biological adaptive processes. Keeping abreast millennia of technological know-how amassed then more easily through efficient communication networking, human societies forming at the threshold of the Neolithic were actively embarking on the acceleration and expansion of their objective world by creating new patterns of productivity. I say "patterns" because, with retrospect, we can easily discern the continuity of this process of escalation (through acculturation) provided by the implantation of such potent adaptive evolutionary strategies as massive abstract communication systems and the establishment of large social units. Technological inventiveness enabled from the huge foundation of expertise amassed throughout the Pleistocene was then flourishing as never before.

In previous chapters, I explained how the human technological tendency gave way to our present condition of technodependency through different phases of experimentation of the potential existing within technological structures (or normalized technical systems). Thus, we have seen how human inventiveness combined with biological development (especially cerebral) led our species to experience different phases of technological advancement for which, in turn, we have necessarily created specific socialization processes to facilitate their integration through learning (culture). Within this spiraling evolutionary process, we have also seen how archeologists have identified cycles of stability that have been recognized historically as a succession of cultural units designated by specific denominations (also referred to as traditions). With this long-term perspective on cultural change, we can now more easily recognize that, through time, different traditions replaced one another with the new technological systems requiring revised socialization processes for integration. Repeatedly, this led to the implosion of existing civilizations and their replacement by new traditions presenting novel cultural features (while the previously existing ones were often "absorbed" – that is to say, their "useful" technocultural aspects were integrated to form the new cultural unit).[298] The liberty to experiment is prerequisite to the development of potentially advantageous technostratagems, which, in turn, facilitate the emergence of change and the consolidation of latent possibilities into concrete technoforms of creation. *Homo* is the only genus to have willfully embarked on this type of process. Acceleration is the structural gist of the human ingenuity process, feeding, as it were, on ideas nascent within each successive technological system. Akin to the *Big Bang* hypothesis explaining universal creation, we can see that, in fact, the structural homogeneity described as the emergence phase of first technologies (during the very earliest Oldowan),[118] actually bore within – from the very beginning – all of the elements with which to construct, destroy and reconstruct the different universes of objective realities that we call culture. The formal attributes of these ever-changing human "realities" necessarily reflect the infinite combinations of the synapses of the human brain that are, in themselves, maintained in a constant state of expansive flux. This process led to our present-day constructed inner operational unity, relying, as it has, on (now globally) shared sets of symbols transmitted through complex systems of communicative networking.

Hunter-gatherer societies flourished during the (relatively short) duration of the Epipaleolithic and Mesolithic periods (generally some 5,000–10,000 years in length, depending on the geographical location). This period that follows the Paleolithic and presages the Neolithic thus varied in chronology and tradition in accordance to the different regions. Epipaleolithic and Mesolithic peoples thrived throughout Eurasia in warming climatic conditions, living in caves, rock shelters and open landscapes and practicing hunter-gatherer subsistence. Epipaleolithic cultures appear as the continuation of the Upper Paleolithic without significant archeologically verifiable change. The oldest of these civilizations appeared more than 21,000 years ago in the Near East (Syria, Jordan, Lebanon, Israel). The particularities of this geographical grouping has justified its attribution to the area-specific cultural entity named Kebaran (Early Near East Epipaleolithic) after the eponymous Kebara cave site situated south of Haifa.[299] Epipaleolithic hunter-gatherers perfected microlithic and hafted tool technologies and creatively explored their symbolic universe through a widening range of artistic expressions. They continued to make and use bone and stone tools, the most characteristic of which are the serrated composite tools mounted with the geometric microliths crafted from flint blades. These peoples hunted small to medium-sized game using hafted tools such as javelins but also fished using harpoons. Because many of the changes seem to appear in continuity with tendencies observed at the end of the Upper Paleolithic, the establishment of an intermediary phase separating the end-Paleolithic from the Neolithic is not without controversy. While some specialists even use the terms interchangeably, others contend that Epipaleolithic should be used to designate those cultural entities that did not subsequently undergo the Neolithic transition and that Mesolithic should refer to the cultural entities existing within the short temporal interval separating these two main technocomplexes.

Around 12,500 BP, nomadic hunter-gatherer populations were replaced in the Levant by proto-agrarian peoples of the Natufian cultural complex.[300,301,302] Elsewhere after the end of the last glacial maximum, a range of post-Upper Paleolithic cultural entities was settling in different frameworks in quasisynchronous time frames. Yet regardless of any diachrony they may show (which appears minimal when compared with previously existing cultural transitions), a certain universality is observable overall in the shift from Paleolithic to Neolithic technosocial lifeways. Pre-Pottery Neolithic peoples succeeded the Natufian in the Levant and Anatolia. In contexts far removed from African and Eurasian "homelands," such as Australia and North and South America, end-Pleistocene human groups also thrived as hunter-gatherers in post-ice age environments. Meanwhile, throughout Eurasia, change was oriented to adopting semiagrarian lifestyles as population densities continued to expand. While Epipaleolithic peoples maintained nomadic/seminomadic lifestyles,[303] the archeological record overall bears witness to the construction of more consequential walled structures (see Figure 7.1). Hunting practices turned manifestly to smaller game and, in some areas, grinding stones and pollen data show that humans were beginning to gather and process wild cereals, incorporating

Figure 7.1
Walled structures from the Epipaleolithic (Natufian) site of el-Wad Terrace (Nahal Me'arot
Nature Reserve, National Park and UNESCO World Heritage Site, Mount Carmel, Israel)
dating to around 12,000 years ago. The site is the object of ongoing excavations directed by
M. Weinstein-Evron, D. Kaufman, and R. Yeshurun of the Zinman Institute of Archaeology
in Haifa. (Photo by Deborah Barsky)

them as supplementary provisions into the resources they were obtaining from hunting
and gathering.

In contrast to the traditional Paleolithic hunter-gatherer subsistence strategies, the
shift to more sedentary lifeways presented certain advantages in terms of feeding the
larger numbers of individuals composing the social groupings (at least so long as
there were no catastrophic climatic events that could annihilate crop yields).[304,305] In
much of Europe and the Near East where this process is visible at an early date, the
expansion of semisedentary populations increased like stains expanding on absorbent
fabric. Meanwhile, populations living in other parts of the globe were undergoing
analogous transformations in different time frames. The outcome of these changes
was that peoples (progressively) needed to avoid social chaos to ensure optimal
survival rates. It was thus during the Neolithic that human groups organized themselves into more clearly established social units with hierarchical societies probably
based on the capacities (or propensities) of the different group members and in
synchronicity with the needs and desires of the group. We may assume from
protohistoric and historic records postdating the Neolithic Period that each striving
social unit would have increased in pace with the number of contributing individuals.
Even more important, perhaps, are the (concrete and abstract) boundaries that were
formed to separate the different rungs of the hierarchical ladder as subsistence
distribution patterns to each benefactor came to be established (most likely) in

accordance to his/her position in the social grading. The organizational patterning that was falling into place as societies grew and adopted lifestyles that were more sedentary evidently precluded a logistical strategy of task distribution. The new contexts evolving into the Neolithic required changes in patterns of socialization beginning with rulemaking to guide the behaviors of the evermore numerous contributing members composing each group. New rules would have emerged, for example, concerning the sharing and distribution of resources that were more massively produced, and these rules must have been determined by taking into account a range of evaluative criteria in terms of individual investment or contribution, such as time, capability, talent, expertise and so on. This individual contribution (by traders, artisans, politicians) was molded by social role-playing, ensuring that each member was contributing optimally to society *as a whole* in order to secure the survival of the group. This safeguarding of the success of a social unit permitted it to thrive and expand. It also attributed each unit with specific defining features that could be contrasted with those of other social entities, reinforcing the already established land-linked identities (from the later Acheulian).[208] Competition between successfully developing groups was likely to have intensified with population increase and ties to the land, justifying the "us versus them" paradigm. In other words, this was a time when the development of trades by skilled artisans became linked with administrative (i.e. political) propensities, arranging peoples into hierarchically distributed societies characterized by the specific features of their own evermore complex material and immaterial cultural traits.

Another way of ensuring this process was by strengthening symbolic significance – of natural occurrences (astronomic, climatic) or of items existing within the material world (specific types of stones, plants, etc.) – infusing them with meanings whose referents were communally recognized and understood. This common symbolic language, which also took the form of rituals or myths, gestures, externalized formal symbols or actions and so on, imbued intergroup specificities with even more intense meaning, defining and sharpening the boundaries separating each social unit. Instilling items, events or even actions with imaginary significance was not only an advantageous strategy to concretize hierarchical guidelines within each group but also was (is) used to justify the enforcement of obedience within the newly defined world order. Thus, items chosen within the material world came to serve as catalysts for prompting predictable behaviors in order to guarantee the perpetuity of a given hierarchical setup with the tacit understanding of all members in a given group that this "way of being" would best ensure the survival of the social unit as a whole. Acting in certain ways thus became a "responsibility" toward other group members that was expressed archeologically by objects and structures with technospecific features. It is, in a way, Darwin's "survival of the fittest"[9] projected from the biological to the material realm and, at the same time, from the individual to the group level. I see this mutation as indicating humanity's divorce from a more natural condition of social organization (should one exist) rooted perhaps more deeply in biological laws relating individuals to their optimal reproductive strategies rather than one founded on the distribution of nonsustenance-related material goods. Thus imparting objects – *things* – with hypothetical value had "graded" levels of meaning for humans whose existence had succumbed then to these extrasomatic creations. In this sense, we became victims of our own collective codification system within which only a few individuals dominate far more persons filtered into functional units.

As we have seen on numerous occasions throughout the past, climate change had its role to play as a prompting force behind some of the upheavals taking place in human societies through time. In the context of the shift from the Pleistocene to the Holocene, as we have seen, a global warming trend followed the last glacial cycle, and this is seen as a factor favoring (rather than limiting) the global expansion of the human clade. However, it is evident that if humanity had not reached the stage of technocultural and spiritual readiness from at least the beginning of the Upper Paleolithic that I have described, then none of the major lifestyle changes heralding the Neolithic would ever have occurred. In fact, I have already suggested that, in my opinion, humans had long since overcome the dictates of climatic change and that (from at least the later Acheulian) they perfectly dominated the landscapes in which they were experiencing a (mega) population explosion. In this discourse, I wish to underline two major trends, which I believe are causal to the "new world order" as it was to take form from the beginning of the Holocene. First, the pattern of exponential acceleration that is observed in demography and technological prowess lies in the very matrix of the human production process that I have described in previous chapters (testing potential within existing technosocial structures followed by systemic exhaustion and stagnation of a techno-logical stage followed by renewed phases of testing giving way to the development of new potential generally leading to social upheaval and cultural transformation). Second, the expansion of communication networks was selected as an adaptive strategy with which to buttress the growing technological substructure through the development of externalized forms of abstract thought (symbolic communication, including complex language and art) as social indicators. Since the earliest phases of human technological invention, complexification and standardization proved to be key trends in the accumu-lation of this know-how and its social integrative processes that were (and continue to be) endlessly incorporated into each new phase. In the distant past, this evolutionary patterning combined with cerebral expansion, translating biologically into highly evolved abilities to assimilate and process imagery, symbolism and language. Thus, by assimilating both physically and socially, the efficacy of knowledge transmission since the invention of first technologies, our species successfully took on the challenges brought into play by our evolutionary choice to invest heavily in developing techno-logical capacities, enabling us to multiply in numbers and, ultimately, to attain our present state of world dominance (see Table 7.1).

Table 7.1

Examples of Mesolithic cultural complexes in different geographical areas reflecting regional cultural diversity based on human material culture

Localization	Cultural Denomination	Age Range (BP)
Western Europe	Azilian	14,000–10,000
	Tardenoisian	10,000–5,000
Portugal		7,600–5,500
Irish and British Mesolithic		11,000–5,500
Western and central Europe	Sauveterrian	10,500–8,500
Netherlands	Swifterbant	7,300–5,400
Northern Europe	Maglemosian	11,000–8,000
Norway	Fosna-Hensbacka	12,000–10,500
	Komsa	12,000–10,000
Scandinavia	Nøstvet, Lihult, Kongemose	8,200–5,200
	Ertebølle	7,300–5,900
Central and Eastern Europe	Neman	9,000–5,000
Balkan Mesolithic	Iron Gates	13,000–5,000
Greece, Aegean		15,000–7,000
Baltics and Russia	Kunda	10,500–7,000
Central Asia middle Urals		12,000–5,000
East Asia		
Japan	Jōmon	16,000–1,350
Korea	Jeulman pottery period	10,000–3,500
South Asia	South Asian Stone Age	12,000–4,000
North Africa	Caspian	12,000–8,000
Upper Paleolithic Mesolithic	Iberomaurusian	24,000–10,000
East Africa (Kenya Mesolithic)		8,200–7,400

Source: en.wikipedia.org/wiki/Mesolithic

NEOLITHIC PEOPLES AND THE CONSOLIDATION OF SOCIAL BOUNDARIES

The oldest evidence of pre-Neolithic and early Neolithic societies has been found in and around the area referred to as the *Fertile Crescent*[306] from around 15,00 to 11,500 years ago, such as (respectively) Israel's Natufian culture[300] and Anatolia's Pre-Pottery Neolithic A site of Göbekli Tepe.[307] This period is particularly marked by the ultimate global domination of *Homo sapiens* after the demise of our last "cousin" species. During and especially following this time frame in Eurasia, there was continued reinforcement of technological and social developments in support of more sedentary lifestyles including the cultivation of wild cereals and progressive domestication of some animals. The archeological record shows the spread of comparable practices in Asia Minor, North Africa and northern Mesopotamia. In fact, after around 12,000 BP, innovations (animal husbandry and agriculture, development of more permanent settlements with larger numbers of individuals, etc.) that we attribute to the Neolithic appear archeologically to have occurred independently *in at least seven parts of the world*.[303] However, ideas about the exact unfolding of this new world order continue to be amended in pace with new discoveries. As pointed out by Jared Diamond,[46] the Fertile Crescent historically has been the most widely studied in terms of the emergence of the Neolithic as defined by first indices of agriculture and animal husbandry,[303] so this could explain the abundance of evidence brought to light in this part of the world. Indeed, we observe the same phenomenon for the East African Rift Valley where idyllic conditions for archeologists combine with an abundance of evidence making it a preferred study area and doubtlessly creating a sort of geographical bias in terms of our ideas about the emergence of particular cultural entities and their spread across the globe. Yet the Fertile Crescent, which includes the modern-day countries of Iraq, Syria, Lebanon, Cyprus, Jordan, Israel, Egypt, southeastern Turkey and parts of western Iran,[308] is considered to have been *naturally favorable* for the emergence of agriculture because of its particular climatic conditions and their influence on some herbaceous plants, especially some species of wild cereals. The proliferation of some annuals under certain conditions made them a natural choice for conversion into cultivated crops by the then seminomadic peoples who were already exploiting their caloric benefits.

The artifact record shows us that some Neolithic peoples met the needs of agriculture by manufacturing axes out of polished stone (the Neolithic is known as the *Age of Polished Stone* in contrast to the preceding Paleolithic or *Age of Knapped Stone*). In numerous Neolithic contexts, pottery was a newly acquired ability that spread rapidly and became a highly significant cultural innovation. There were many uses for pottery in serving the daily requirements of emerging sedentary societies who needed a way to store all types of accumulated materials. The surplus food production and the everyday requirements of sedentary living would have greatly increased the requirement for stocking and transporting both liquid and dry goods, thus establishing pottery making as an indispensable and highly valued new skill. Interestingly, pottery making appeared in some areas very early on (in Asia, for example), developing independently in different time frames (especially after around 10,000 years ago [Ka]). As is the case for the other innovations we have considered together in this book, humans dabbled with clay over millennia before developing the art of pottery (the nearly 15,000 year-old clay relief depicting bison from the Tuc d'Audoubert site in France is one very ancient example). Globally, the use of pottery blossomed, giving way to new creativity and inventiveness as utility combined with artistic expression. Using clay to create a variety of vessels and artistic items is one of the most important hallmarks of numerous (postpottery) Neolithic civilizations who distinguished themselves stylistically in the creation of these objects. Indeed, even the utilitarian was decorated, thus being both functional and ornamental. As we have seen in the case of lithic tools, the technical and stylistic features of pottery are useful indicators for archeologists seeking to establish chronology and to identify the different cultural complexes in their regional contexts. This is especially valuable during this time of high mobility because it enables archeologists to recognize population movements and the spread of different civilizations by the distribution of clay material culture. Luckily for archeologists, pottery resists the passage of time, and it is a commonly discovered element in archeological contexts dating globally from the Neolithic period and beyond. Even when clay artifacts are found broken or partial (in sherds), specialists to restore them can be found to complete missing parts using catalogs of known forms and decorations (now also with the help of three-dimensional imagery techniques). Also significant are the highly specialized techniques developed for clay-based pottery making that required new manipulations and mastery of firing at high temperatures in specially designed pits (or kilns). Through experimentation, early potters developed special techniques to mix the clay, combining it with sand, gravels, crushed shell fragments and even plant chaff to allow steam to escape and thus avoid breakage from shrinking as the pottery dried during heating. Before the invention of the pottery wheel, early potters mounted their clay vessels either by pinching mounds of clay into the desired form or by joining coils of clay together to build up shapes. Pottery-making civilizations sometimes established their dwellings on or near a source of clay raw material, organizing specialized production areas within their habitats. In sum, pottery played a highly significant role in the formation of early human semisedentary and sedentary civilizations, allowing social groups to display their cultural cohesion (identity) by embellishing functional objects with decorations imbued with symbolic meaning.

Compared with most Paleolithic occurrences, Neolithic archeological sites in some regions of the world can be numerous and archeologically dense, a trend that we observe as we move through time. Higher complexity in spatial organization is another feature observed in the archeological record dating to this period, a reflection of the wider variability of domestic tasks being performed by different group members as they organized themselves into "villages" whose inhabitants became truly productive agents serving, as it were, the greater cause of the community that accommodated them. Indeed, task-related social organization created the need for a regular workforce of specialized persons capable of maintaining new responsibilities relating, for example, to agriculture and animal husbandry as well as to actually maintaining social order. When humans made the choice to become producers rather than foragers, new stresses evolved because resource acquisition and, by extension, group survival came to depend on successfully harnessing both resources and invested labor. This also engendered the need for order within each social entity, dividing it into specialized sectors founded on individual capacities to optimize and integrate techno-logical and even spiritual know-how and related practices.

Important changes thus took root after humans made the choice to favor production as a preferred lifestyle and accommodate living in larger group entities. While some maintain a progressivist viewpoint for this phase of the human story, this interpretation is questioned by others who uphold a more revisionist view (for example, J. Diamond who qualified it as "The worst mistake in the history of the human race").[305] Research suggests that, in fact, this choice engendered various detrimental effects on populations living after the establishment of sedentary communities. For instance, ethnographic comparisons carried out with surviving hunter-gatherer populations in Australia and Tanzania indicate that more time was actually required for individuals in agricultural contexts to perform tasks relating to food acquisition than in foraging contexts. Overall, the sedentary agricultural condition took place in constructed environments and entailed important changes in diet and lifestyle such as decreased mobility. All of this has a considerable impact on human health, transforming human anatomical features along with those of the domesticates.[309] For example, skeletal remains from Greece and Turkey dating to the end of the last ice age showed marked size reduction compared with those of preceding populations.[310] In addition, the adoption of farming has been blamed for an increase in some paleo pathologies in postdomestication societies with the evidence pointing to negative effects on human teeth and bones.[311,312] The shift from hunter-gatherer to agricultural lifeways, for example, at Dickson Mounds (Illinois) around 1150 Common Era (CE), registered episodes of nutritional stress and infectious disease undergone by Paleo-Indian peoples after they adopted farming:

> At Dickson Mounds, located near the confluence of the Spoon and Illinois rivers, archaeologists have excavated some 800 skeletons that paint a picture of the health changes that occurred when a hunter-gatherer culture gave way to intensive maize farming around A. D. 1150. Studies by George Armelagos and his colleagues then at the University of Massachusetts show these early farmers paid a price for their new-found livelihood. Compared to the hunter-gatherers who preceded them, the farmers had a nearly 50 per cent increase in enamel defects indicative of malnutrition, a fourfold increase in iron-deficiency anemia (evidenced by a bone condition called porotic hyperostosis), a threefold rise in bone lesions reflecting infectious disease in general, and an increase in degenerative conditions of the spine, probably reflecting a lot of hard physical labor.[310,311]

The anatomic alterations recorded in human remains corresponding to this temporal phase are explained in the concept of "human domestication."[309] This biocultural process taking place from the later Pleistocene and accelerating over time occurred in synchronicity with the human domination over Nature and her associated changes in lifestyle (diet, workload, etc.).[309] Recently, other forms of human domestication reinforced by DNA studies have been found to relate to cerebral processes.[313] Accordingly, research suggests that as humans moved progressively into organized and hierarchically arranged social units, they were more frequently required to make concessions to others, thus making less aggressive tendencies more advantageous overall. By 12,000 BP, humanity's crushing domination over Nature was underway, signaled in the Fertile Crescent by the subjugation of some animal species (dogs, sheep, goats) with the development of controlled breeding of selected animals such as cows and pigs soon following (around 10,000 BP). The capacity to alter the original state of Nature and to mold it in accordance to one's will (or even whim) took an accelerated pace from this point. With hindsight, we observe this capacity beginning in the Neolithic as a sort of *subtle tampering* that today in the face of mass production to provide for the needs of millions of human souls has exploded into obsessive and even crazed mediation on the natural world order in total disregard for the well-being of the species being exploited.

By following the successive events leading to the horrific situations of animal abuse and subjugation that we are facing today, we can more clearly discern when and how specific inventions allowed us to consolidate human domination over all other living beings on the planet. Furthermore, when we consider the archeological evidence, we can identify the trends that have led us to the verge of our next phase of cultural overload (now very close or upon us): the breakdown of the present human system. In contrast, Upper Paleolithic artistic creations evoke a very different, somehow more spiritual image, in which we detect profound respect for animals that people encountered, captured and killed. In the (remaining) myths and legends of indigenous peoples (Canada, Australia), such respect is often woven into a belief in the interconnectedness of all things.[314,315] Yet there is only a relatively minor time interval separating this holistic universal vision from the one majoritarily adopted after the onset of the Holocene where animals became simply a means by which to fulfill and maintain the ever-increasing human appetites for domination. Still, we can also relate this development to a period of learning after which humanity adopted specifically oriented technological innovations to devise ways to achieve ultimate domination over animals (capture, imprisonment, artificial insemination, industrial breeding) in the aim of satisfying the basest of human needs and desires (food, protection, companionship, leisure). The shortness of the time interval separating pre-domestication societies from farming civilizations in Europe is such that colonial era documents report about the hunting practices of indigenous peoples still being grounded in spiritual and ritual and often imbued with a deep respect for the animals. In numerous cases, this respectful behavior involved sacred beliefs that inspired fear of reprisals from the spiritual realms in the case of abusive, nonmindful killing. In fact, such profound respect for Nature still persists today among some of the remaining indigenous populations in spite of their near annihilation following global colonization processes from the Middle Ages into modern times.

Presently, we can directly observe how human relationships with the animal kingdom changed radically during and after the Neolithic Period as we intervened on animal and plant reproductive processes to optimize production. Today, we persist in our search to invent new ways to manipulate, modify and control animals and environments. Landscapes were (and continue to be) modeled in ways considered optimal for human survival, meaning, reducing species' variability, for example, in favor of monocultures designed to feed the ever-growing number of human mouths. Indeed, in 2019, a global United Nations-backed assessment reported that at least 1 million animal and plant species were threatened with extinction in the upcoming decades. While it is true that other species (beavers, for example) intervene on or model their environments to better suit their needs, modern humans do so in ways that are harmful to themselves and to other living species of plants and animals. This difference in niche construction[131] practices constitutes a major alienating factor separating humans from all other life forms. Looking at our actual situation, this discourse is useful because it shows us that our own disregard for Nature can be related to a process that began with the invention of – and eventual reliance on – technology as a means to interact with the outside world.

The consequences of this behavioral choice are cumulative, and we are only just beginning to realize the importance of acting responsibly to address the repercussions of our divorce from – and raping of – Earth's natural balance. Come what may, artificially created human environments are most clearly contrary to adequate natural selection processes because they destroy the delicate balance orchestrated by the unity of interactions of all living and nonliving entities on the planet (ecosystems) and even in the universe. The *feedback loop*[316] underlines the interconnectedness of all things that can be recognized in today's world where we are now constantly being reminded that, by pushing the artificial modeling of nonsustainable environments to the brink, we are harmfully affecting both human and nonhuman natural selection processes, finally causing them to convert into negative forces. Thousands of years from the Neolithic Period, our unbridled artificial niche construction has finally resulted in the drastic transformation of natural environments that will be the next generation's ecological inheritance to which our children and all future generations will fall heir. This fits well with the foreboding principles outlined for demographic growth by T. R. Malthus[317] who argued (as early as the beginning of the nineteenth century) that exponential human population growth in relation to the possibilities for the Earth to nourish them would ultimately lead to disaster unless the process was checked by socially imposed reproductive limits or by war, famine, disease or other catastrophic scenarios. Ultimately, we have collectively created over time an abusive, anthropocentric model of the world that has upset the spectacularly complex universal balance built up naturally over millions of years. Inevitably, this will lead us once again to seek a new structural balance that will dictate the fitness of the human species if we are to continue to play a role in the future of the planet Earth.

EFFECTS OF THE NEOLITHIC TRANSFORMATION

Like other prehistoric periods, the Neolithic is recognizable by specific categories and styles of artifacts with new levels of perception materially expressed by more complex technological and sociobehavioral characteristics built onto the foundations of accumulated know-how and skills evolved throughout the millennia. While Neolithic societies continued to practice microlithic traditions, their tool kits also contain an abundant array of armaments, a foreboding of newly acquired needs for control in the new social order, for it is also during this period that there is accrued evidence for unprecedented intraspecific violence.[318] Some specialists establish a link between the development of more complex social interchange – consequential to sedentary lifestyles – and the phenomena of ritual fighting behaviors.[319] In earlier periods, human skeletal accumulations showing signs of humanly induced trauma are scarce, and there is little evidence proving that humans voluntarily incurred physical injury in any significant way on each other or on neighboring populations. However, it is argued that large-scale warlike violence emerged after the Neolithic because of changes made after this time to the basic social organizational setting and the new settlement configuration it entailed. Might we conjecture against Kantian precepts that warlike behavior arose during this stage because humans were increasingly estranged from Nature and because they existed in large-size sedentary competitive groups? Or is warfare a natural behavior inscribed in our genetic makeup that emerged to deal with the new social configurations arising out of the Neolithic? The effects of the Neolithic transformation laid the foundations for the organization of human societies into sedentary units composed of numerous individuals and readied them to face the challenges of intensive nonrespectful environmental exploitation as they alienated themselves from nonconstructed surroundings. This new, exploitative relationship (both within the human groups themselves and without toward other living beings) was abstractly justified (as it still is today) through a process of social selection. One such strategy that we humans have developed is to promote fear response modes as a way to achieve homage to a specific social order (fear of reprisals, of the unknown, of hunger, etc.). This strategy involved exponential increases in the central groundbreaking process of widening the range of abstract and symbolic communication venues of all types. It is not surprising that one of the earliest modes of communication designed to manipulate the masses was the supreme symbolic expression that is writing, and it is also not fortuitous that the oldest recognized written documents were elaborated mainly to track and control production and exchange. With relative rapidity, permanent houses replacing seasonal occupations were finally arranged into hamlets and villages. Deceased peoples were buried in different contexts (even inside houses or in nearby grave fields called necropolis), establishing a durable presence and cementing the concept of *ancestors* specific to each population, thus consolidating, once again, ever-stronger ties to land-based identities.

The notion of property stands out as an obviously significant development stemming from new social arrangements tested during the Neolithic period. Then the sense of "belonging" as an abstract concept developed meaningful spatial limitations highlighting "group" over "individual" interests. Personal value was measured in terms of what an individual could contribute to the community: how much he or she could produce, or even how much control a person could hold over the populace. Ideologies needed to be *arranged* to better fit the needs of each working part of the whole. They developed, in turn, into sets of rules with their own hierarchical diversification: for the working populace, women, men, spiritual leaders, children, the sick, the elderly, and so on. Social bonds had to be regularized and codified to fit the growing complexity of relationships formed both within (single communities) and without (contact groups). Trading networks were founded on variability and availability in accordance to what was produced (or producible) in different areas and on value-imbued materialistic standards. All of this interconnectedness resulted in a snowball of cause and effect that, in many ways, favored the continued selection for improvement in communication venues over time. Combined with a growing symbolic database building up common collective consciousness, the potential for writing – stemming certainly out of signs and symbols widely used since the Paleolithic – was logically brought to the fore as the subsequent

2 cm

Figure 7.2
Can-Pey Cave (Can-Pey level 3, Montferrer. Pyrénées-Orientales. France). Flint arrowhead
with notches and stem (Late Neolithic, Véraza Group, 2470 ± 120 BC and 2110 ± 200
years BC). (Excavations and photograph by Henry Baills)

phase. Within a relatively short time, the first pastoral peoples progressively mastered
new technological advances that were to dramatically alter the human way of life for
thousands of years to come (Figure 7.2). These changes, however multifaceted, have a
common denominator: production and personal accumulation of goods. Becoming the
center of human concerns, optimal productivity and consumption of produced goods
became the essential aim of human existence. From a Darwinian standpoint, more
effective production maximizes reproductive potential and constitutes a viable strategy
to challenge exterior pressures in order to optimize survival. Different from the animal
world, this specific human response demonstrates increased reproductive potential by
virtue of the humanly created extrasomatic capacity for technology. Through time,
innovations such as agriculture and animal husbandry led human populations to opt
for large-scale sedentary lifestyles, contributing in different ways to reinforcing the
emerging notion of property. This, in turn, generated new forms of competitiveness on
a now multilevel social scale. Complex human interactions became more and more
stratified as peoples distinguished themselves as individual members within the larger
circumvolutions of social complexes through professional, religious and/or political
differences. The watchword was to sustain human life at any cost.

8

COMMUNICATION NETWORKING AT THE END OF THE PREHISTORIC ERA

METALLURGY: A NOVEL HUMAN EXPERIMENT

The innovation of mining and the transformation of metal ores (smelting, casting) reshaped the nature and organization of human societies as a whole and heralded a new phase of acceleration in technological progress. This is especially noteworthy because it consolidated the emerging set of values based on resource distribution and material investments, stemming from the sociocultural changes proceeding from the Neolithic. Combined with the intensification of communication networking in the rapidly developing sedentary societies, humans cultivated their material response modes (of course without time for significant biological or anatomical changes to follow). As demography exploded in pace with technological inventiveness, storytelling continued to grow as a widespread strategy adopted by humans to manage expanding population densities. Sharing stories as a way to support cultural cohesion provided humanity an edge for sustaining survival in groups of ever-increasing numbers of individuals. The relatively complex preparatory stages involved in exploiting different types of metals emerged through various phases of testing and data sharing through time. The cherished arts of mining, metal refinement and metallurgy were thus mastered progressively as proficiency increased through the necessary stages of learning. As always, this new phase of human experimentation and knowledge did not appear "out of nowhere"; it was rooted deeply in long-term observation (visual, tactile) during which raw materials found in natural contexts inspired human curiosity. In previous chapters, we saw how curiosity in relation to the mastery of fire led humans to test the reactions of raw substances by heating them to varying degrees (smelting), blending them to form different substances (alloying) and shaping the by-products into different types of tools or ornamental objects (forging and casting). Buttressing this process were renewed symbolic methods of social networking favoring optimum communication whose expanding efficacy explains the relative rapidity with which this novel expertise spread. To be sure, none of these endeavors could have taken place had humans not reached the required state of readiness prerequisite to these inventions in terms of accumulated technological know-how *and* the efficacy of social diffusion networking.

Proficiency in manipulating fire by controlling and maintaining its temperature enabled the exploitation of metal ores. In itself, the handling of fire constituted a wide-ranging experimental adventure for humankind begun, as we have seen, many thousands of years ago in the Levant[194] and probably even earlier in Africa.[320] During the Late Acheulian and Middle Paleolithic and beyond, humans had gained widespread intimate experience with fire over thousands of years. Experimenting with its uses, humans used fire to heat different materials to varying degrees to investigate their physical reactions while seeking utility in its resulting transformative features. Metallurgy, like pottery, is a fire-related art and humans therefore were aware and prepared for its use. When compared with past milestones in human technological evolution, it is interesting to underline some distinctive differences that characterize the first metal-producing civilizations. While the founding of urban centers and the development of large-scale warfare are among the most outstanding and spectacular features of the Metal Ages, it is important that we examine the more foundational reasons for the changes observed in the material culture left behind by these civilizations. From their accrued technological experience and know-how, Metal Age peoples of the world reveled in their newfound skills and externalized culture in multifaceted ways. Meanwhile, the complexity attained in human productivity was such that it necessarily branched off into separate yet interconnected and interdependent areas of specialization. I suggest calling this phenomenon a *fractalization* process because each branch reproduced the very same evolutionary patterning dictated by the limits of the source of the branches, maintaining the range of expression of the human brain itself: in a continuous process of experimentation, stagnation and excess. In the fractalization scenario (as in the evolutionary biological process of natural selection), the introduction of any even minimal element of change, alteration or adjustment would have exponentially great consequences by virtue of the ensuing, infinite phases of reproduction (see Figure 8.1).

> A fractal is a never-ending pattern. Fractals are infinitely complex patterns that are self-similar across different scales. They are created by repeating a simple process over and over in an ongoing feedback loop. Driven by recursion, fractals are images of dynamic systems – the pictures of Chaos. Geometrically, they exist in between our familiar dimensions. Fractal patterns are extremely familiar, since nature is full of fractals. For instance: trees, rivers, coastlines, mountains, clouds, seashells, hurricanes, etc. Abstract fractals – such as the Mandelbrot Set – can be generated by a computer calculating a simple equation over and over.[321]

Figure 8.1

This aerial view of a natural landscape provides an example of fractal patterning characterized by the eternal reproduction of a specific design no matter the scale. Fractals reflect mathematical realities of assembled repetitive patterns that are identical even when infinitely reduced in size. Examples of fractals are numerous in nature as in the branching of a tree, the bifurcations of a snowflake or even the convolutions of the human brain itself. The introduction of an anomaly into a fractal system will inevitably alter its eternal patterning on a tangentially large scale. (http://paulbourke.net/fractals/googleearth/)

This process of technological development into isolated pockets of specialization in fact closely echoes what was happening in the socialization process that was itself transformed after the implementation of sedentary lifestyles and the changes incurred in this important shift from hunter-gatherer to production-consumption regimes, implying communal living for far more numerous individuals within each single social unit. Especially after the Neolithic Period, new societal arrangements were grounded in complex symbolic communication structures and composite material culture imposing both distinct land-linked identities (as we have seen) but also establishing *artificial laws of hierarchy* whose obeisance was requisite to group cohesion. Artificial states of equilibrium had to be maintained to reach functional social equilibrium in a falsely hierarchical system. The latter state (stagnation) must be seen as a structure; it is an intentionally constructed set of composite social and material features that defines a given cultural unit. In (pre)historical processes, stagnation inevitably ensued following the effects of redundancy (state of exhaustion). Intensified phases of production in excess led inevitably to the collapse of each successive social system (sometimes through violence and anarchy) to achieve a renewed phase of testing and build a new set of paradigms[298] that would be repeatedly characterized by their own specific material and behavioral morphotypes, now commonly referred to as "culture." Culture therefore renews itself through material innovation and, as such, is a property unique to humankind.

Let us turn now to the archeological record to place these events into a tangible chronological and geographical context. For the overwhelming majority of humanity's existence – nearly 3 million years – stone tools constituted the primary base of our technocultural expression. The Paleolithic era thus culminated here ("here" meaning at a specific "evolutionary stage" rather than a specific time or place) with the management of new materials – namely, metal ores – modeled using relatively complex transformation processes to suit human needs and desires. Metals and metal alloys were certainly not unknown to previously living human populations, nor was the concept of "mining" foreign to former Paleolithic peoples. Minerals such as ochre and hematite, for example, were mined for various uses from quite early in the Middle Paleolithic, well before some other substances were appreciated as metal ores for smelting (e.g. iron ca. 3000 BP in Europe).[322] In contrast, hematite, a mineral rich in iron ore (ochre), was mined in South Africa as far back as the late Middle Stone Age (the oldest evidence is from The Lion's Cave in Swaziland dating to nearly 45,000 years ago [Ka]).[323] Mining nonmetal materials such as flint largely predated intentional extraction of metal ores (Acheulian).[324] Meanwhile, salt mining is evidenced in Western Asia (Azerbaijan) from the Neolithic Period,[325] and clay mining for pottery production is recorded in Anatolia from around 9,000 BP.[326] Besides quarrying, other types of activities oriented toward collecting attractively colored stones for ornamentation such as malachite (a green-colored mineral) are documented in the early prehistoric register.[327] Neolithic peoples prized metamorphic rocks such as serpentine, which they polished into durable axes intended for agricultural tasks. Among the sources of iron ores available in natural contexts, the European and Southeast Asian artifact record shows some exceptional evidence for the exploitation of nickel-rich iron in the form of meteorites and telluric (basalt) sources.[328] Besides metals, a wide range of different raw materials, were known therefore to our early human ancestors for a very long time – at least in their unrefined form– from their explorations above and below the Earth's surface. By improving their technological capacities over time, humans developed not only the tools needed to more effectively mine these curiosities but also to manipulate the physical qualities of such materials These resources allowed humanity to further improve and expand living standards. All the while, their discoveries made them wonder about the transformation potential of these novel materials, which they explored through endless experiments.

It is fitting, therefore, that we distinguish "metallurgy" from "mining," which is a much older activity. We can acknowledge the use of metal ores for producing tools and cultural objects as one of the earliest authentic handicrafts because it involved the use of specialized equipment and specific training and could be practiced only by experienced and qualified individuals. Around 7,000 years ago in geographical Europe, metal, in many ways more effective than stone, began systematically to replace it when some communities began experimenting with copper, eventually shaping it into knives and sickles adequate for emerging activities. Initially worked by cold hammering and folding, metals were eventually melted and molded into shape thanks to the invention of furnaces designed to reach high temperatures. Metallurgy overcame some of the uncertainties of stone tool production, which was comparatively risky because of possible failures caused by raw material imperfections or simple lack of mastery. In contrast, metal offered the advantage of manufacturing series of identical high-quality tools. These advantages led to a surplus of production, hoarding and enrichment of resources and manufactured goods. Old World populations continued, however, to rely on stone for much of their small tool manufacture, even as pottery had entered so significantly into the material repertoire of their daily lives. The fascination with metals took hold with astounding convergence throughout much of the world. Although the transition from stone to metal appears to have occurred as a brief "moment" in the archeological register, it involved different phases that generally succeeded one another in the global trend of developing technology.

Copper, a relatively common substance on the Earth's surface, was worked in the early phases of metallurgy, and its cultural referent in Europe is commonly referred to as the *Chalcolithic Period*. This composite denomination is derived from the Greek words *chalcos*, meaning copper and *lithos*, meaning stone. Copper's refinement is relatively easy because its melting point is relatively low. At first worked by cold hammering, this metal was soon melted and molded into desired forms. Smelting was made possible (Near East, during the seventh millennium BP) thanks to the development of furnaces, which could reach high temperatures (>1,000°C), for firing pottery. In order to remedy the relatively fragile nature of pure copper, alloys with other metals such as tin were used to create bronze, a relatively harder substance (tin is a scarcer metal substance whose admixture requires precise dosage). The *Bronze Age*, beginning in Europe around 5,000 BP and continuing in some areas up to around 2,500 BP, was a period marked by flourishing civilizations that appeared in relatively close chronological range in widely distant geographical areas of the world (the Near East, India, China, Mesoamerica) to the extent that, in each geographical context, there are many different cultural expressions that have been attributed with different denominations.[329] Iron came to be preferred to bronze for its superior qualities and resistance between around 3,000 BP (modern Middle East and Ancient Near East) and spread throughout the Mediterranean region.[330] With its ore available across the globe, iron unseated bronze as a preferred material even though its smelting is more difficult (its melting point is higher and it therefore requires a large supply of oxygen and special furnaces). Metal objects were often stored in caches or deposited as grave goods, practices that underlined their special worth. Of course, this is only a very rough outline of a process that was very complex indeed and whose subtle transitions and many different facets were recorded in archeological records. Taken on their global scale, rough equivalents of these cultural entities were found in many different parts of the world. And so, once again, as in the previous phases of human development that we have reviewed together, we cannot help but observe the parallel occurrence of analogous social change and recognize how it is so deeply rooted in technological innovation. Structural evolution of technosystems created civilizations

Figure 8.2
Bronze arrowhead (Tautavel, France). (Courtesy of Denis Dainat, EPCC-CERPT)

with similar material and social referents in widely distant areas of the world, and, in some cases, in time intervals too short for transmission to have occurred through direct exchange between the populations within which they appear. See Figures 8.2 and 8.3.

We have seen such parallelisms in older cultural units whose specificities seemingly appeared in comparable chronologies in widely distinct parts of the globe (for example, Acheulian bifaces on large flakes, Levallois flake production methods, stone blade production, hafting technologies and art). It seems obvious to me that only the explanations that consider the fundamental, structural aspects of human cultural evolution related to anatomic and cerebral processes common to *Homo* are useful for understanding the advent of one or another breakthrough in the evolutionary processes of human behavior. To be effective, this analytical strategy must consider trends observed over very long periods so that we can recognize similarities and differences from one to another major technological achievement. Thanks to long-term retrovision offered by prehistory, we can recognize systemic human material and social change that can explain how and why analogous developments marking the human evolutionary process occurred in different areas of the globe where transmission by direct contact between populations was unlikely. In the time line followed by this book, we observe the impacts of the evolution of technology on the (rather dire) present-day human condition, basing our observations on the huge evolutionary force of the technological process that was born in the Oldowan. Technology can thus be seen as a sort of runaway branch of our own evolutionary process caused by the uniformity of change expressed in the human species. Today, technological evolution appears to be dictating the

Figure 8.3
Serralongue Tombe 9: En Camp de las Olles (Serralongue, Pyrénées-Orientales, France).
Cremation grave around 2,700 BP. (Courtesy of Henry Baills)

outcome of our own destiny as we follow its changing course into the future, a trajectory guided by cumulative and technospecific possibilities for change from within each successive strategy.

And so, although there are discrepancies in the timing and geographical settings for the emergence and development of different types of metallurgy around the world after around 7 Ka, it is noteworthy that successive phases defined by the use of different types of metals and metal alloys (copper, bronze, iron) followed more or less consistently in different parts of the world (although all phases are not always represented in each part). We also note the obsessive use of gold, the most noble of metals, for the creation of objects. Apparently favored very early on for its resilience, malleability and beauty, gold quite rapidly developed as a preferred metal for ornamentation in those areas of the world where it was available (for example, South America, Egypt), and it rapidly became a commodity for the developing trade networks. Likewise, each evolutionary phase of metal refinement was commonly accompanied by the setting up of analogous structural relationships: building fortified cities, erecting large-sized monuments (megaliths, fortifications, tombs), expanding creative processes and art, integrating trade into the social fabric, intensifying commerce and large-scale warfare. The political joined the spiritual to "guide" peoples through intense social upheavals and herd them into functional hierarchical social schemes. Stimulated trade and communications were further marked over time by unprecedented (independent) inventions (the wheel, sailing ships). Meanwhile, it has been pointed out, importantly, that the timing and geographical situation of each innovation was largely dictated by complex external impact factors (such as landscape and vegetation, climate), not by fictitious ideas postulating inequalities in the degree of intellectual advancement of different civilizations.[46] As I pointed out in earlier chapters of this book, human inventiveness is also contingent on "cultural readiness," that is to say, in terms of where a specific society was in the fractalization process: whether it had reached equilibrium in a specific behavioral patterning or if it was rather in a saturation or experimental phase.

It is noteworthy that only twenty-four of the eighty-six currently known metals had been discovered prior to the nineteenth century and that half of these had been recognized in the eighteenth century. In other words, sixty-two of eighty-six metals known to humankind (nearly 75 percent) were encountered only in the last hundred years or so.[329]

ESTABLISHING LONG-RANGE SOCIAL INTERCONNECTIONS FOR TRADE AND WEALTH PRODUCTION

A plethora of objects continued to be manufactured for trade, producing wealth, even as farming and herding sustained the exploding urban populations. The human fascination with metal substances offered by the Earth constitutes a true scientific venture by humankind – an ongoing manipulative, transformative process performed by mysterious alchemistic enterprises made available to humans through thousands of years of cumulative technocultural inheritance. What we have seen together throughout this book is that it is precisely this very human essence of enterprise that ultimately freed humans from the obligation of redundantly performing time-consuming survival-related tasks. Through the prism of cumulative knowledge and innovation, humans scrutinized the properties of natural substances inspired by our innate curiosity to explore their limitless forms by testing their combinations and perfecting methodologies acquired through our accrued mental and technical capacities. From the first ages of metal refining onward, trade, commerce and communications acted as catalysts to rapid developments on all fronts. Thus, even though there may have been a few thousand years separating one or another breakthrough leading up to modern civilization, the time lapse separating each achievement is nil compared with the major technosocial changes that we have seen to have occurred in the more distant past. In the present overview of our shared prehistoric existence, I have stressed that one of the most observable trends is the increasing rapidity of the time spans separating each major sociocultural transformation worldwide (with only a few exceptions concerning geo-graphically isolated peoples in cultural equilibrium). As we have seen, each of the recorded cultural upheavals is of increasingly shorter duration (from the Oldowan to the Acheulian, the Acheulian to the Mousterian, the Mousterian to the Upper Paleolithic cultural succession, etc.). The evidence clearly shows that although periods of cultural stability (or stasis) that once lasted for hundreds of thousands of years were progres-sively reduced in duration, it is no secret that humanity continues today on the same (now frenzied) evolutionary path, inventing and transmitting technologies and trans-muting them into symbolic culture at astonishingly rapid rates.

Special emphasis should be given here to underline the parallelism with which communications developed evermore complex systems of networking in synchronicity with the growing trends of material production and the founding of territorial markets. Any gaps in the rapid assimilation of new cultural tendencies were soon filled as the world readied itself for the absolute and unabridged domination of a human populace obsessed with amassing and exchanging material goods. These metalworking peoples belong to the phase of human development referred to as proto-historic, meaning that they possessed early forms of writing. Compared with "historic" peoples, proto-historic written forms of communication require at least some degree of knowledge-based interpretation. Primordial forms of writing usually involved the use of signs (or simplified symbolic representations) called glyphs, which are readable by individuals sharing a common set of visual referents. These forms are mnemonic systems designed to designate objective reality by offering suggestive imagery in the form of simplistic graphic representations made to stimulate the memory, evoking objects, ideas or even emotions. It is certain that writing developed from these earlier pictographs and ideographs. The earliest evidence of written documents are the cuneiform texts from ancient Sumeria and Egyptian hieroglyphs, both dating to around 5,000 BP. Meanwhile, writing systems independently emerged in lands separated by huge territorial expanses (once again) excluding the possibility of transmission by direct social contact; for example, they were invented in Central America by the Olmec peoples of Mexico, perhaps as early as around 2,000 BP, and in faraway northern China around 3,000 BP.[331] Symbolic representations came to denote not only meaning but also sound. Becoming more and more stylized, glyphs progressively lost their iconicity, developing phonetic expression and becoming logographs representing words or phrases, a process that took thousands of years. Today, the shape of most written symbols has little to do with their meaning.

For archeologists, interpreting ancient written documents is challenging as it must be carried out using data from the universe of the artifact record or from the reading of geo-sedimentologic contexts. Of course, written documents constitute a huge development for understanding and interpreting early human behavior and lifeways. Writing and basic mathematics were both created as pragmatic tools that could be used for recording data and keeping inventories, for example, of livestock or other agricultural goods, a need that emerged logically out of the newly founded reliance on production-consumption activities. These valuable tools provided modes with which to quantify accumulated material goods and to determine/compare their scarcity/abundance with that amassed by others, thus inevitably underpinning another new concept, that of wealth. This begged competition, setting individuals and groups against one another because of differences originating from the accumulation of goods (what types, how much). In addition, writing enabled individuals to relate their personal stories and to express group interests, gradually serving as a vector for reporting activities or even vaunting violent warfare achievements. In a nutshell, the invention of systemic writing is the ultimate expression of the degree of complexity attained by the human capacity for abstract thought. It is the consecration of humanity's choice to select the nonphysiological attribute, which is the ability to communicate through symbols, as a formidable adaptive strategy.

HOW IDEAS CAME TO TRANSCEND TIME

Societies chose symbolic communication as a way to expand on their shared experiences, fortifying collective consciousness as a key factor facilitating the expansion of complex symbolic databases and making them understandable to other humans at first within single groups and later universally. By inventing writing and strengthening intercommunicative processes, humanity accelerated every detail of its cultural adaptation strategies, facilitating the assimilation of even very complex activities and thought processes by the masses. In this way, each phase of technical innovation and its accompanying social transformations could, on the one hand, contain within itself all of the knowledge accumulated during the fulfillment of each experience and, on the other hand, give way to more frequent and larger-scale pioneering exploits in material manipulations. Importantly, writing became the means by which to record and share human exploits (the birth of history), a species-centric mode of collectively naming and memorizing events, achievements and/or downfalls of our species (and modeling them to emulate land-based identities). Transcending time and space, writing allows the communication of experiences that occurred in the past or the present to subsequent generations and to postulate likely (or unlikely) scenarios for the future. Writing thus accelerates knowledge acquisition and constitutes a formidable tool for transmitting and learning culture. In the context of increasing demography, writing provides estranged individuals with the capacity to seclude themselves from the social context to express ideas, opinions and emotions and to share them (or not) with other individuals of one's own or even future generations.

Abstract human ideas now instantaneously transcend space and time. Today, communication continues to be the network through which humanity is guided and controlled. The explosion of multimedia, currently chiefly represented by the Internet and other virtual realities, represents the vehicle through which ideas are transmitted to the largest possible audience. Billions of messages are sent daily over the entire planet, making information instantaneously accessible to populations all over the world. The Internet serves as a communication tool, which decreases distance in time and space; the entire planet has become accessible; the world has become small. As a vector of consumer culture, the Internet is the ultimate tool for mass media controlled by corporate entities, which continue to guide resource exploitation and distribution planetwide. It serves the power-holding minority by dictating choices in production, consumption and economy. With multimedia, humanity is becoming evermore homogenous as distances separating populations are being closed by media contact. Presently, multimedia further serves the purposes of war in the race to control resource distribution in societies seeking to differentiate themselves and justify their hegemony. In our world, war over territories or ideologies takes place on a communicative level. The enemy, without face or name, is an abstract concept. Hitting first and transmitting messages after, we attest to wartime activities via television, the Internet and radio. War takes place on a technological level and occurs spasmodically – any place and any time – and like the enemy, its logic is uncertain. With the revolution of digital imagery (we live in a world of visual imagery designed to stimulate consumption and manipulate thought processes), words are referents pregnant with symbolic meanings now shared by huge masses of individuals all over the world. Interconnectedness is the keystone of present-day society as it moves with dramatic rapidity toward a new process of homogenization or postliteracy, as a way to survive the mass, worldwide phenomena of our astounding reproductive success as a species.

Although it began earlier, communicating abstract thoughts by way of diverse mediums was conducted by our early ancestors: pre-Neandertals, Neandertals and then anatomically modern humans, creating and emulating art and music. Systems of communication have been boundlessly revolutionized, time and again, in parallel with social expansion over time. Underlining once again our alienation from the natural world, our communication networking, established through external, material means, is just another type of tool: a strictly human adaptive response mode. From cave paintings to the incised stones of the first pastoral peoples, the pictographs of the first proto-historic societies, the engraved clay tablets and papyrus documents, the creation of acrophony (when the names of the letters composing an alphabet begin with the same intonation as the letter itself) and other alphabetical systems, scripts and hieroglyphs – all are moldable expressions of our complex cerebral processes that continue to find enunciation in an apparently endless variety of communicative modes. Because it has been modeled so, over time, by each and every social entity that has existed throughout the world, language, both written and spoken, is a fundamental manifestation of human cultural diversity. But today's developments in computerized language systems are causing us to do away with this apparently superfluous variability. Language diversity and complexity are being reduced by the process of globalization and its consequential homogenization: language development is, for all intents and purposes, in the saturation phase of the human evolutionary process.

9

GLOBAL WARMING
Natural Climatic Trend or Humanly Induced Phenomenon?

CLIMATE CHANGE THROUGH TIME

Throughout the Quaternary Period, humans have encountered, adapted to and survived through more or less intense phases of cyclical climatic change. For at least 2.5 million years, our genus has withstood even the most forceful oscillations in temperature and humidity affecting the Earth's atmosphere, oceanic circulation and hydrological cycles. *Homo sapiens* endured the pressures of the last ice age and prospered throughout the transition to warmer, more temperate conditions, marching arrogantly into to the Holocene and collectively engendering the Anthropocene Epoch. The story of humanity has taken place on an ever-changing stage of radically different settings, causing life to remodel itself, both unconsciously (physically) and consciously (culturally and socially) to find ways to adapt and survive in the face of continuously changing environmental conditions. Thanks to technology, we humans have sharpened our adaptive capacities through time, developing ever-greater flexibility by increasing our foundation of technoforms to face up to even the toughest of adaptive challenges. From the very dawn of human existence nearly 3 million years ago (Ma), climatic change has caused upheavals in animal and human life, altering landscapes all over the planet. This key moment of inception close in time to the emergence of *Homo*, as we have seen, began with a global trend toward cooler and dryer climatic conditions. In the first chapters of this book, we saw how cyclical climatic change driven by orbital forces established Pleistocene climate periodicity while expansions and contractions of the polar ice sheets perpetually altered climatic conditions. The contingency of the repercussions has fashioned the evolutionary pathways of all living beings in a constant waltz of changing settings, implicating processes of survival-extinction-migration-adaptation for all living beings. In this brutal and beautiful world in constant mutation, each species has relied on the successful ability of their own potential to change as the mechanisms of natural selection seek biological solutions from within each specific gene pool in the aim of achieving reproductive success, no matter the degree of intensity of external pressures. Yet only humans have chosen to so massively counter these forces with culture, a superlative adaptive response. Up to now, our seemingly never-ending spiral of technological innovation has assisted us in confronting climatic forcing, enabling us to live and prosper even in the most inhospitable landscapes and to colonize the planet's most inaccessible territories. Thanks to our material culture, we have subsisted, reproduced and prospered.

Only more recently in the face of dwindling land integrity and exhausted resources has this trend led us to an existence like a parasite, with human technologies overtaking and transforming the planet to the detriment not only of other living species but also of the most destitute of our own species. Thanks to such innovations as tool making and the control of fire and the evolutionary processes guiding the spiral of technological and social developments, humanity has gained liberty to the point of brutal stagnation, developing social rules and models to our guise, laughing in the face of Nature – but who will have the last laugh? Today we ask why our technosocial success has been transformed into a planetary nightmare. Have we passed the point of no return in terms of niche construction? Is planetary equilibrium altered beyond repair for the next millennia? We turn to the past and wonder how today's situation differs from what has gone before. Is it true, as some postulate, that global warming may soon lead to the destruction of human and other forms of life? Based on the evidence now available to us thanks to our technologies and largely to our (relatively recent) capacity to record past events, we can observe and predict developments guiding the future of climate change (with, as we are realizing from new data on oceanic temperature trends, relative precision).[332] I am not of those who deny the reality of anthropogenic climate change.[333] Obviously, the difference with today's situation compared with past trends is certainly one of degree or extent because human intervention on the planet's natural equilibrium is far higher than it ever was in the past. Our choice to use technology as an adaptive tool has greatly distanced us from Nature (at least in the abstract sense), and modern humans have increasingly (through time) caused (now) highly visible and (in some cases) irredeemable scars on the planet and its life forms. Over the millennia and forward from the Industrial Revolution, we have increasingly distanced ourselves from our natural, biological heritage.

Not surprisingly, the denatured lifestyle we have been leading engenders fear, insecurity and guilt in modern human populations. Individuals living in this modern context of cement, metal, plastic and polyester are experiencing feelings of discomfort and fear that they cannot remedy even by taking refuge in the subsidiary social matrix because it too is now so tightly structured to favor production-consumption behaviors without regard for such cares. These distortions in the face of our very nature are causing sickness within the modern social configuration, which is now being addressed by a newly adopted human response: unbridled consumption of artificially created placebos. Manufactured goods (and virtual realities) presently constitute the nongenetic material basis from which we are being guided to act in response to new psychosocial pressures provided by the corporate few who dictate our extrasomatic selective processes. Beyond the environment, huge social external pressures are being created, rendering our reactions as far from Nature as the plastics in which they are wrapped. For many individuals, this state of angst has inspired the desire for a "return" to a utopic past (idealized prehistoric situation) when humans (may have) lived harmoniously with other life forms, moving mindfully within the landscape, aware and respectful of their surroundings. Today, the evidence of our influence on the planet is all around us, rendering moot the discussion of whether humanly induced climate change is a reality or not.[334] But we can still try to discern how our present-day situation differs from that of the past at least in terms of our ability to deal with climate change. In any case, it is evident that today's choices in response to climate change can come only from the very same source as the disaster causality to which we are assisting: human technological prowess. In spite of climate change denial, many technological "solutions" are being developed today as an ominous indication that, rather than changing direction, humans are choosing to deal with a future without naturally generated resources. To remedy humanly induced planetary degradations, we are turning to our technologies to attempt implausible feats of "biomimicry," such as creating pollinating drones to replace the bees that are facing huge die-offs around the world[335] or developing underwater agriculture to deal with the disappearance of arable land resulting from exploding human demography and irreparably damaged terrains rapt with pollutants.[336]

ASSESSING CLIMATE CHANGE IN THE ARCHEOLOGICAL RECORD

Archeological sites provide us with precious paleoclimatic data critical to gain knowledge of climatic variability through time and establishing trends beyond what is measurable in the present. At the same time, climate-dependent phenomena dictate the preservation or not of archeological occurrences while also providing natural "archives" of climate information. In some cases, natural disasters (such as volcanoes, flash floods and mudslides) actually favor the preservation of archeological sites and the artifacts they contain. As we saw in Chapter 2, archeologists obtain useful paleoclimatic data from many different sources (tree rings, to ice cores, corals, continental and oceanic sediment, pollen, speleothems, etc.) that furnish information for evaluating chronology and fixing climatic events within their successive framework over time and space. Thanks to advances made in so many different fields of knowledge contributing to

Figure 9.1
General view of the Caune de l'Arago (Tautavel, France) late Acheulian cave site (indicated by the arrow in the upper right of the photograph) at the mouth of the Gouleyrous Gorges. The hominins inhabiting the cave over a period of some 600,000 years exploited local alluvial sources for lithic raw materials to make their tools. They even sometimes sourced fine-quality rocks from up to 30 kilometers away. They hunted and butchered different types of animals that thrived in a variety of ecological niches situated around the cavern. (Courtesy of Denis Dainat, EPCC-CERPT)

multidisciplinary archeological analysis, the global picture of climate change is constantly being revised as we fill in the gaps reaching far back into the distant past. These paleoclimatic reconstructions are types of scaffolding that are constantly being built up, reviewed and adjusted as data is added and cross-checked across the different disciplines while new knowledge is continuously being integrated to improve accuracy. In this circumstance, multilevel archeological sites serve as useful contexts to illustrate how humans have dealt with climate change in the distant past and how it might have differed from what we are experiencing today. One case in point is the Late Acheulian site of the Caune de l'Arago cave situated in southern France near the border with Spain, in the sleepy little village of Tautavel. While numerous examples of (post-Oldowan) multilevel archeological sites exist, I have chosen to discuss this particular example because my own doctoral research (at Perpignan University) was undertaken on the lithic assemblages from this site. The Caune de l'Arago provides a long and quasicontinuous stratigraphic sequence allowing us not only to follow physical changes that affected climates and landscapes over time in a single regional context but also to observe how early humans adapted their cultural and social responses to these changes. The cave is perched near the summit of a limestone cliff at the opening of a steep gorge carved out by a small river (see Figure 9.1). Its deposits, accumulated between 690,000 up to 90,000 years ago, document the passage of time like so many pages of a book and record successive glacial and interglacial events distinguishing this phase of the Middle

Pleistocene.[337] Excavations at the cave have been underway for more than half a century under the direction of H. de Lumley from the Institut de Paléontologie Humaine (Paris, France) and his collaborators at the Établissement public de coopération culturelle – Centre Européen de Recherches Préhistoriques de Tautavel (EPCC-CERPT). Throughout the years, layers of sediment composing the cave's 15-meter-thick depositional sequence have been progressively and systematically excavated to study each of the ancient hominin occupations buried within (Musée de Préhistoire de Tautavel; EPCC-CERPT).[338] The cave has yielded a very significant record of archeological finds including thousands of stone tools, large and small mammal remains and hominin fossils attributed to an evolved form of European *Homo erectus* (or *Homo heidelbergensis*), also referred to as *Homo erectus tautavelensis*.[339] In 1971, the discovery of a partial skull in a level dated to some 450,000 years ago rocked the world, revealing the facial features of this "first European" (later far older fossils were discovered at Atapuerca and Orce). Missing portions of the skull were completed in the laboratory based on other finds, allowing specialists to study the skull's interior bone surfaces using endocranial casting methods.[340] The skull's cerebral volume estimated at 1.150 cm^3 is considerably less than that of modern *Homo sapiens* (around 1.350 cm^3), and its overall morphology and configurations were also different (the frontal region of the skull is hardly developed with a receding forehead complemented by a supraorbital brow ridge and an outwardly jutting – or "prognathic" face – and strong, thick jaws).

The archeostratigraphic sequence enclosing the different layers of the Caune de l'Arago cave[337] bears witness to dramatic climatic changes occurring through time registered by the fluctuating nature of the sediment composing the infill and enclosing the artifacts and by significant changes in the types of faunal spectrum attributed to each archeostratigraphic unit. The hominins hunted a range of herbivorous animals that they brought into the cave to be consumed there. Meanwhile, different types of carnivores (notably bears) occupied the cave when the hominins were absent. During the colder glacial phases, sands blown by strong winds entered the cave from the overlying plateau while during warmer and more humid phases, clay deposits accumulated by percolation from the erosion of the encasing limestone. The faunal assemblages represented in layers deposited during cold phases (reindeer, muskox and arctic fox) differed dramatically from those of the layers reflecting the warmer ones (red deer and other forest-dwelling animals).[341] The presence of numerous stone tools in all of the levels indicates that the hominins were adapted to living in strikingly different climates and landscapes. Soundings in the cave's deep sedimentary sequence confirm the nearly constant presence of humans in the cave for a period spanning nearly 600,000-years, including during the very cold phases (there are no structured hearths in the cave). The cave's sequence thus covers much of the period in which Acheulian humans are known to have occupied Western Europe. Meanwhile, the lithic assemblages unearthed from each successive layer changed little over time, suggesting relative cultural stability in adequacy with the environmental contexts throughout this very long period.[40] In spite of this, studies of the lithics have brought to light subtle cultural differences attributed to a complex evolutionary scenario in which hominins adapted their tools to accommodate external forces (climate change, shifts in available resources) and in relation to changing functionality of the site (type of habitat, for example, temporary, seasonal or long term).[40,183,208,341,342] Dating of the stratigraphic sequence has been established by radiometric dating methods and biochronology of large and small mammals.[341,343,344,345,346,347,348]

In this context, it is appropriate to consider once again (as we have throughout the different chapters of this book) the extraordinary archeological records from the Sierra de Atapuerca sites in Spain. The Atapuerca complex encloses a series of multilevel sites whose human occupations have (thanks to years of excavation and research) been accurately dated to different periods covering a combined duration of more than 1 million years.[41,349] The Atapuerca complex includes the Sima del Elefante, Galería and Gran Dolina sites, with their paleontologically and archeologically rich and very deep Early and Middle Pleistocene infills. These sites are situated in the so-called Trinchera del Ferrocarril, a 500-meter-long trench that was dug out in the early twentieth century to accommodate a local mining railway. The nearby Cueva Mayor-Cueva del Silo contains the famous Sima de los Huesos, Galería de las Estatuas and El Portalón sites that are Middle Pleistocene through Holocene in age. On the southern slope of the Sierra de Atapuerca, the El Mirador cave contains an important infill with levels dating from the Early Neolithic to Middle Bronze Age. Also, the Arlanzón, Pico and Vena valleys, have revealed sites with archeological finds attributed to different periods.[350] The Atapuerca sites have yielded not only an exceptionally complete archeo-paleontological and geological record, but also important hominin finds attesting to the very long human presence in this region – even in the face of climatic fluctuations recorded within the sedimentary contexts of the sites. The sites have yielded hominin finds, including the first hominin of Europe[138] from level TE9 of the Sima del Elefante site (dated to 1.3 Ma by palaeomagnetism, cosmogenic nuclides and biostratigraphy).[351,352] For the moment, this hominin is attributed to Homo sp.[353] As discussed in Chapter 4, excavations in level TD6 of the Gran Dolina site produced the remains of Homo antecessor (0.9 Ma),[165] a hominin proposed as the last common ancestor to modern humans, Neanderthals and Denisovans.[163,166,354,355,213] Moreover, thousands of hominin fossils (attributed to twenty-nine individuals)[356] have been exhumed from the Sima de los Huesos site (along with numerous bear remains and a single handaxe),[287] resulting in the largest and most complete fossil hominin assemblage of Middle Pleistocene age in the world (ca. 430,000 years ago [Ka]).[357,358,359] This site is a chamber within the Cueva Mayor-Cueva del Silo karst system[357] that can be accessed only by a sloping ramp contiguous to a deep vertical shaft (this extraordinary context is discussed further in Chapter 12). While the Sima de los Huesos (SH) fossils were initially assigned to Homo heidelbergensis,[357] their affiliation with this taxon has since been reconsidered[359] and the definitive taxonomic determination for these "pre-Neandertals" is still pending.[359] At

Galería, Homo *heidelbergensis* is represented by a skull fragment and a mandibular fragment,[360,361] and a foot phalanx attributed to Homo *neandertalensis* has recently been documented at Galería de las Estatuas.[362] To complete this evolutionary odyssey, numerous modern human remains have been excavated from El Mirador cave where they were buried in relative abundance and where there is evidence for cannibalism during different periods of the Neolithic and Bronze Ages.[363,364]

Beyond all of these important hominin finds, the Atapuerca sites provide high-resolution records of stratigraphy, large and small mammals and human cultural remains (stone tools, pottery remains), all associated with a wealth of information gathered from widely published multidisciplinary studies[41,349] (see Figures 9.2 and 9.3). Scientific data from the Atapuerca complex continues to be meticulously collected and analyzed, providing a window through which to observe paleoclimatic conditions and the timing and modes of human evolution in a single geographic region (see Figure 9.2). Therefore, relative to the aims of this chapter, the Atapuerca record provides us precious information about how early humans and other life forms adjusted to climate change in order to continue occupying the same space even in the face of shifting environments. Multidisciplinary research at the sites by researchers collaborating from different institutions continues to yield key information about human evolution that is shared with both the more specialized scientific community and the general public (articles, books, videos, documentaries).

> The Atapuerca project is one of the most outstanding research programs to study world prehistory in terms of economic investment, relevance of excavated sites, number of scientists engaged, organisational complexity, and volume of scientific production. From 1978 to 2016, more than 1,000 people participated in excavations at the Atapuerca sites. Subsequent research generated publications in highly rated international scientific journals, including 6 papers in Nature, 6 in Science and 15 in PNAS. In addition, the project has generated a significant social impact with a total of 2,349,052 visitors to the facilities related to the project between 2010 and 2015 (the archaeological sites, the archaeological park and the Museum of Human Evolution).[365]

The teams working at the Caune de l'Arago and the Sierra de Atapuerca sites are exemplary for their many initiatives regarding the study of human evolution. Their contributions embrace the elaboration and teaching of excavation techniques with established field schools as well as site preservation and patrimony awareness through dissemination of scientific results. Over the years, these sites have offered training for students interested in prehistory and promoted research opportunities in the different scientific disciplines in the field of prehistory. Today, the research centers and museums built around these sites continue to work collaboratively with other institutions and universities around the world, some of which are following suit by creating analogous site-based structures to stimulate interest in prehistory among students, scientists,

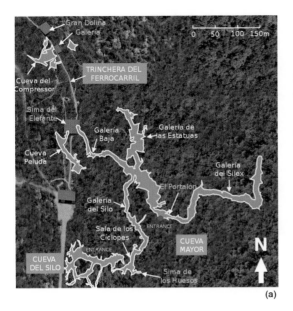

(a) (b)

Figure 9.2

Sierra de Atapuerca (Burgos, Spain) main archeological sites declared World heritage by UNESCO in 2000. (a) Map showing the situation of the archeological sites in the karst system. (b) Aerial view of the Trinchera del ferrocarril railway trench sector of the Sierra de Atapuerca site complex. The archeopaleontological sites of the Atapuerca complex record more than 1 million years of the human evolutionary story in a single region. They have yielded an abundant and highly significant record of human fossils in association with cultural materials as well as numerous small and large mammal remains. (Map: https:// upload.wikimedia.org/wikipedia/commons/2/22/Atapuerca_map.jpg and photograph of the Trinchera by Gerard Campeny courtesy of the IPHES-CERCA). The area was explored in the 1950s by the local Edelweiss speleological club, which sighted fossils in the Trinchera and later (1976) reported hominin skulls in the SH. In the same year, a mining engineer (T. Torres) informed paleontologist E. Aguirre of human remains at the SH. Aguirre initiated excavations at the Atapuerca sites, which he continued until his retirement in 1991. His succession in the direction of the research, the three co-directors: J. M. Bermúdez de Castro, J. L. Arsuaga and E. Carbonell (respective institutions: Centro Nacional de Investigación sobre la Evolución Humana (CENIEH) in Burgos and the National Museum of Natural Sciences in Madrid, the Universidad Complutense de Madrid - Instituto Carlos III and the Rovira i Virgili University and IPHES-CERCA in Tarragona), founded the Atapuerca Foundation. These scientists and the research teams they have formed continue to jointly manage the Atapuerca Project, and their contributions to the world of science are materialized by major cultural institutions (CENIEH currently directed by M. Martinón-Torres) and the Museo de la Evolución Humana in Burgos; the Centro Mixto de la Universidad Complutense de Madrid and the Instituto de Salud Carlos III de Evolución y Comportamiento Humanos (UCM-ISCIII) headed by J. L. Arsuaga with his team and the Institut de Paleoecologia Humana i Evolució Social (IPHES-CERCA) in Tarragona, founded by E. Carbonell and presently under the direction of R. Sala Ramos. Excavations at Atapuerca continue to this day under the auspices of the Junta de Castilla y León and the contribution of the Atapuerca Foundation.

Figure 9.3
General view of excavations at Sima del Elefante at the Sierra de Atapuerca (Burgos, Spain) in 2013. (Jordi Mestre, courtesy of the IPHES-CERCA)

politicians and the general public. All of this demonstrates great developments in the discipline of prehistoric archeology, underlining the importance of locating, excavating, analyzing and preserving archeological evidence and transforming it into shared human cultural heritage. Indeed, prehistoric archeological sites teach us important lessons about how human life has dealt with cyclical climate change through time. While the archeological record does register short-term and even relatively intense climate oscillations, the main trends observed in the past show relative cyclical regularity and a dominant tendency for gradual transformation through time. We might assume that this would have enabled biological adaptations to occur or provided the time necessary for other reactionary processes such as cultural adaptation or migration flow. Archeological data is today providing a basis for understanding how, when and why we have come to alter the pace of physical and cultural transmutations through time and space. Reconstructing past environments from the archeological record allows us to gain insights into human behavioral ecology through the notion of exchange: the effects that humans had on their environment and vice versa. From this, it has been deduced that detrimental human niche construction really began to have significant implications for the environment from the Late Pleistocene onward[366] when humans began to have effects on their surroundings with gradually increasing intensity. Human impact on the planet and its resources is thus very difficult to assess in such ancient time frames and are only beginning to be evidenced from the archeological record dating to after the appearance of *Homo sapiens* thanks to our own developing technologies applied to archeology and research.

Mounting evidence indicates that these Late Pleistocene dispersals, and the increase in global human populations with which they are associated, were linked in complex ways with a variety of species extinctions, extirpations, translocations, and new modes of niche modification. Evaluating Pleistocene anthropogenic impacts remains challenging, but novel methods and approaches are providing solutions to long-standing problems posed by limited preservation and chronological resolution.[366]

Thanks to collaborative research among the numerous disciplines relating to prehistory, data recorded from archeological sites contributes precious information that is useful to construct a global climatic evolutionary framework. Finally, all of this information must be contrasted with other important climate-sourcing sciences whose aim is to reconstruct long-term climate change on a global scale. Useful climatic data is also provided from analyses of the relationship existing between two oxygen isotopes (O^{16} and O^{18}) recorded in the world's ocean sediments. Core drilling brings up samples from deep within the earth to catalog changes in the ratio of these isotopes documented in the carbonate shells of tiny marine organisms accumulated on the ocean floor over time. The method (developed in the mid-twentieth century by the paleo-oceanographer C. Emiliani) is based on the observation that fluctuating ratios between these isotopes depend on changes in water temperature.[367] Because O^{18} is heavier than O^{16} (it contains two more neutrons), it tends to condense into precipitation after evaporating into the atmosphere while the lighter O^{16} forms water vapor in the troposphere. In the global water cycle, vapor accumulated in the subtropical oceans moves toward the Earth's polar regions, progressively releasing O^{18} into the oceans (in the form of rain or snow) while the O^{16} is absorbed by the polar ice sheets. During warm climatic phases, higher amounts of O^{16} are released as meltwater from ice caps, and the ratio of it relative to O^{18} is increased. Inversely, in colder climatic conditions, the O^{16} remains locked within the polar ice caps, and the ocean water reflects higher proportions of O^{18}. In this way, deep oceanic drilling to obtain cores of sediment containing these fossil remnants provides a useful method for measuring climatic change over time, constituting a continuous and global documentation: the marine isotope record. It provides a global chrono-climatic backdrop with which to situate data obtained from the archeological record. These isotopes contained within calcareous fossil foraminifera serve as practical bioindicators for observing changes in oceanic acidity and are used to carry out other types of analyses (biochronological and paleoenvironmental reconstructions).

Global temporal climatic reconstructions are particularly useful for establishing trends that help us to answer questions relating to what we are observing today, notably, about how changes in the quantity of humanly induced carbon emissions released into the atmosphere are affecting the delicate balance of the Earth's systemic atmospheric functions, which, in turn, affect all forms of life. Throughout the Quaternary Period, progressively shifting climates had repercussions on animal and plant life, shaping different environments and prompting biological change through natural selection. However, more rapid or especially dramatic climatic oscillations forced species to migrate or even to die out. Through all of this, humans survived and spread, thanks largely to their adaptive flexibility gained through the adoption of the technoresponse mode. Cultural evidence from multilevel sites (such as the Caune de l'Arago and the Sierra de Atapuerca complex) attests to the fact that later Middle Pleistocene hominins readily faced up to climatic change, surviving over successive generations thanks to their advanced cultural innovations and social networking, organized hunting and group survival strategies.[40,184,368] As we have seen, it is likely that the Acheulian populations present in Europe during the Middle Pleistocene already possessed the tool kits that enabled them to live in complex group frameworks tightly knit into a wider, regional scale of nomadic tribes. Acheulians certainly exchanged and shared their knowledge about the environment and the resources that were (or were not) available to them in each regional ecological context to which they returned seasonally to hunt and to reproduce. In order to maintain the necessary gene pool variability to sustain reproductive viability as nomadic groups of limited size, they would have been forced to exchange mates with other (nearby) populations, perhaps in ritual meetings between regional groups. In this process, they might have shared stories and exchanged information, forming the foundations that would sharpen traditions, mold identities and strengthen regional ties. In spite of cultural multiplicity,[176] the relative cultural conservatism demonstrated by these populations designates a certain stability in which Acheulian hominins pooled their vast technological and social savoir faire. We may even postulate that they shared their knowledge of plants in primal medicinal procedures and even (surely) spiritual beliefs. The data from stratigraphic sequences of long duration shows us that, while the types of animals represented in the archives of each successive archeological level vary in accordance to climatic changes over time, the human factor remained constant; this means that these hominins had already demarked themselves in numerous ways from the animal world. Yet these peoples thrived without visibly scarring their environment in lasting ways that could be observed in the geophysical record. The capacity of Acheulian peoples to thrive even in very harsh climatic conditions is further confirmed by their presence at sites situated as far north as England.[369] In sum, Acheulian hominins had sufficiently evolved their technological and social abilities to face up to climate change even as they maintained their colonization of Europe nearly 1 million years ago.

WHAT IS HAPPENING WITH THE CLIMATE TODAY?

But what about the rapid changes occurring in today's climatic conditions? Modern technologies, such as computer simulations and digital modeling techniques, announce global trends that differ from anything we observe in the past. The Intergovernmental

Panel on Climate Change (IPCC) has officially pronounced that the main cause for recent global warming is the increase in anthropogenic carbonic gas emissions (from automobiles, industry), enhancing the so-called greenhouse effect in which carbonic gas acts as a screen capturing thermal solar energy and trapping infrared radiation, subsequently raising the Earth's surface air temperature. The acknowledgement of this phenomenon is certainly not new; Swedish scientist S. Arrhenius first predicted it as early as 1896, more than 120 years ago.[370,371] In fact, humans have long been aware that the massive amounts of toxic pollutants released daily into the water and air as a result of our technological and social activities have harmful planetary repercussions that cause climate change.[371] What we see today, however, is that this situation, which has been ignored for so long, has worsened exponentially, reaching the point where we are being forced to deal with it. In the framework of the present book, it suffices to say that there is sufficient scientific data and clearly perceptible evidence that the climate is now changing drastically and that humans have had a huge impact on the planet in terms of landscape transformation and lack of respect for animals and plants. We can actually observe that human technologies have led us to produce unprecedented levels of toxic carbon emissions from burning fossil fuels released into the atmosphere, especially over the last century – and even more markedly since the 1950s.[372]

As of today, NASA reports that carbon dioxide in the air has reached the highest levels in 650,000 years.[373] Thanks to new technologies, the effects attesting to the reality of greenhouse gas–related warming are now well documented. Meticulously monitored on satellite, the melting of polar ice and other land glaciers is now reducing Artic ice formations to their lowest levels on record while warming temperatures are driving the Arctic greening. Biodiversity, the crucible of future evolutionary success for life on Earth, is diminishing all over the planet. In addition to cruel animal industrialization, hapless anthropomorphization is driving other unprecedented disturbances to animal life as stated in the recent global assessment report Intergovernmental Science-Policy Platform on Biodiversity and Ecosystem Services (IPBES), showing that more than 1 million animal species are presently in danger of extinction. The causes for this dire situation range from habitat degradation due to deforestation, pollution or other humanly induced causes to dramatic reductions in their populations by human hunting, overfishing, poaching and other activities. Information published reveals that two-fifths of all plants now qualify as "at risk of extinction" (assessment of the State of the World's Plants and Fungi project based on research by more than 200 scientists in 42 countries). But this is only a very incomplete inventory of some of the human-driven climate disasters that are painting a very bleak picture for the future not only for human life, but also for the millions of life forms on the planet. This reality is made even more palpable today by the increasingly frequent and robust weather events (cyclones, heat waves, wildfires, etc.) destroying homes, environments and livelihoods and displacing millions of humans and animals, with people in underdeveloped countries being four times more affected overall.[374]

Figure 9.4
Aerial view of intense fires in the boreal forests of eastern Siberia that continue to burn.
(NASA image courtesy of NASA Goddard Flight Centre, Jeff Schmaltz, MODIS Rapid
Response Team at NASA GSFC accessed at https://commons.wikimedia.org/wiki/File:Fires_in_
Eastern_Siberia_(4860546639).jpg)

The IPCC currently projects that average global surface temperatures will likely continue to rise by two degrees Celsius (C.) per decade, reaching unprecedented highs during the twenty-first century if we do not take drastic actions to reduce our emissions. Considering the magnitude of temperature increase projected for the very near future, the planetary scenario is indeed terrifying. Globally, the last decade has been the hottest on record with the highest temperature ever recorded (54.4°C) registered in August 2020 in Death Valley (New Mexico). The same year, wildfires spread out of control in the southwestern United States and Canada, displacing thousands and leaving others homeless. In Australia, fires killing or harming an estimated 3 billion animals are classified as "one of the worst wildlife disasters in modern history" by the World Wildlife Fund for Nature (WWF). Gigantic fires attributed to the warming climate are raging over many kilometers in Siberia, melting permafrost, releasing huge amounts of stored carbon dioxide and methane into the atmosphere and further exacerbating global warming (permafrost emissions; see Figure 9.4). Currently, these huge fires have affected at least 3 million hectares. The fires are releasing massive amounts of carbon into the atmosphere and are permanently damaging vast expanses of permafrost. Smoke from the fires has affected air quality over thousands of kilometers. Scientists agree that the cause of the fires is human induced climate change. In June 2020, Siberia experienced the record-breaking temperature of 38°C. The World Resources Institute has warned that rising sea levels (178 millimeters over the past 100 years)[375] will bring about large-scale human destruction and the displacement of more than 2 billion people presently living on or within 100 kilometers of a seashore. This catastrophic scenario (currently in progress) is expected to produce a massive climate-related migrant crisis, the gravity and proportions of which would far exceed the one the world is presently facing. Currently, human migratory pattern is largely based on established inequalities in access to resources where countries are justifying the closing of their borders to the thousands of poverty and war refugees by manufactured notions of birthright and populist or nationalist arguments. How will the world deal with climate refugees? Given that nearly half of the world's population living on or near the coastlines of the planet could potentially become the world's next refugees, they will be of all origins, colors and religions – all migrating in massive numbers to escape natural disaster. Natural cataclysmic events due to extreme weather events are leading to the upheavals in the planet's natural balance. Observed deviations vary from expanding tropical weather systems to desertification, altering agricultural yields even as the human species reaches nearly 8 billion souls. Planetary species' extinction (already in progress with unknown repercussions to the Earth's natural equilibrium) and disease are affecting the world's populations. As scientists look to the past for answers, it is widely acknowledged that humanly induced global warming is a reality whose long-term effects remain uncertain. While it is true that in the past, the Earth has experienced important (and sometimes rapid) warming, in some cases due to greenhouse gases naturally released into the atmosphere (for example, by volcanoes), there is now global scientific consensus that the current situation is indeed the result of human expansion and industrialization.[376]

Global warming and the ensuing climate deregulation are experienced today in different ways in various parts of the globe as an increase in both hot and cold temperature variability and extreme weather conditions with an overall increase in the temperature of the globe. Applying computerized systems, the IPCC and other scientific institutions are working to integrate data from the past to predict future climatic scenarios. All agree that the *very real* increase in temperature over most of the Earth's surface (including ocean temperature) due in very large part to anthropic greenhouse gas emissions will continue to increase the risk of drought in some regions such as the western United States, Canada and Australia where farmland is experiencing difficulties from the severe lack of summer and winter precipitation. Global warming is already increasing the frequency and intensity of mid-latitude tropical storms and cyclones, resulting in stronger winds and unusually high levels of rainfall leading to massive flooding events. Countries affected by monsoons are already dealing with higher rates of precipitation in some areas or extreme dryness in others. Areas affected by record-breaking temperatures and the resulting dryness of vegetation face devastating wildfires and severe water shortages. In today's world where all of these consequences are already happening, some are asking whether these natural disasters are really occurring more often than in the past. Although some scientists beg to differ, the majority do concur that there has been a progressive increase in the average measured temperature of nearly 1° C of the Earth's near surface air since the mid-twentieth century. In spite of widespread acceptance of the human impact theory on global warming, some scientists (and politicians) still suggest that these claims simply reflect modern communication networks that increase global awareness of climatic events occurring all over the planet in "real time" (television, radio, Internet). According to this premise, rapid information transfer explains the perceived increase in the intensity and frequency of catastrophic climate events taking place on a planetary level. But this denies the science, which, thanks to sophisticated technologies, presently takes into account long-term trends in climatic conditions over the entire planet. In contrast to the relative exclusion of peoples and continents in the past, today large areas of the industrialized world receive and emit information about what is happening all over the planet each and every hour of each and every day. World events are transmitted instantaneously and shared with a rapidity never before achieved. Global participation in natural catastrophes triggers empathy and sensations of empowerment to the populace of unaffected regions even as people are solicited to provide material assistance to the victims of catastrophic events occurring hundreds or even thousands of kilometers away. Televised debates following such tragic events often invite scientists to discuss ways to prevent or at least more effectively predict their incidence. Not surprisingly, specialists from the field of prehistory are now frequently called on to contribute their views on the causes and effects of natural disasters precisely because of their ability to provide the large-scale hindsight necessary to interpret them.

HUMAN RESPONSIBILITY AND ACTIONS ON CLIMATE CHANGE

In recent years in efforts to reverse these climatic trends, governments have ratified international pacts such as the landmark Kyoto Protocol adopted in Japan in 1997.[377] The United Nations Framework Convention on Climate Change officially recognized the reality of the anthropic nature of the recent increases in the greenhouse effect, fixing real limits to emissions on a global scale by implementing a series of rules (the Marrakesh accords, Morocco, 2001)[378] with a first period of global commitment from 2008 to 2012. This initiative was followed in 2012 by the Doha Amendment to the Kyoto Protocol,[379] revising and updating the precedent and fixing a new commitment period for thirty-seven countries with the European Union vowing to increase its pledge to reduce greenhouse gas emissions by 5 percent compared to the 1990 levels of the first commitment period and by 18 percent in the second period (from 2013 to 2020).[377] Then came the Paris Agreement officially introduced in 2015,[380] proposing to step up the measures through global collaboration to actively combat climate change. Ideally, upper-middle and high-income countries should take the lead role in the effort and assist lower-middle and low-income countries to achieve the main goal of maintaining the global rise in temperature well below 2° C above the preindustrial level. Because of the gravity of the present situation, the Paris Agreement hopes to deal with some of the more drastic effects of climate change by calling on modern technological know-how to help people to adapt to the new paradigm of planetary damages we have generated. Of course, the fact that the United States, the largest contributor of greenhouse gas pollution on the planet and a cultural unit led by climate change deniers during these crucial years (2017–2021), withdrew from the agreement in 2017, dooming it to failure in spite of some promising efforts by other participating countries. As I write this book, the forty-sixth president of the United States, Joe Biden, stated (on his first day in office) that the United States is joining the Paris Agreement again, providing some optimism for the future of world collaboration on this important issue. As the IPCC continues to issue ominous reports assessing the situation of climate change and its catastrophic effects on the planet, it is of the keenest interest to humanity to heed to the fact, as many point out, that the climate deregulation "tipping point" has already been reached. The 2019 IPBES report informing of worldwide plant and animal loss[381] must serve as a warning to all of us: environmental catastrophe is upsetting the world's natural balance and triggering new dangers poised to destroy clean water and air supplies. This situation increases the likelihood for more frequent and intense climate disruptions (that we are already experiencing first hand) and the unleashing of unprecedented global pandemics rooted in the resulting dysfunctional social and demographic trends (such as the Covid-19 pandemic that the world began experiencing in 2019).

Yet in spite of these ongoing conventions regarding what, if any, action should be taken to reduce or reverse future planetary warming or to develop technologies to adapt to its expected consequences, it remains unclear whether even drastic measures will have significant bearing on the climatic and environmental changes already in progress. The consequences already underway on the planet's ecosystems will continue to be felt over the next millennia regardless of the type and extent of global action that may be taken in the next years. In other words, yes, we have reached the point of no return in terms of sustainability, and it seems that humanity has already made the choice to adapt technologies to face the future of this reality rather than trying to remedy it by conservation efforts or significant changes in human lifestyles. While the Earth's natural systems are subject to cyclical change, as we reach this tipping point, its natural trends will no longer be valid or predictable. In other words, we are sailing into unknown waters in terms of the future of our planet. In the face of rapid climatic change and the degradation of the quality of the atmosphere due to a myriad of forms of pollution, not to mention the rapid disappearance of space available for species other than humans and their domesticated herds and crops, many wild species are disappearing. Episodes of massive die outs recorded in the archeological record of the planet are not unknown. In fact, we know of five really major extinction episodes in the past that in some cases led to the disappearance of more than 90 percent of land and marine life on Earth.[382] Today, some specialists are proposing that we are heading toward a sixth extinction,[383] only this time it will be the first one to be induced by unnatural causes brought on by humans. The reality of the global situation *that we have created and that we are responsible* for must now be managed if we are to avoid unpredictable repercussions on the Earth's ecosystems leading humankind, perhaps, toward the next massive extinction event.

And so, humankind is preparing for the future, one that will be very different from all that has come before. The Anthropocene Epoch[29] is dominated by constructed environments filled with manufactured goods. This polymorphous mass of humanly created items (now beyond "culture" as defined in this book) is currently most adequately referred to as "the technosphere,"[384] the nonbiological sphere of human existence that we have chosen to create and on which we now base our survival. Currently, a new political landscape is being implemented by the most powerful nations of the world, prevalent emitters of hazardous greenhouse gases into the atmosphere in a setting of climate change denial that deliberately seeks to increase – instead of decrease – the use of fossil fuels. We stand by and watch helplessly as the world's nations continue to play with planetary life in a contemptible struggle to obtain brief hedonistic and capitalistic monetary gain and in complete disregard for science and the well-being of all life forms on the Earth. Our physical and cultural evolution has and will continue to be intimately linked to changing climatic conditions. The archeological register in general (and multilayer sites in particular) has shown us that our early ancestors used technology and socialization to irrevocably free humanity from the dictates of natural climate forces. And so, although climate change might have acted as a trigger for early human adaptation/innovation, the technological selective route we have taken has provided us the liberty to develop exponentially our material and social foundations to overcome effectively the external pressures of perpetually changing environmental settings. Decrypting the procedural evolution of the human technoselective choice evidences our distancing from environmental dependency and toward intensive, harmful and potentially dangerous niche construction. But on the upside, our cerebral capacities that have evolved alongside our technologies provide us with the long-term perspective necessary to understand present-day developments and to predict the forms they may take in the very near future. The cumulative vision provided from our knowledge of prehistory contributes precious information about the human trajectory, telling us finally that the survival strategy that we will opt for in the very near future will not come from the biological sphere but rather, from the material means provided by our technologies.

10

TECHNOLOGY AND HUMAN ALIENATION
FROM NATURE

REFLECTIONS ON THE HUMAN CONDITION

Our distinctively advanced cognitive capacities originally assumed through the agency of natural selection developed exponentially in proximate synchronicity with the invention and evolution of technology. Over time, technological selection has been at work shaping human evolution. The growth of technology and its associated cultural facets has enabled our species to attain unprecedented levels of achievement, ultimately granting us full reign on the planet and all it encompasses. By manipulating both the objective and the subjective realms and shaping them according to changing mental templates, we create and recreate environments that reflect the circumstances of our inner world. The models we produce in the objective world are not random, but rather they are subject to the very patterning of the human brain itself, reproducing its predisposition to categorize even as it stocks the masses of information it absorbs over lifetimes, generations, centuries and millennia. The unique anatomic development of cerebral lateralization has enabled the human brain to increase its volume very significantly in proportion to our body mass (the "encephalization quotient" measures relative brain size in accordance to the ratio of brain mass and body size). *Homo sapiens* has the highest encephalization quotient of all species of mammals.[385] This was achieved by a unique evolutionary event affecting the human brain by dividing it both vertically and horizontally into separate but interconnected lobes, enabling it to compartmentalize different (if sometimes overlapping) motor, sensorial and cognitive tasks.[386] The expansion of the outer cortex of the brain (also called gray matter or neocortex) was made possible through anatomic strategy that set up an asymmetrical operating system. This scheme has been a key factor in giving us the ability to absorb, process and share extensive amounts of information, which we proceed to filter through complex, non-biological social constructs. The human cerebral neocortex is an evolutionary marvel of unimaginable intricacy and efficiency that has evolved coetaneous to our nonbiological modes of resource acquisition (technology), an evolutionary choice that came to demand an enormously heavy burden of social learning.

The brain's amazing complexity is what has allowed us to develop and intimately link the extremely numerous and complex symbolic thought processes needed for us to interact functionally in large group settings relying on composite sets of technological devices. Our cerebral organization allows us to act in situations in which complex prerequisite technological know-how will trigger automated responses that are adequate and socially acceptable to the overall functioning of individuals in each specific group setting. Exchanges taking place through the synapses in the cerebral convolutions enable us to rapidly react and perform tasks that have become essential to our survival, such as those requiring interactive competences (planning and predicting behaviors, spatially organizing and expressing symbolic language). Knowledge about the functioning and the organization of the brain indicates that hominins developed complex symbolic thought-communication abilities in synchronicity with the growth of the neocortex and, notably, the expansion of the brain's frontal lobe. The exact timing of the emergence of language, often seen as the ultimate expression of culture and advanced symbolic thought processes, is difficult to pinpoint in the archeological record. Indeed, even some of early hominin forms appear to have been – at least physically – prepared for spoken language by being equipped with the pharynx and larynx in a language-appropriate position, a deep enough palette to emit a suitably large range of sounds and sufficiently developed Wernicke and Broca areas of the brain. Yet it is possible that truly developed language capacities, although anatomically conceivable very early on, remained as a latent trait until the selective force to develop and use complex signs and symbols brought it to the fore. For this reason, some propose that early hominin language capacities could have been similar at first to those accomplished by some primates, such as chimpanzees, whose genetic makeup differs little from our own.

The physical transformations linked in particular to the development of the brain that we have undergone have led us to evolve almost in spite of ourselves toward technical and social complexity. In addition, our choice to overcome physical dependence has inclined our species to develop an exceptionally high degree of intellectual dependency-interdependency through complex communication networks combined with techno-logical innovation. Today, as we link ourselves to the digital world, we transform our physical selves into little more than shells for the transport of the brain, which now remains the ultimate tool to access and experience constructed realities. We are already facing some of the repercussions of this inward escape, for example, by way of physical deformations observed in modern industrialized societies such as obesity and the absence of a calibrated musculature. Despite the fact that this condition results from a completely normal evolutionary process, it dehumanizes us because it does not originate from natural causes but rather from a new world order that is external and alien to Nature. Such unnatural conditions cause physical discomfort and even disease (heart and cholesterol problems, rheumatism, arthritis) brought on by the sedentary lifestyle of the computerized age in the developed world. Of course, we humans are not exempt from natural selection, and our bodies still continue to undergo physical change, however imperceptible, in successive generations. So what are the changes we might expect in the future? Should we continue to privilege digital existence over physical exertion, we may assume that doing so will cause continued development of the brain coupled with a relative neglect of the postcephalic musculature that will ultimately result in increased corpulence coupled perhaps with hyperencephalization.

Human cognitive complexity involves intricate patterns of cerebral networking that allow us to carry out linked sequences of actions such as those involved in stone knapping. This capacity took on particular significance during the Acheulian when hominins demonstrated complex understanding and prediction of volumetric models.[61,169] Unlike simply experiencing sensations or reacting intuitively to a causal trigger as animals do, humans are capable of assessing sequential actions or ideas based in cause and effect connectedness and involving meditation and planning.[118] Returning to the case of toolmaking (object manipulation), the cause and effect relationship is rooted in the physical nature of the materials themselves. Therefore, in order to modify a stone, one must be capable of adequately predicting what its physical reactions to specific types of gestures and forces will be. In stone-reduction processes, humans learn to make the best (or most suitable) choices through experience and culture. Seemingly simple stone toolmaking can in fact be conceptually complicated, sometimes involving multiple levels of choice (position, pressure, angle) and taking into account a large range of variables (raw material type, quality, shape, desired formal template). In contrast, a planned social act stemming from rudimentary desires or needs (hunger, sex, fear) will be executed in accordance with another set of learned variables, each very different from the other, depending on the context of culturally learned norms of action. These include, especially, the ability to predict the reactions of individuals that will be involved in an action as well as the impact that their reaction(s) may have on each one's own situation (inner mental image or socially visible consequence: shame, fear, guilt, jealousy, etc.). In fact, any social situation or action triggers both innate (biological) and learned (cultural, social) responses that will determine their outcome. As observed in the works of Z. Bauman,[387] this underlines the paradoxical nature characterizing the planning of a human social act as, on the one hand, determined by an individual's desire for originality or uniqueness (standing out, being noticed) while being conditioned by the desire to fit in with one's social group (be effaced, be one of the crowd). Both animals and humans communicate their inner mental processes either physically, using expressions and gestures, or vocally, emitting sounds. These emanations will be understandable by the receptive party(ies) from within the social unit to which the individual belongs and who, therefore, *have followed an identical social learning process*. For this reason, the specificities of the physical and vocal gestures emitted are the hallmark of one or another social grouping (i.e. language). In fact, the template of physical/vocal expressions from which an individual will make his/her choice when planning an action (social or material intervention) is simply a set of shared, symbolic prototypes socially transmitted through learning. They are dictates for the sets of behaviors that are acceptable (or not) in a given social context. In sum, these premeditated socially formulated templates are shared physical and verbal vocabularies that constitute the basic elements differentiating one social unit from another and, therefore, are the very foundation of what we commonly call Culture.

TOOLMAKING, LANGUAGE AND THE EVOLUTION OF COMPLEX SYMBOLIC THOUGHT PROCESSES

As our database of technological information gradually enlarged, so too did our need to amplify the act of processing and communicating information socially in order to transmit the growing compendia of acquired knowledge. This strategy of effectively sharing knowledge accumulated through socially learned processes has had the obvious advantage of allowing each successive generation to begin assimilating new knowledge from a progressively more advanced starting point. Humanity thus moved beyond sharing only instinctively acquired cognitive triggers, such as fear, hunger, empathy, affection and danger, to sharing readily processed information, such as music, philosophy, rational concepts and art, acquired by previous generations through social learning. This incredible achievement was made possible over time, as we have seen, thanks to the enlargement of specific capacities, including not only technology but also the development of concepts such as identity and belonging within a well-defined social entity. This impressive feat was accomplished thanks to the human choice to massively adopt and exploit symbolic behavior and expression as an adaptive strategy. The choice to elaborate and socialize complex symbolic behaviors is *the* supremely human developmental trait that distinguishes the significance and impact of our species' technoforms, transforming them into culture, and making the distinction between what is human and what is animal very clear.

The capacity for *Homo* to communicate on a symbolic level has evolved similar to any other trait – anatomic or mental – through natural selective processes. On the cognitive level, this is perhaps best illustrated by evoking some examples from ongoing research that is establishing links between language capacity and the ability to make stone tools.[61] This theme is being researched to understand when and why symbolic thought patterns evolved and how they developed into composite modes of communication. It is significant that the language-relevant frontal cortex of the human brain also participates in a range of nonlinguistic behaviors, such as the ability to elaborate sequential actions

Figure 10.1
Imitation and emulation are important for teaching simple stone tool–knapping strategies,
but using spoken language allows far better integration of the notions required to
successfully knap flakes from stone. (Courtesy of Francisco Javier Luengo Gutiérrez)

and to predict volumetric reactions in physical bodies, that can be easily associated with
toolmaking. Accordingly, toolmaking is believed to have evolved initially in the context
of manual praxis before being "co-opted" to support other behaviors such as symbolic
communication in general and language in particular.[169] The investigation by Morgan
and colleagues[61] tested the use of different modes of communication to evaluate how
toolmaking technologies are most satisfactorily transmitted (or learned). The results
demonstrate clear advantages for verbal teaching over other forms of learning such as
visual imitation or emulation (see Figure 10.1). Consequentially, early hominins would
have evolved primitive forms of language as a means to teach one another toolmaking
skills, and this behavior was amplified because the technologies required for tool
manufacturing grew increasingly complex. Eventually, both complex toolmaking and
language became fundamental survival skills. From this, it seems obvious that the
accelerations in the advancement of technological complexity that we observe through
time are directly related to the success of the strategic evolutionary choice of adapting
symbolic communicative networks and their synchronic progression. Through social
transmission, these networks permit(ted) humans to facilitate the accumulation of
knowledge sets involving multifaceted actions of object modification.

> Although human social transmission has allowed the cumulative elaboration of a
> vast number of technologies and behaviors, non-human animal social transmission
> has not. It seems possible that this is because non-human animal social transmission,
> which appears to be largely limited to forms of observational learning less
> sophisticated than those of humans, lacks the fidelity required to transmit more
> complex innovations, thus constraining cumulative cultural evolution.[61]

Toolmaking and tool use would thus have contributed to the development of other cooperative activities, such as hunting, in which symbolic communication was useful. Through time, hunting developed into a shared, cooperative (social) activity that was of paramount importance to the survival of human groups. Organizing hunting expeditions (in group contexts) requires experience and knowledge about the desired prey's environment(s) and behavioral tendencies such as seasonality (for example, niche exploitation and conduct). A successful group hunt involves gestural and verbal communication modes that are understandable to the individuals participating. As we have seen, Acheulian hominins (*Homo erectus* or *Homo heidelbergensis*) were indeed capable of organizing complex hunting expeditions.[40,184] I might even propose hunting as a key factor that favored the organization of humans into functional group entities. Hunting can require long periods of absence for stalking prey and sometimes entail danger or extreme difficulties to kill, butcher and transport the game, and a range of skills is necessary for dividing and transporting carcasses and finally sharing the food among other group members. All of this underlines the clear advantages gleaned from organizing individuals into social units founded on task division. Different members of a group maintained distinct responsibilities relating, at least at first, to ensuring group survival (caring for the young, hunting and gathering, warding off predators).

ON SYMBOLISM, IDENTITY AND DEMOGRAPHIC EXPANSION

The obvious benefits obtained from task division were yet another factor accelerating hierarchical socialization. As societies evolved into civilizations in the later phases of the Paleolithic and beyond, the advantages reaped from the technology-communication biome bore their fruits as the human species experienced unparalleled demographic growth, snowballing the need to intensify this praxis. In turn, the need for symbols grew because they provided a system to rapidly convey and understand messages, facilitating the control and channeling the growing numbers of individuals, fitting them into the constructed ranking in the hierarchical social ladder specific to each group. Over time, symbolic role-playing by shamans and other ritual figures was actually woven into the social tissue as another means by which to control and mediate behavior and mold it into communally acceptable norms.[288] This strategy – however deeply rooted as we have seen in nascent civilizations at least 15,000 years old – has only strengthened over time as our numbers have grown exponentially. Controlling symbolism persists in modern societies where role-playing is still ubiquitous by, for example, politicians, dignitaries, nobles, religious icons such as the pope or the Dalai Lama and performers in music, theater and television. In the modern world, an individual's identity depends on his/her ability to read and interpret many different sets of symbols (visual, vocal, gestural, digital) emitted by members of their own social entity. Through time, growing population density eventually required individual human groups to acquire interpretative capacities that would enable them to relate to other social units they encountered as they expanded their territorial range. In the prehistoric context, we have seen how unique sets of symbolic expression distinguished one social unit from another and how they became indicators of distinct cultures. We must not forget that, from the later Acheulian at least, each sociocultural group was defined by its own expression of a specific developmental stage of the global technosocial construction in relation to the territories in which it evolved. Just as some animals mark their territories using odor, scratch marks or other physical behaviors, humans marked theirs by distinctive symbols and symbolic behaviors. This conduct still dominates in our modern world, and we struggle instinctively to maintain it, actively or subconsciously, in a context where frontiers are becoming more and more meaningless. Through the process of globalization, we are evolving toward becoming a single and homogenous social unit in which the need or meaning of culture is itself becoming moot even as some strive to conserve it by way of constructed nationalisms. Hence, symbolism, as it is so supremely expressed by the distinctive linguistic and gestural communication patterns invented by humans, was opted for initially as a survival strategy relating directly to resource acquisition through object manipulation (technology), lending our species a considerable edge for survival and egging on human reproductive success. As we discussed in previous chapters of this book, demography of ancestral human populations shows a definite growth patterning from the later Oldowan, becoming truly phenomenal after the Late Acheulian, and finally transforming into a global explosion after the emergence of Homo sapiens in the later phases of the Paleolithic. This archeological reality (the so-called Human Revolution)[285] is a phenomenon conveying the spectacular repercussions of complex cultural expression following the emergence of anatomically modern humans: the superb artistic creations, sophisticated hunting gear and incredibly complex technologies that transformed the final Paleolithic peoples into the first proto-historic civilizations. Lacking a hyperdeveloped frontal lobe, ancestral hominin species still evolved symbolic behavior from the Acheulian onward with the superb symmetrical bifaces made by Homo erectus or Homo heidelbergensis, for example, and followed up more conspicuously by the works and behaviors of the elusive Homo neandertalensis.

Gradually, increasingly higher degrees of physical, temporal and intellectual inversion were needed to maintain the developing human brain. In response to these requirements, our species chose to invest heavily in evolving communication networks and social learning systems in the aim of reaping the full benefits offered by complex technologies. Symbolic behaviors, such as producing music and art, provided a formidable means by which to externalize thought processes existing deep within the human mind and to share elusive systems of thought, binding peoples together into strongly knitted social units and ensuring their functional efficiency despite the great influxes of individuals composing the overall social web. Archeologically, Neandertals using ochre, feathers and shells for body decoration and reverently burying their dead, provide evidence of the existence of complex symbolic communication in the Eurasian late Middle Pleistocene archeological record nearly 100,000 years ago.

Meanwhile, it is certain that even stronger forms of abstract expression intensified with frequency in the Upper Paleolithic context. This behavior is the hallmark of anatomically modern humans, such as those living in South Africa during the Middle Stone Age in the same time frame as the Neandertals were roaming throughout much of Eurasia (as discussed in Chapter 5). And so symbols and symbolic behaviors have grown up out of this very ancient tradition that we refer to today under the generic label "culture," developing progressively into valuable social standards communally used to inspire emotions, channel desires, indicate social status or ranking, unify social entities, or direct basic instincts, such as altruism or sexuality. This fundamental social role-playing still serves in today's world to legitimize powers and maintain order in the context of an increasingly deteriorating social fabric.

HOW CULTURE CONSOLIDATED THE HUMAN DIVORCE FROM NATURE

I wish to conclude that our perceived and real alienation from Nature can be traced back to stone toolmaking, the original sin *par excellence!* What truly differentiates humans from all other animals is, therefore, certainly not biological but rather is *technological*. Human technologies have allowed us to tip the balance of natural equilibrium, alienating the human species from all other living beings inhabiting the planet, for only humans manipulate the material world as they please, satisfying personal or group needs and appeasing our wildest desires. Technology enables us to go beyond immediate gratification of basic needs, changing our lives in ways never before imagined and freeing ourselves forever from the sustenance-based lifestyles that all other animals submissively acknowledge. We once also lived thus. By embracing technology, we have changed our destinies in ways never imagined and, as we lose our hold on the reigns of its parallel evolutionary force, its mutations become evermore unpredictable. Looking at techno-logical advancements, it becomes evident that by liberating ourselves from the inertia of a lifestyle dependent on the vagaries of Nature, technology has heralded our species into an era of autonomy whose self-same social complexity is now impeding the making of appropriate, evolutionarily sustainable choices. As a consequence, we must concede that technology is what threatens our own and other species' ultimate survival because it has given us the capacity with which to reap large-scale destruction unless it is checked or guided by what the human mind and hand have learned over time. The new world order suggests further vertiginous and unrelenting technological developments whose only reasoning seems to be that of following through on our experiments if only to discover just how far we can go. Do we not feel today that, somehow along the way, our nonbiological creation has gotten out of hand? We must not forget that we have lived like beasts, kneeling in fear before the forces of Nature, withstanding rather than wielding, surrendering rather than opposing, being fearful yet defiant. This state of being is not yet entirely overcome. We as a species have morphed through sociological conditioning and, while we once believed ourselves liberated from the basal constraints of Nature, we are now finding ourselves still and forever subject to Her angry vengeance. In retrospect, we need to transform the potential of technological advances into assets for our species rather than scenarios of horror and desolation. Let us not forget that, no matter how far-fetched they may appear today, the fantastic possibilities opened up by human technologies are and must remain guided by scrupulous civilized conduct. The emerging new world order begs the continuing, dizzying and relentless development of technology without suitable planning or vigilance regarding its impact on other life forms. It is now for us to master it once again, to understand its advancement and to tether it to that other aspect that makes us human: empathy, not only for other human beings but also extended to all living beings with which we share the planet. Only then can we begin to anticipate a sustainable future.

Establishing behavioral patterns and evaluating cognitive capacities and placing them within a temporal, environmental and spatial framework are procedures presently used in prehistory for understanding human evolution. That said, we should evaluate intellectual aptitude from levels of technological achievement and then consider the status of empathy in relation to these achievements as a measuring stick by which to judge our true degree of progress. For no matter how far humankind has strayed from Nature, we remain inseparable from Her. The rapidity that characterizes change in modern societies has engendered in many individuals a desire for return, a wish to go back in time to an imaginary, utopian past human condition. Some conjure up prehistory as a time when humans lived simply and sanely in ideal harmony with Nature and in undefiled fusion with their environment. Prehistoric humans thus exist in the modern collective imagination in an idealized context as Utopian beings, rulers of a world without conflicts tearing up nations, without catastrophes due to human fault that disturb the delicate balance of our planet's equilibrium and without the dizzyingly rapid pace of technological progress. Yet truthfully, archeology shows us that we are the products of a denaturalized selective process that began so long ago with the first *Homo sapiens*, conquerors and colonizers with limitless ambition and a not-so-minimal degree of cruelty. Even though I would prefer to argue against this defeatist evolutionary viewpoint, it gains strength when we observe the redundancy of our acts through time: over and over the same scenarios relentlessly repeating themselves through war, cruelty, greed, power – only the faces and names change. Yet there is in all of this beauty, art, sympathy and goodness, and these too are human qualities that we so desperately need to cultivate today. These too are behavioral aspects that we can choose to develop if we are to adopt a more appropriate manner of exploiting all that we have learned throughout our hominization process.

The reality of events that have occurred in the past explains what we are today. But what are the real facts, and how can we understand the transformations, subdued or deliberately provoked, of human society? Since its inception, science has sought to build up an objective reality. More specifically, the science of prehistory seeks to reconstruct, as accurately as possible, past realities through the observation of artifacts and structures.

These material remnants of the past thus become valuable physical witnesses to the lifeways of ancestral forms of human beings and the choices they made. However, inferring truths from inanimate objects and structures is a constant struggle that cannot indeed escape our socially molded subjective minds; there is no observation without interpretation. Furthermore, our vision of the world is filtered by the way our brain allows us to perceive and interpret it. The question arises as to whether there are alternative realities. And if there are, which reality is the correct one? Alternate realities are indeed perceived by other animals or even by people experiencing dissimilar cerebral messaging. The very synaptic processes occurring within the human brain shape the ways in which we are *able* to perceive reality. We are (biologically) forced to categorize our perceptions in a species-specific way to make sense of the information we amass. All information received by our brain is processed, therefore, by our own biological system, which then triggers an "appropriate" reaction that itself is filtered and conditioned by current sociological norms practiced by the human group to which we belong. Viewed thus, only scientific advances can prove that our species' sensorial world vision is truly the accurate one.

11

WHO ARE WE?
Ancient and Modern Human Migrations

A PREHISTORIC PERSPECTIVE ON RACISM AND NATIONALISM IN THE MODERN WORLD

Nations willingly modify their historical past to provide stories based on interpretations that favor their own group members and rationalize transformations that are unjust to "others" *even though they are all members of the same human group.* These stories serve to rationalize policies that are exclusive to peoples existing outside of a given, shared constructed reality: the social identity. The modern tendency to build and perpetuate such constructs is deeply rooted in our animal nature in the instinctual Darwinian disposition to favor choices that promote *the survival of the fittest.* After all, we are now more than ever competing with one another and with other life forms for access to resources, now both real (water, food, sand, forest) and imagined (money, popularity, accumulation of material goods).[304] In the face of unparalleled demographic increase, the race to dominate resources has only reinforced the links between identity and territory established at least during the later Middle Pleistocene. Human identities are cultural and as such, do not have any real grounding; they are purely symbolic creations. Yet, identity-based criteria are presently guiding almost all of our major decision-making processes. These criteria are what lead us to favor specific nationalist policies even though they may be harmful to other human beings. Consequently, it is difficult (or impossible) to objectively understand reality unless we base our notions on advances in the natural sciences, which will help us to replace the manufactured human reality by a more factual, evolutionary (pre)historical veracity of the human species underpinning its true potency.

> Under the terms of the Treaty of Westphalia (1648), for example, a number of countries received territories, or were confirmed in their sovereignty over territories. This led to the creation of a legal landscape whereby rights came to be accorded to individuals on the basis of their status in an existing nation state. As a matter of course, some states provided better protection to others, depending upon their relative wealth and military power. Early international law ensconced rights of movement across borders, favoring colonization and conquest, and when those who were colonized sought rights from the more powerful nations, suddenly the right to "absolute sovereignty" was used against them, on the basis of their belonging to "barbarian" races, blasphemous religions, or conquered territories.[388]

In today's so-called developed world, the resurgence of nationalisms[389] is feeding far-right sentiments of exclusionism, and newfound tensions are emerging and spreading in response to increasing shortages in resources and the corresponding rise in the cost of living complicated by job shortages, overpopulation and poor management of ecosystems. In the meantime, the abyss separating the high- and upper-middle–income countries of the world from the needy, undernourished populations of war-ravaged and disease-plagued low-income countries is purposefully being maintained and deepened.[390] Most underprivileged countries are former colonies of bygone empires whose lands and peoples have never fully recovered from the outrages of abusive exploitation undergone in previous centuries (and are still ongoing in some cases) and whose own bounty has provided the means by which this inequality was established in the first place. Having provided the raw materials to create the riches reaped during (and after) the technological revolutions that transformed the industrialized world, low-income countries remain in a state of limbo sustained by corrupt politicians and a lack of suitable infrastructure that begins with (and is sustained by) unacceptable (or nonexistent) educational and medical facilities. Meanwhile, under cover of democracy and false paradigms of equality, this situation is being upheld through fake news and mass cover-ups, inhibiting the masses of material-dependent peoples living in capitalist societies from rationalizing about the origins of this state of extreme inequality. Presently, nationalist sentiments are underpinned by the grave situation of the Covid-19 pandemic sharpened by inequalities in medical facilities and access to basic sanitary rights (for example, to vaccinations that are presently being bought up and hoarded by richer countries that, unlike poorer nations, also have the infrastructure required for their rapid distribution). A. Guterres, the ninth secretary-general of the United Nations (since 2017), has underlined the need for countries to work together to fight the advance of this disease, which is affecting the world's populations without heed to geographic barriers, race, color or creed. With the catch phrase "we are all in this together," he has communicated on social media via Twitter that "Covid-19 is a public health emergency – that is fast becoming a human rights crisis. People – and their rights – must be front and center."

With only around 20 percent of nonanthropized territory remaining on the planet today (and not all of it arable),[391] it is in the highest interest of modernized countries to maintain the paradoxical situation of inequality between nations in order to reclaim upon demand the lands of (previously or currently) colonized countries as their own, to feed their own exploding populations when the need arises. Therefore, reinforcing symbolism as a shared common denominator is with hindsight a most effective method by which the dictating privileged minority can continue to wield power (in the form of propaganda distributed via mass communication and digital networks) and to manipulate and unite huge masses of peoples under imaginary banners. Thus, myths promulgated in nationalist constructs are fed to the masses by way of simple and effective symbolic representations (transmitted by evermore efficient technological systems), constituting a highly effective means of mind control enabling the justification of even the cruelest of high-power political decision-making. This scheme is especially potent in justifying the rejection of peoples from nonprofiting nations wishing to enter into the already overloaded capitalist systems of the richer countries in search of a better life. Over millennia, racism and nationalism have been paramount among the manipulative tools used to justify the crushing of peoples considered "alien" to comparatively "richer" territories occupied by other groups of individuals as if by birthright of the latter. This has been demonstrated over centuries of forced domination of the "have-nots" by the "haves," often spearheaded by charismatic leaders (Alexander the Great, Julius Caesar, Genghis Kahn, Napoleon, Hitler) who created vast empires in the aim of absorbing the wealth, lands and cultures and dominating (or enslaving) the peoples living there. We may see "richness" in this case as proportionately related to the degree of technological development because that is precisely what has permitted the accumulation of massive amounts of material goods circulating in the world of capitalist society,[392] a hierarchical organizational strategy into which the privileged *Homo sapiens* have currently organized themselves. The accumulation of material goods is presently the measuring stick by which individuals and societies gauge themselves in a seemingly never-ending process metaphorically akin to fractal reproduction (as discussed in Chapter 8).[393]

The rich-poor paradigm is as essential to sustaining our present worldview as good is to evil because such opposed values give mutual meaning to each other. And so, as modern societies struggle to justify the brutality of turning away migrant peoples infiltrating into "their" lands to escape the vile lives that have been imposed on asylum seekers over centuries of unjust dominating processes, so nationalist discourse relieves the peoples of the burden of responsibility for their acts. Nationalist sentiments inspired by the original identity-territory paradigm born of cultural specificities defined since the Acheulian (as I show in Chapter 4) have served through time to carve out imaginary territorial boundaries, inventing rules to make them impenetrable to those who do not share the same symbolic inheritance. In today's version of "survival of the fittest," access or not to territories is dictated by mutual cultural denominators whose power is mentally transposed to the masses through symbolic concepts such as religion, language, socialized taboo, ritual and so on. Those who do not therefore fit the template of a given cultural unit cannot easily gain access to the territory to which it corresponds. They are "outsiders" from another realm imagined to be at odds or somehow incompatible with integration. In addition, on the global level, only some cultural templates are considered "acceptable" within the framework of larger territorial divisions so that only individuals corresponding to a predefined hegemonic norm may gain access to the range of (member) territories. As resources have grown scarcer and populations denser, so have human movements from one to another territory come to be the most strictly regulated human activity of the planet, although consumer goods cross national borders even during their production with complete impunity. The regulatory process implanted over millennia and deepened over the last two decades by globalization[394] is deeply rooted in the idea of cultural belonging instilled in peoples from birth through social and familial educational processes that are deeply homogenized on a territorial level. Thus, individuals are taught from birth to adopt those behaviors and rituals that are deemed appropriate and to reject (or denigrate) those that are not in order to fit into the mold of their assumed social unit. This enables members of a given social unit to obtain a series of material "proofs" in the form of administrative documents that are essential not only for moving within one's assigned territorial space but also for gaining access (or not) to other areas of the globe. Based on their standing within this hierarchical system, only a limited number of individuals are responsible for granting (or not) those documents by which members of a society can prove their own birth, educational background, religious affiliation, family relationships and other such personal stories, highlighting an individual's capacity to follow the rules defined by a given social context. In this way, when traveling abroad, an individual issued such documents is (or is not) a qualified representative of his/her social origin. Any individual who does not conform to this strict regulation – generally based on birthright – will be denied the necessary documentation and, by extension, refused access to the territorial areas they wish to occupy.

MOVING CULTURES: HUMAN MIGRATIONS THROUGH TIME

Of course, we cannot fully know the workings of ancient migration systems of the distant past. Looking to prehistory, we can only observe and extrapolate meaning from the very partial material data available to us from the archeological record. The overview provided in this book shows only how human culture was born out of the Oldowan as a selective operative choice to adapt with the aid of innovative extrasomatic means through the invention of the first technologies. This choice gave an edge to our species, demarking it from all other animals with which we share the planet. The relative scarcity of Oldowan sites and their generally low artifact density allows us to propose that, throughout the nearly 2-million-year duration of this technocomplex, populations were probably restricted to isolated groups composed of few individuals. The lifestyle and life expectancy of these early hominins, who we presume to have been nomadic scavengers, suggest a limited number of individuals per group and, at least initially, occupying different regions of the planet in relative isolation. It is also assumed that without the controlled use of fire, those territories situated in the northern hemisphere would have had been difficult to populate, at least until this innovation was fully acquired and acculturated. Interestingly, the archeology further indicates to us that Oldowan hominins were not members of a single homogenous biological grouping, but they were different species, all sharing a semitropical territorial range. They thrived at first in open savannah landscapes, always near water systems, such as lakes, rivers and river deltas. Stone-tool producing hominins emerged in Africa nearly 3 million years ago,[24] but they were present outside of Africa 1 million years later in western Asia[146,150] and even as far away as China.[141] Even though we presently assume a single point of origin (Africa), we can accept that these hominin groups were moving uninhibited through huge geographical areas and, incredibly as it may seem to us today, actually encountering and sharing the lands they roamed with other hominin species. By the later Oldowan, the demographic and reproductive success of our early ancestors is recorded in areas such as Western Europe, for example, which begins to show a relative density of archeological sites from around 1.2 million years ago.[68] It seems that during the Oldowan, hominins were indeed free rangers, depending on natural dictates such as water availability, the movement and abundance of large and small animals and their capacity to establish a niche in relation to other large carnivores in the different landscapes in which they lived.[395] Still relatively restricted, their simple cultural objectification did not yet dictate to them any abstract rules guiding their movements within and beyond different areas of the globe. Apparently their nomadic lifestyle and the lack of standardization of their culture had not yet created any identity-based criteria with which to claim a given territorial bond.

This all changed once Oldowan technologies had advanced to the point of developing complex standardized systems of production and their associated sets of normalized tool kits. According to the conceptual framework defined in prehistory, these achievements are the hallmark of the Acheulian, a cultural division characterized, as we have seen, by a new set of hominins with bigger brains (members of the Homo erectus clade) and wider and denser global representation, ranging throughout much of Africa and Eurasia for some 1.4 million years.[176] Wielding fire and hunting large and small game, Acheulian peoples confronted even the harshest climatic conditions, eventually establishing seasonal base camps in the most favorable areas. This very long cultural period is especially marked by human migrations manifest not only from the exponential increase in the number and density of sites but also from discernible similarities in the technologies that appear to suggest cultural transmission in some cases by interpopulation contact through time and space. However, I have demonstrated how technical features of the Acheulian likely emerged out of preexisting and well-established hotbeds of Oldowan culture, such as South and East Africa, India and the Near East.[176] After this emergence phase, the advantages of the newly invented Acheulian tool kits claimed prominence and spread through social networking pooled by increasingly dense hominin populations, reaping the successes of their newfound technological magnificence. In the archeological record, this phenomenon of adaptive success is sometimes perceived as migration waves.[396] While hominin species' diversity is manifest during the Acheulian, it seems to be in a different way than in the past Oldowan period in the sense that we observe speciation in different parts of the globe rather than just cohabitation of different species (for example, in Eurasia from ancestral *Homo erectus* to *Homo heidelbergensis* or from ancestral *Homo antecessor* to *Homo neandertalensis*, *Homo sapiens* and Denisovans).[166,209,213]

I have also described how, toward the later Middle Pleistocene, cultural distinctiveness born of the multiplicity of Acheulian technological systems gave way, for the first time, to the tool kits whose features are distinctively linked to specific geographical areas of repartition, *signaling the first identities with physically defined territorial boundaries* (Tayacian, Clactonian, Micoquian). However, there is no clear evidence in the archeological record for intentionally inflicted physical violence or warfare on the human skeletal remains dating to this time frame. Might we assume peaceful integration of peoples into lands already occupied by other groups of individuals in spite of the developing cultural differences? It is likely that Acheulian groups occupied specific regions for generations, establishing themselves as highly mobile groups whose survival depended on their reproductive interactions with other populations sharing the same territories. Based on actual behavior observed in the rare remaining tribal cultures of the world, we may assume that they established ritual encounters, which took place in seasonal synchronicity (meetings with other groups, perhaps on a yearly basis, specifically for the reproductive exchanges necessary for their survival).[342] Migration patterns throughout the Quaternary Period are often considered to have been regulated by shifting landscape configurations due to cyclical glacial-interglacial climatic oscillations, although, I believe that this influence was minimal from the later Acheulian (onward from ca. 700 thousand years ago [Ka]). That said, it is true that land bridges created by receding sea levels and isostatic continental movements during the different climatic phases would have provided opportunities for humans and other animals to move into new, otherwise inaccessible lands. Likewise, during interglacial periods, physical isolation occurred when islands formed by the submersion of land bridges, which, if lasting for long periods, would result in speciation (the uniqueness of *Homo floresiensis* from the Island of Flores in Indonesia being one example). Because of overall low population density during the time frame covered by both the Oldowan and the Acheulian, we may assume that the movements of peoples across the lands and their colonization of territories that were perhaps already occupied by other groups (or types) of hominins did not incur any serious inconveniences (at least in these early phases). In fact, this process seems, on the contrary, to have produced a complex networking that was most fertile to cultural and biological exchange.

Toward the end of the Middle Pleistocene (Late Acheulian), however, we discern a more complex situation from the relative abundance of archeological sites and the density of their artifact records. The archeology indicates higher concentrations of peoples with cyclical fidelity to specific areas as well as larger groups displaying distinct cultural features. In addition, these groups were sharpening their technological capacities to access resources and overcome the burdens associated with day-to-day survival, ultimately giving them more free time to invest in their inner, spiritual world, thus even further demarcating their specific social identities. That there were attachments to specific territories is discerned in the archeological record dating to the end of the upper Middle Pleistocene by the specificities we recognize in the signature manufacture of the tool kits. As we have seen, this phase was followed (from some 400,000 years ago) by the remarkable phenomenon of the Neandertal peoples' spread throughout the Near East, Siberia, western and central Asia, and their nearly total occupation of Western Europe until their mysterious extinction only 28,000 years ago.[211] Around the same time, the "Human Revolution"[285] was underway on a large scale in places such as South Africa where Homo sapiens was preparing to explode onto the scene on a worldwide scale. The situation during the Middle Pleistocene was extremely complex with the world occupied simultaneously by perhaps as many as six different species of hominins. Unlike in the Oldowan, during this later time frame, all of these hominins possessed significantly advanced cultural capacities and practiced developed symbolic communication networking – still there is no clear sign of a clashing. Nevertheless, migration was manifest and the final domination of the single species Homo sapiens,[288] imminent.

INTRAHUMAN DOMINATION THROUGH CULTURE

Because the only archeological signals for war and other forms of interpopulation violence become obvious only after the total domination of Homo sapiens (to the exclusion of all other hominin species) and the founding of sedentary cultural units, the notion of property appears viably causal to the ensuing amplification of clear-cut hierarchical social systems enforced by different expressions of symbolic culture. Problems relating to humans belonging to one cultural unit migrating into territories already claimed by another one are, therefore, certainly not new. Proto-history, history and even the modern human condition clearly demonstrate the never-ending succession of flourishing cultural units claiming territories of the weaker ones.[298] The power of symbolic unification ultimately provides the (abstract, imaginary) foundations for justifying the cyclical discriminations of peoples toward one another in the guise of color, creed, religion, tradition and so on. In fact, the only evidence we have so far of difficulties encountered in prehistoric migration processes, either interspecific of hominins belonging to an entirely different clade or intraspecific of groups moving into territories occupied by other groups of a same species, seems to indicate that it began on a significantly large scale after the appearance and expansion of modern Homo sapiens. Of course, even if prehistoric interrelational behaviors must remain at least for now in the realm of conjecture, we can consider only the most outstanding feature of the present human condition: we are alone[288] in that we are the only hominin species to have survived among at least five other hominins living only some 200,000 years ago – nothing in geological time. Today, as we are on the verge of becoming 8 billion souls sharing the planet and its resources, we do not have to deal with excluding other species of hominins, which could provide competition. No. We have turned to *creating difference* through culture, continuing thus to practice the survival of the fittest paradigm on a nonbiological level.

Our scientific achievements have proved that we are all *one and the same species*, that there is no difference that could justify subjugation of some individuals and favoritism toward others. It is only our constructed reality that acts as a catalyzer to mobilize the masses to react in accordance with the basal (animalistic) attitudes of fear and hate required to favor one group of individuals versus another. Culture is, therefore, utilized to create triggers to inspire basic human instincts on a massive scale to perpetuate the dominant situation of have and have-nots. Today, the *survival of the fittest* paradigm favors only a handful of individuals – those who exist to uphold the pattern of forceful and merciless predominance of the few in utter disregard for the multitudinous. What better way to uphold the system than by convincing the masses to cooperate for their own benefit? Carrying flags, singing patriotic songs and practicing complex rituals in every detail of their day-to-day existences, peoples of the world's countries (territories separated by imaginary frontiers) find meaning in their existence by upholding this relationship in their own specific cultural constructs. They are ready to die (or to send their own children to die) to uphold their country's imaginary boundaries, to protect it tooth and nail from "invaders" from other lands and to prevent it from becoming "polluted" through any (created and supposed) differences. Fear of losing material gains to peoples deemed alien to the values cultivated within a specific group context is wielded as a supreme weapon by which to generate the hate needed for excluding the designated "others" and, ultimately, justifying the maintenance of their lives in the vilest of circumstances. Therefore, it seems once again that culture – expressed as technology coupled with complex systems of symbolic communication – forms the instrument responsible for modern patterns of abuse maintained toward all peoples wishing to move from a position of dire need to one of decent living environments. It is obvious that this situation is only worsening with the increase in populations on both sides of the coin and the corresponding decrease in natural resources aggravated as it is by our complete disregard to opting for sustainable life rules. Through time, the Homo sapiens' ideal of domination through violence and mercilessness toward the week and the needy has certainly allowed us to become the only hominin existing on the planet to wield with incredible forcefulness our power to dominate the entire animal kingdom, making it servile to our needs. Our "success" is total. Ironically, however, this success now appears limited only by the very natural elements that we have so effectively raped and disregarded. Our so-called success has become so total, in fact, that it is now tipping the balance of planetary equilibrium in our disfavor. Beyond the disappearance of all other forms of hominin species that modern humans might have encountered under shrouded circumstances in the prehistoric context and the extinctions documented in the animal record in different areas of the globe after colonization by modern humans (see Chapter 6), there is also ample evidence from the Neolithic and proto-historic periods suggesting that modern humans began cultivating patterns of merciless eliminating behavior not long after we began to cultivate plants and round up some animals into domesticated groupings to serve the needs of sedentary lifestyles as people organized themselves into social units each fixed, finally, into specific territorial groupings.

> Scientists are fond of running the evolutionary clock backward, using DNA analysis and the fossil record to figure out when our ancestors stood erect and split off from the rest of the primate evolutionary tree.
>
> But the clock is running forward as well. So where are humans headed?
>
> ... Paleontologists say that anatomically modern humans may have at one time shared the Earth with as many as three other closely related types – Neanderthals, *Homo erectus* and the dwarf hominids whose remains were discovered last year in Indonesia.
>
> Does evolutionary theory allow for circumstances in which "spin-off" human species could develop again?
>
> Some think the rapid rise of genetic modification could be just such a circumstance. Others believe we could blend ourselves with machines in unprecedented ways – turning natural-born humans into an endangered species.[397]

Once established as the unique inheritors of the richness of the planet, we humans have continued to blatantly cultivate patterns of exploitative existence within the animal kingdom and, somewhat more subtly, within our own species. Organized into discrete social units with specific cultural idioms, the modernization process began by sharpening hierarchical frameworks within each social unit. With the development of city-states, this behavioral strategy was defined as requisite to the survival of larger numbers of peoples-producers of wealth. In turn, trade was established, enabling effective production to take place on massive levels by attributing cultural objects with a more or less fixed worth or value. Eventually, through alienation, peoples that did not possess the technologies to enter into the game of trade were progressively estranged from the system. Meanwhile, when contact was finally made with peoples who existed in territories situated outside these areas of production-consumption/trade-value, the peoples' total lack of shared symbolic referents made them easy prey to exploitation by those in possession of different, more powerful technological systems.

As the hunger to possess the more "valuable" goods being issued from the evermore complex networks of production and import/export grew, so were different forms of slavery invented as a means by which to achieve more wealth.

> Slavery is any system in which principles of property law are applied to people, allowing individuals to own, buy and sell other individuals, as a de jure [i.e. de facto] form of property.[398]

Early on, slavery became an outcome of value attributions that came to have meaning even within the hierarchical social systems themselves, and roles played by members of a community were also attributed with different levels of worth. Slavery has existed in virtually all major civilizations since the dawn of recorded human history, from ancient Sumeria to the Roman Empire and (up to the latter half of the nineteenth century) in the United States. Modern slavery continues to thrive in Libya, for example, where migrants from all over Africa who hope to find new lives in the developed world are tortured, humiliated and killed in transitional holding camps and survivors are piled into danger-ously precarious boats (often rubber dinghies) to risk their lives at sea, generally after having paid dearly for this "privilege." People born into specific social units on the one hand are attributed with worth in accordance with their birthright or their supposed usefulness or merit for the optimal functioning of the society to which they belong. This abstract concept of "social worth" has grown to be evermore ferociously upheld as the scramble for technological production took on increasing importance. It is hardly necessary to contextualize temporally the events that I am sketching here because in contrast to the relatively long time frames we have been dealing with until this point in this book, these events have all occurred only within the last 5,000 years or so. In fact, they are still taking place. My aim here is to demonstrate the central role played by "value" as a socially constructed concept that goes beyond the world of monetary goods: people and animals can be valuable or not as can property, time, symbols and other abstract notions. Value is also linked to usefulness in this discussion in terms of what an individual can contribute to either the larger collectivity of peoples or the more "valuable" few. So, cultural difference established for peoples existing outside a given social unit − in the modern sense in low-income countries − was and remains an effective way by which to justify the enslavement of "less valuable" peoples considered to be such by their very alienation from the social unit of reference.

In order to uphold these inequalities, modern humans will soon need to establish new referents of hate to justify the exclusion of a − much larger − upcoming rush of climate catastrophe migrants predicted (by the World Bank and the United Nations among others) to be generated by climate change in the next years (140 million people are estimated to become climate migrants in the very near future[399,400]). Up to now, race and religion have provided effective measures for maintaining exclusion and

Figure 11.1
Sea Watch, a nonprofit organization, carries out search and rescue missions in the
Mediterranean Sea assisting migrants. This image shows an April 2018 rescue of people
stranded near the coast of Libya in a rubber dingy. Since 2014, at least 20,000 migrants and
refugees have perished at sea while trying to reach Europe from Africa. (©Tim Lüddemann,
flickr.com)

enabling the masses to turn their backs on the suffering populations and thousands of
horrific deaths occurring each day as peoples from the lower income countries of the
world attempt to escape their fates by crossing deserts and oceans in astonishingly
terrifying circumstances. Even more desperately vile, *Homo sapiens* are making profit from
the dire situation of these migrant peoples who have already lost everything, enslaving,
torturing and raping them even as their lives are lost to intense misery. Is this the true
nature of the "last survivors"[288] (see Figure 11.1)?

12

ON RELIGION, WAR AND TERRORISM IN THE GLOBALIZED WORLD

WHY DO RELIGIONS STILL EXIST?

From time immemorial, emotional states of anxiety and fear have spawned from our species' complete inability to explain death and by our powerlessness in facing up to the cruel and paradoxical injustices prompted by our own conspecifics. As our species followed through on its evolutionary processes, we expanded all the while our symbolic brainpower, triggering the appropriate social and physical developments that, in turn, permitted the remarkable expansion of the brain's neocortex and associated apparatus. In spite of our phantasmagorical technological feats, none of our inventions has thus far been able to address adequately our existential angst in the face of the unknowable. Our brain synapses are "programmed," as it were, to provide answers to the myriad of questions generated by our complex sensory network as it gathers information throughout the day and night. But it is simply incapable – at least for the moment – of satisfying our arrogant need for eternal existence or explaining how to come to grips with the concept of infinity. Such questions are simply beyond the modeling capacities of our synaptic inner universe. In response to this conundrum, humans have responded by creating alternative realities by designing parallel universal templates to replace this void in the real world. In ancestral *Homo*, such models are understood as nascent spiritualism, a phenomenon that is difficult to recognize in the archeological record, especially for the older phases of our evolutionary process. In any case, this particular evolutionary choice ultimately led modern humans to the establishment of religion (eventually institutionalized) as a surrogate social response with which to fill this emotionally disturbing void. By adopting the strategy of socially reinforcing the validity of alternative realities through socially created rituals, the poignancy of religion was finally ratified on a massive scale.

Fear of the unknown universally produced spiritualistic responses regardless of vast interpopulation differences in life experiences. Early civilizations worldwide elaborated stories to explain the initial stages of the universe and how animal and, especially, human life, came to be.[401] These stories grew into myths around which a certain consensus developed, further intensifying (once again) the sense of belonging in groups of peoples affiliated to one or another social entity. This formidably reinforced those imaginary borders I have discussed in previous chapters of this book by further separating groups of peoples in accordance with their different beliefs and their associated traditions.

Virtually all religions are grounded in cosmological stories describing the birth of the universe and the arrival and role of humans and all other living things existing in the world. These are called "creation myths" and are mostly simple, symbolic narratives shared among peoples of a same civilization. Their role in the social order is to explain – figuratively or literally – the emergence of the universe and all it contains (including us humans). Creation myths are characterized by their far-fetched quality and general lack of scientific grounding. In spite of this, they are common to virtually every known cultural complex recorded since the dawn of history. Most surprising of all, perhaps, is that many of these stories continue to be upheld even in today's modern world in total disregard of the advances made in science that completely annul their credibility! Up to this day, the world's religions continue to be founded on different versions of such creationist myths: Why is this still a human standard? While we continue to seek answers to our existential questions, we concur that science rather than religion more adequately provides satisfactory answers within the range of its (ever-expanding) scope.[402] Nevertheless, even modern science has not succeeded in solving the enigma of death in a way that would be satisfying to individuals who cannot fathom an end to their personal identity-existence. People are striving to gain immortality, to effectively become the gods of their own creation.[304] As yet, science has not assuaged this burning human desire for afterlife. Neither has science thus far provided fitting explanations to justify the doomsday scenarios we humans continue to carve out for ourselves. It cannot explain why war and all the horrors it entails continues to be the hallmark of our species. Why in today's society do digital images of murder, rape, animal cruelty, pedophilia, and other forms of basal pornography continue to rank among the most sought-after virtual search objectives? Why do religious institutions housing make-believe representatives of people's emotional and spiritual guidance become havens for individuals with difficulties in coming to terms with their own ambiguous sexual compulsions? (The Catholic Church currently led by Pope Francis is presently dealing with this problem as thousands of cases of sexual abuse of children and other behaviors considered aberrant by modern civilized society – but tacitly accepted by church clerics – are finally coming to the fore).

In previous chapters, I illustrated occurrences of cultural convergence for very ancient stages of prehistory (some examples are Acheulian handaxes, Mousterian Levallois knapping methods, Upper Paleolithic blade technologies, Holocene farming and megalithic structures and the invention of writing). In dealing with the "why" of religion, it is interesting and significant to recognize cultural convergences in the puzzling similarities existing in many of the world's myths and their associated symbolism. Indeed, numerous mythologies contain surprising correspondences regardless of their (likely) independent emergence in different parts of the globe in different time frames. One explanation is that common elements occurring as myths may be remnants of factual geological or atmospheric disturbances that took place in the past. Subjected to natural stresses and lacking scientific explanations, our human ancestors would have "reasoned" catastrophic events by creating explanatory stories that could serve as satisfactory replacements for truth. Through time, these stories were transformed into myths that were orally transmitted and transmuted into traditions, weaving them into the tissue of the human collective consciousness. When closely examined, this storytelling strategy can provide information about the nature of such disturbances, which sometimes resulted from cataclysmic phenomena (flooding or violent volcanic eruptions), that would have significantly altered landscapes and subsistence patterns, perhaps even prompting major migration events. Diluvium myths are among the most noticeable examples because they have been recorded from many early contexts, such as the ancient Mesopotamian preurban settings, ancient Greek city-states, Meso-American indigenous sites, Australian aboriginals, Norse folklore, Chinese and Hindu mythologies and the Bible's Old Testament. Sometimes these stories were strengthened by discoveries of fossilized marine animal shells in situations distant from existing coastal areas. Could the universality of the stories that recount a massive flood event actually be narrations elaborated to explain the global rising sea levels that followed the last glacial maximum? In this sense, collective consciousness can be seen as a powerful survival strategy used by humans to reason happenings by transforming them into myth and endowing them with mutual significance.[403] This shared human consciousness continues to play an essential role in our existence today, constituting an indispensable database for the survival of each individual in the present, supporting the endurance of our species into the future. On a larger scale, our capacity to solve increasingly complex global problems depends, therefore, on our ability to make sense of these shared symbolic realities as so many lessons for survival learned from the past and accomplished through experience.

Our responsibility as scientists working in prehistory therefore, is to fulfill the global and social necessity for people to distinguish between what is real in the past and what has been created by the human inner realm. If we are to understand the present human condition and effectively rectify our evolutionary trajectory, then the truthfulness of the "stories" we share is crucial. They must be firmly grounded in scientific facts in the real world, past and present. Applying science to the study of the past as we do in prehistoric archeology provides us with reliable reconstructions of our collective past experiences, pooled, as it were, into communal awareness of what it truly means to be human. Over millennia, cumulated culture has amassed in our brains as common denominative symbols for which we have developed seemingly innate responses enabling us to thrive in large social units. Fatalistically, myth alleviates individual responsibility for drastically cruel outcomes of catastrophic events, be they humanly or naturally induced. By transferring the responsibility to an imagined deity (divine human) or a natural source (divine Nature) beyond human control, some events (cannibalism, mass killings, torture, climate catastrophes, etc.) become unavoidable destiny; they exist outside the realm of human influence. When catastrophic events (entailing indiscriminate death) are reasoned and shared through myth, they are more easily assimilated and processed so that peoples can find the motivation to move on in their lives. Even though religious or spiritual inclinations tend to stem from some type of explanatory story of the past (generally void of any real temporal scale), they do not establish any coherency in recounting the present human condition because their explanations are not rooted in any tangible evidence. Unlike scientific explanations, therefore, they cannot be tested or refuted. Furthermore, none of the different religious stories describes the true past human condition, nor do they provide any *information* about our prehistoric past or about the evolution of our species. This paradox is upheld in spite of the masses of scientific information (fossil and artifact evidence) being accumulated daily by people working in the disciplines of the Earth and human sciences. Paradoxical to our technological spiral of innovation, digitalization and otherwise rapidly accumulated scientific-technical expertise, religions are flourishing in the contemporary world, still fulfilling their role of caulking the vacuum left by the boundaries of our (now joint) cerebral-computerized operative systems (see Figure 12.1).

DEALING WITH DEATH IN THE PREHISTORIC CONTEXT

To understand this phenomenon of death in prehistoric time more thoroughly, let us turn now to that time. The roots of religious or spiritual activities practiced by humans can be traced back to a time well before the first urbanized cultures, before agriculture and settling of grouped humans into outsized social units requiring control mechanisms provided by the upper levels of hierarchy wielding fear-of-death manipulative strategies via progressively entrenched religious standardization (institutionalization). Although they do not fossilize, spiritual outlooks, considered the stuff of specifically human behavior, can still reach us in the archeological record in the form of elusive clues that prehistorians decode as early symbolic consciousness, enabling spiritualism and leading eventually to what we call today "religion." A common example used to demonstrate spiritualism in the archeological record concerns evidence from our prehistoric past evoking special handling pertaining to the dead. This is interpreted as a signal for an

Figure 12.1
Ardh Kumbh Mela religious pilgrimage in Allahabad (India). In 2019, some 120 million
Hindu devotees assisted in the religious pilgrimage that took place over a period of 55 days
in Allahabad, India. The cyclical event involves a dip in the "holy" waters at the confluence
of the Ganges, Yamuna and Sarasvati Rivers. (Courtesy of Jennifer Barsky).

important milestone in our recognition of the emergence of spiritualistic thought
processes in the human ancestral record. When humans began to select specific contexts
in view of depositing their defunct congeners, then we assume that they were experiencing some type of conceptual discomfort, or awareness, regarding *the idea of death* or
perhaps life after death or the unacceptability of death as an end of a life, of an
individual, of an identity: infinite nothingness. Of course, in the prehistoric context,
it is not easy to establish the *intentionality* of a deposit of fossil human remains. But when it
is possible, it is highly significant because the timing and situation of these deposits have
deep implications that can help us to ascertain when in the evolutionary process
hominins began to demonstrate metaphysical consciousness and what its first manifestations were like. We thereby demonstrate the first inkling of some strain of spiritualistic
conduct or indicators for displays of a conscious belief in an afterlife that today we can
link to "embryonic religious thought."

> Thus the history of the treatment of death, well beyond its scientific significance, is
> also of extreme importance for the History of Life, of Man, of philosophical and
> religious thought, that of consciousness.[404]

It is generally accepted that *Homo neandertalensis* were the first to express emotional states
(in a more or less tangible way) that could be qualified as "spiritual" or even "religious"
(in a nonformal way). We saw (in Chapter 5), thanks to the advancement of archeological research, how Neandertal aesthetic values have progressively come to light from
the many different aspects of their material culture. Indeed, Neandertals demonstrated

complex symbolic behaviors (and their associated thought processes), for example, by using feathers as body ornamentation and practicing budding forms of artistic expression.[227,253,254] The finds show us that Neandertals had moved beyond the purely functional aspects of technological manufacture and into the realm of the aesthetic while imbuing the material world with abstract meaning. Undoubtedly, one of the most outstanding features of the Neandertal realm of spiritual expression is the practice of intentional burial of their congeners.[404] Beyond special treatment of the dead, the archeological record has occasionally revealed the possibility that "offerings" were buried with the Neandertal cadavers (flowers, stone tools or animal remains).[262,263,404] While the oldest (occasional?) evidence for intentional burial is more widely associated with the Middle Paleolithic Neanderthals, the Lower Paleolithic Pre-neandertals found at the Sima de los Huesos site (Sierra de Atapuerca, Spain) constitutes an exceptional and significantly ancient archeological context indicating special handling of the dead.[357] As we saw in Chapter 9, years of meticulous excavations at this site have exhumed thousands of hominin fossils (attributed to at least twenty-nine individuals, men, women and children) "deposited" in a karstic pit some 430,000 years ago.[356,358] The bodies appear to have been intentionally dropped (or deposited) into the chamber (or pit) through a deep karstic shaft and a narrow sloping ramp. This unlikely and very difficult access indicates the likelihood of an anthropic accumulation.[357] In addition to the human remains and bear bones, a single stone tool was found: a beautifully crafted quartzite handaxe that could, given this extraordinary context, represent some type of funerary offering[287] (see Figure 12.2).

Human burials are relatively frequent during later Paleolithic, although they show no universal patterning in the positioning of the defunct or in the orientation of the graves.[405] Middle and Upper Paleolithic burials are often associated with red ochre and may contain grave goods (such as shell beads, fossils or other forms of adornments). Once exhumed, human fossil finds studied by paleontologists sometimes reveal cases of secondary manipulation of the bones, such as de-fleshing, cremation and even cannibalism. Concerning the latter point, it is noteworthy that the eating of humans by other humans (or anthropophagy) has been recognized in very ancient (pre-Acheulian) prehistoric times (this is the case of level TD6 at Gran Dolina, Sierra de Atapuerca that dates to 0.9 million years ago [Ma]).[406] Without a doubt, cannibalism is a behavior that through time was likely to have been imbued with heavy symbolic meanings, perhaps also tied to ritualistic conduct.[407] In very different time frames, we may conceive of anthropophagy as being somehow linked to basally inspired spiritual beliefs, for example, as an act that could enable the human flesh–consuming individual(s) to acquire the qualities of the deceased victim (bravery, luck, wealth). Funerary archeology (linked with physical anthropology) deals with the characteristics of human burial practices and their evolution through time. Meticulous excavation techniques are required to document and exhume single or multiple human bodies from widely variable depository contexts; these include plotting, drawing and

Figure 12.2

Handaxe ("Excalibur") from the Sierra de Atapuerca's Sima de los Huesos site in Spain. This singular quartzite handaxe was discovered with the human remains of some twenty-nine Pre-neandertal individuals as well as some bear bones, dating to around 430,000 years ago. This discovery has very profound implications. How and why did these people end up at the bottom of this deep pit nearly half a million years ago? The presence of this tool in this apparently purposeful "deposit" of human bodies might be the earliest evidence of ancestral symbolic reflection. (© Susana Sarmiento-Pérez; property of the photographic collection of Professor José María Bermúdez-de-Castro Risueño at the Atapuerca Foundation in Burgos, Spain).

photographing the finds, observing the disposition of the bones in relation to one another and their conservation and possible anatomical connections, looking for associated artifacts, sampling the sediment and so on. In primary inhumations, skeletons are found undisturbed in their original tomb while in secondary ones, bone accumulations are disposed within another delimited spatial context.[54]

Collective burials became more frequent during the course of the Neolithic Period, perhaps in relation to sedentary lifestyles, heavily impacting the significance of people's perception of their identity in relation to the land. Relationships to specific territorial contexts became strongly imbued with meaning as people buried family, friends, leaders and other members of their social unit in the same areas over generations, inspiring cults based on the notion of "ancestors." In this, we discern once again the building blocks of land-linked identities and their inseparability from the past. At this time of yet unrecorded events, linking peoples to each other and to the territories they inhabited, the role of myth and ritual must have strongly reinforced ties and land-based identities, providing some degree of comfort in the face of the unknown. During Neolithic and protohistoric times, some burials were accompanied by large monuments of varying regional styles (dolmens and other megalithic structures). These monuments were generally associated with ritual practices, sometimes cyclical and (seasonal) or linked to astronomical phenomena, uniting peoples of a single tribe or from multiple tribes within each regional context. The use of earthenware urns as vehicles for secondary burial practices was widespread from the Neolithic onward in different areas of the globe (Asia, Europe). In the post-Paleolithic world (Roman or Greek, for example), human bones were frequently removed from their original burial place, de-fleshed/incinerated to remove soft tissues, and then redeposited in a secondary burial situation. Grave goods may or may not be associated. In some cases, only specific parts of a skeleton or the remains of two or more individuals were selected and redeposited in the funerary urns. Each urn could contain the cremated bone remains of one or more individuals along with a selection of offerings (pottery, shell jewelry). In much of Europe toward the end of the Bronze Age and into Roman times and beyond, funerary urns were discovered grouped together into a necropolis.

HOW RELIGIONS EVOLVED

Proto-historic ideograms and historic documents teach us that religions evolved out of spiritual beliefs initially intended to explain the unexplainable: to fill the gap in human conceptual capacities by providing (as it still does) a tool for controlling populations as they increased in density and organized themselves into distinct social groups. Other structured (but non-institutionalized) religions, such as animism, highlight human-animal tendencies and relationship with Nature while incorporating supernatural beliefs to soothe fears and provide hope for immorality. Attaining states of altered consciousness through trances or consuming medicinal (drug-inducing) plants was/is often a prerequisite for entering into contact with supernatural forces. Different expressions of this practice are common in modern societies where various trancelike experiences are still available facilitated by medicines, treatments and prescription drugs or otherwise, allowing for temporary escape from reality. In today's world, we need not look very far to find examples of rituals punctuating the lives of virtually every living civilization on the planet. They are expressed by a myriad of events guiding our lives or as remnant traditions whose roots are deep into the past, calling on symbolic behaviors understood as participatory events individualizing one culture from another. This begs the question of why religion/myth is so forcefully maintained among contemporary human societies. Perhaps it is the distancing that humans have taken from Nature and what now so visibly and irredeemably scars the planet that has enforced the fears, insecurity and guilt required for its maintenance in modern human populations. In today's insecure living contexts, the cyclical rituals provided by the world's religions continue to serve a cathartic role for people seeking meaning and security in their lives and guaranteeing continuity in the future for our children. As modern as it is, our present civilization is profoundly spiritual. Be it among the most "industrialized" nations or the most reclusive peoples, this deeply entrenched modern human feature continues to play a vital role in all human societies.

But how can we presently explain the fact that religions based on myths and consequently antiscientific and antimodern belief systems persist and are even gaining momentum in modern societies? The religious fervor that marks and even defines U.S. society today is an interesting example. In this country, religion is inseparable from the governmental structure. The key phrase "In God we trust" inscribed on U.S. currency underpins the full integration of Christianity into the lifeways of this capitalist and market-centric society. Biblical creationists characterized by their complete negation of evolutionary theory are thriving like never before. Meanwhile, costumed individuals, such as the Pope in Rome, imbued with huge religiously based powers continue to implement rites and rituals conducted by millions of human lives. After the death of Pope John Paul II in Vatican City in 2005, millions of people from around the world as well as more than 200 of the most important state representatives, mobilized to attend the funeral. This was an impressive global gathering. The pope's body was viewed by thousands lining the crowded streets, evoking ancestral ceremonies even as millions of people awaited the outcome of the election of a new pope being held behind closed doors by members of a secret society – elected representatives who represent god on Earth? Is this anachronistic behavior not disconcerting in contemporary society? The power of such a man (because no women are among the candidates) seems unimaginable in our world unless, paradoxically, examined from the point of view of our evolutionary trajectory. As otherworldly designees, powerful religious figures of the world (shamans, popes, imams) are often upheld in great opulence, a condition contrary to the masses of peoples they control. These designees are thought to embody "righteousness," in the strictest sense, heavily underlining the nationalist sentiment and intolerance of any behavior seen as deviant from the defined norms. These individuals embody the mysterious power of Nature still beyond our scientific grasp. Currently, their role is often to maintain defined religious precepts as a powerful psychological tool to reinforce nationalistic sentiments grounded in racist precepts, homophobic principles and antifeminist tendencies. On a par with powerful abstract political entities (embodied by a few individuals), religion rallies together huge masses of peoples performing rites founded in completely nonscientific stories. In India's 2019 Maha Kumbh (in Allahabad), more than 100 million people from 222 countries participated over fifty-five days in the world's largest religious festival that every 12 years unites sadhus and other devotees to bathe in the "holy" waters at the confluence of the Ganges, Yamunas and Sarasvati Rivers. In retrospect, we may acknowledge the human inability to grasp death that first provoked the awakening of spirituality at the root of our modern-day institutionalized religions. Humans are rational beings. We need to be able to explain the world around us and to understand its workings. Death, however, dwells in the realm of the unknown and the unknowable. It is, therefore, the fear of death that led humans to invent religion.

RELIGION AS THE SWATHE OF WAR AND TERRORISM IN THE GLOBALIZED WORLD

After discussing the prehistoric origins of the human religious mental response mode, we can quite easily move on to understand why throughout the recorded history of humanity it is inexorably linked to war and terrorism. Some 30,000 years have gone by since Neandertals shared territories with anatomically modern human populations, finally disappearing in shadowy circumstances. We have discussed the possibility of genocide to explain the extinction of the Neandertal species. No concrete proof of their systematic extermination by *Homo sapiens* actually exists today (i.e. there are no significant accumulations of Neandertal bodies perforated by stone armaments or bearing other traces that can be attributed to intentionally inflicted physical trauma). There are only isolated cases tentatively interpreted as suggestive of some form of human-generated wounds – but were they due to inter- or intraspecific violence?[408] Of course, it may be that the scarcity of information about human inter- or intraspecific violence in the early archeological record is attributable, at least in part, to difficulties in recognizing its traces in the archeological record. It is important to remember that prehistoric hominin skeletal remains are sparse, especially those pertaining to the older evolutionary stages. There are in fact very few hominin remains available for study and their often fragmentary nature reveals little about the populations they represent. That said, another example from the exceptional site of Atapuerca's Sima de los Huesos, the so-called Cranium 17, is believed to witness a 430,000-year-old individual case of Middle Pleistocene murder[409] after study of two perimortem fractures detected on the frontal bone:

> The type of injuries, their location, the strong similarity of the fractures in shape and size, and the different orientations and implied trajectories of the two fractures suggest they were produced with the same object in face-to-face interpersonal conflict. Given that either of the two traumatic events was likely lethal, the presence of multiple blows implies an intention to kill. This finding shows that the lethal interpersonal violence is an ancient human behavior and has important implications for the accumulation of bodies at the site, supporting an anthropic origin.[409]

This indicates that at least some intraspecific violence has a much older origin than previously believed. Compared with the animal kingdom closest to the human lineage, chimpanzees have been observed on occasion to inexplicably kill and eat their conspecifics. In 1975, the famous primatologist Jane Goodall reported witnessing a "cannibalistic killing spree" in which a female chimpanzee kidnapped, killed and ate at least three infant chimps in Tanzania's Gombe Stream National Park.[410] Still, there is no evidence (so far) that massive violent events attributable to large-scale warfare occurred among human populations until after the last glacial period. We may therefore infer that the human capacity to make war was somehow awakened at this time. The emergence of large-scale violence may be likened to that of any other physical or behavioral characteristic on the evolutionary trajectory in that it undoubtedly existed as a latent trait in our genetic makeup until it was naturally or socially selected by some triggering phenomena. The favorable context for its expression arose therefore just prior to the Neolithic revolution – just yesterday from an evolutionary standpoint. The nature of this activating force, however, remains to be determined, and we may assume that it probably did not originate from a single source (there are many plausible causes for warfare including, for example, climate change, resource scarcity, demographic expansion, widespread illness, symbolically generated hate). Yet the oldest evidence for large-scale and indiscriminate killing (i.e. violent murder of victims unable to defend themselves or not linked to violent provocations, such as children or pregnant women) that could be qualified as war is identified from some societies that were thriving in hunter-gatherer subsistence contexts, actually making it difficult to link such behaviors to schemas of property-based human interactions established after the Neolithic Period.[411,412] In spite of the scarcity of archeological evidence, it is important to consider questions of both *degree* and *frequency* when looking at the emergence of large-scale warfare and to contrast our considerations with observations of present-day human conditions, relating this to the development of the notion of "property" and how this concept was significantly strengthened from the Neolithic Period onward into the realm of proto-historic civilizations. The latter periods – and into early recorded history – are profoundly marked by cyclical events of large-scale violence between increasingly larger, more powerful and wider-ranging civilizations as they rose and fell in a perpetual waltz of brilliance and collapse. Over the long-term perspective developed in this book, we can now link these developments to the consolidation of land-linked identities beginning in the later Acheulian, which as we have seen, followed their own evolutionary process when ground-breaking technological capabilities allowed populations to overcome environmental hurdles and establish themselves within relatively fixed territorial boundaries. Underpinning this process, increasing technological complexity imparted these compartmentalized groups of peoples with their own individual specificities and modes of tool manufacture, lending particular qualities to their finished tool kits (defined as culture). We have seen how these phenomena further intensified through time after the demographic explosion of *Homo sapiens* in the later Middle Paleolithic and, exponentially, after their phenomenal occupation of the planet in the Upper Pleistocene.

In the areas of the world where humans settled on parcels of land domesticating plants and animals, technological capacities once designed only to meet daily subsistence requirements and perform domestic tasks were transformed to support larger groups, deepening well-defined land-based parcels that would eventually become nation-states.

The acquisitions of each of these social entities, of course, needed to be protected and preserved to guarantee the survival of all recognized members. Gains had to be guarded and kept from "others" (i.e. peoples living in other areas and with contrasting cultural expression). Technological superiority embracing new forms of weaponry and terror-inducing acts thus became the means by which compartmentalized human populations could protect their material and regional acquisitions. Within these entities, which became units of production and trade, safeguarded nutrition and improved living conditions soon resulted in an increased number of births, higher life expectancy, and decreased mortality rates. These same criteria are among the factors that continue to contribute to the demographic growth we are experiencing today. At the onset of proto-historic times, villages were rapidly transformed into urban settings, which, since the Industrial Revolution, have become home to more than half of the globe's human population (projections by the United Nations based on trends recorded since the later Middle Ages predict that by the year 2050, nearly 68 percent of humanity will live in urban environments).[413]

Cultural conformity, underpinning sameness or oneness among grouped peoples and forming the foundation of modern nationalisms, were strengthened through time by reinforcing the concepts of territory-based identity through the sharing of abstract notions. This sharing was effectively provided by historic cultural myths that were symbolically transmitted at first orally and pictorially and then through written documents to eventually become imposed through obligatory institutionalized education buttressed by religious dogma. This process continues today to nurture racism by highlighting symbolic (imaginary) differences between peoples – where real biological differences are entirely lacking. The recorded history of humanity – the human story – is most strongly marked in its later phases by successive rises and falls of civilizations that sought to enlarge their range of influence by gobbling up other peoples with contrasting sets of stories and traditions. Thus, wars and violence inflicted between nations are grounded in symbolic constructions of difference enforced by dissimilarities of (often religious) stories. The immense destructive force wielded since discoveries of nuclear fission and fusion reactions on the atomic level in the 1930s transposed the human scientific endeavor into a formidable means by which to create the most powerful weapons capable of destroying not only human life but also all forms of life on the planet. Since that time, we humans are living with new types of fear, carving out ever-deeper territorial differences and redefining haves and have-nots in terms of capacity for mass destruction. Is this the logical outcome of the evolution of technology, the darling of humanity? Or do armaments of mass destruction express the culmination of human curiosity – the human trait *par excellence*? Is it curiosity that drives us inexorably to experience our achievements in this way without worrying about their consequences? Are we ready to pay the price of reaping horrific death on innocent peoples and animals simply because we feel compelled to follow the deadly snowball of technological complexity?

Figure 12.3
Tower being hit during the 9/11 attacks (World Trade Center in New York City, United States of America). Passenger airplanes were hijacked and used as lethal weapons in the unprecedented and horrifying attacks on the World Trade Center in New York City and the Pentagon just outside Washington, DC. Another flight heading for Washington crashed in a field in Pennsylvania. The Afghan terrorist group Al-Qaeda was responsible for the attacks. (NIST SIPA/Wikicommons https://theconversation.com/world-politics-explainer-the-twin-tower-bombings-9-11-101443).

Paradoxically, this deeply entrenched feature of modern human civilization globalized today through communication networks has led us to the bizarre phenomena of terrorism as a primitive form of warfare seemingly more powerful today even than our most developed technological weaponry. Even as we struggle with our own irresponsibility in dealing with this godlike power placed on us from our own technological prowess, the rise of terrorism is underlining another type of power whose far-reaching potency is proven to us on a daily basis by simple, violent and destructive acts occurring in a spiral of frequency and potency throughout the world. Terrorism born of inequality, fear and hate is turning the basic items of our daily lives (vans, airplanes, homespun bombs) into lethal weapons, so we are experiencing ever-deeper varieties of fear and insecurity (see Figure 12.3). The incredible cruelty and the terrifying reality of something in our human nature is slowly awakening even the most ignorant of the happy sleepers in the social masses, warning us that the danger is all around and is unavoidable and unpredictable. This is not a new phenomenon but simply the continuation of a process begun in the early Holocene, engendered from the hyperdeveloped symbolic world created out of technology and the global games we are playing on the most abstract of levels.[304] In this game now executed on a global level, no one is safe and the enemy is everywhere. As human history cyclically plays out this merciless competition, the have-not humans strive to overcome their intolerable situations by freeing themselves from suffering unsustainable inequality, striking out desperately and blindly using any means of violence available to them. This is the terrorist who threatens us – the one we have created, the one whose control escapes us absolutely. But the real danger lies in the civic and political impotence of the human masses desensitized by digital paradises created to blind us to the reality of our own destructive force and now manipulated into appeasement by the promise of material gain. This is symptomatic of our time; this is the history we are writing, *and this is our moment*, which is somehow fleeting with dizzying rapidity. History shows us that the terrifying events we are experiencing are not infrequent in their degree of cruelty or in the number of deaths they involve; no, they are distinguished rather by their strange quality of alienation because they exist totally outside of reality. Despite the unbearable horror of the acts we are experiencing and, involuntarily are even generating, we have lost our ability to prevent them.

13

THE ROLE OF PREHISTORY IN UNDERSTANDING THE MODERN HUMAN CONDITION

LINKING UP THE PAST TO UNDERSTAND THE PRESENT AND STEP INTO THE FUTURE

Compared with other fields of knowledge, prehistoric archeology allows us to observe the world from the specific standpoint of comparatively vast temporal and spatial scales. In today's society, most people – including those living in so called "underdeveloped" parts of the world – are accustomed to thinking in generational terms or, even more commonly, in terms of immediate gratification: cause and effect on an individual level. In this book, I shared with you the ways in which prehistory and all of the sciences it embraces presently engenders modern, global thinking. Working with the distant past allows us to consider humanity as a whole, to ponder the wonders of its emergence and evolution and to conceive appropriately of ourselves as a species that, once divided, has evolved into a single, globalized entity. This is where our technological evolution has led us, and we must embrace our situation and take responsibility for it, acting only to preserve and protect all forms of life with utmost respect.

As with all evolutionary processes, the emergence and, ultimately, domination by *Homo sapiens* is fruit of a complex spiral of interconnected events that continue to be unpredictable (at least for the most part). Even though some religions seek to explain life as a story leading to the domination of our species on the planet, this situation is in reality only a result of evolutionary contingency. In his magisterial work describing the Burgess Shale fossil fauna, a virtual explosion of life that occurred millions of years ago in the Paleozoic Era during the Cambrian Period (541–485 million years ago [Ma]), the late evolutionary biologist S. J. Gould taught us essential lessons about contingency, the main driving force behind evolutionary processes.[414] During the Proterozoic Eon, the Earth was inhabited by single-celled and then multicelled soft-bodied organisms. The subsequent appearance and rapid diversification of skeletonized fauna during the Cambrian was a major event in Earth's history. This phenomenon is exceptionally documented by thousands of fossils of multicelled creatures exceptionally well preserved in the Burgess Shale, a rock formation situated in the Rocky Mountains of western Canada (an analogous accumulation is recognized in China at the World Heritage Chengjiang fossil site).[415] These incredibly rich fossil beds bear witness to the huge variability and complexity represented in this early period of animal life on Earth. This incredible diversity is at the root of all existing life forms because it was during this time that virtually all of the major invertebrate phyla (except coral-like animals called Bryozoa) appeared in the fossil record. The Burgess Shale fauna includes several groups of arthropods, sponges, onychophora, crinoids, mollusks, corals, worms, chordates and many other species, some of which cannot even be placed within known phyla. This profusion of early life forms, sometimes referred to as "evolution's Big Bang," was followed by a mass extinction event about 490 million years ago. In his book, Gould presents the reader with Pikaia, the oldest known chordate (possessing a notochord, a feature linked to the development of a spinal column) and "the first recorded member of our own phylum" (the Chordata):

> Pikaia is the missing and final link in our story of contingency – the direct connection between Burgess decimation and eventual human evolution. We need no longer talk of subjects peripheral to our parochial concerns – of alternative worlds crowded with little penis worms, of marrelliform arthropods and no mosquitos, of fearsome anomalocarids gobbling fishes. Wind the tape of life back to the Burgess times, and let it play again. If Pikaia does not survive the replay, we are wiped out of future history – all of us, from shark to robin to orangutan. And I don't think that any handicapper, given Burgess evidence known today, would have granted any favorable odds for the persistence of Pikaia.
>
> And so, if you wish to ask the question of the ages – why do humans exist? – a major part of the answer, touching those aspects of the issue that science can treat at all, must be: because Pikaia survived the Burgess decimation. The response does not cite a single law of nature; it embodies no statement about predictable evolutionary pathways, no calculation of probabilities based on general rules of anatomy or ecology. The survival of Pikaia was a contingency of "just history". I do not think that any "higher" answer can be given, and I cannot imagine that any resolution could be more fascinating. We are the offspring of history, and must establish our own paths in this most diverse and interesting of conceivable universes – one indifferent to our suffering, and therefore offering us maximal freedom to thrive, or to fail, in our own chosen way.[414]

Currently, some predict that the next evolutionary phase awaiting our technospecies will be our total assimilation with artificial intelligence,[304] a process that is (arguably) already underway. I like to relate the implications of this scenario to a future where we will embrace an existence akin to the so-called Borg created by M. Hurley in the famous television and movie series *Star Trek: The Next Generation*. The Borg are alien life forms comprised of individual beings that are all connected into a single, centralized computer (the hive mind: "A group mind, hive mind, group ego, mind coalescence, or gestalt intelligence in science fiction is a plot device in which multiple minds, or consciousnesses, are linked into a single, collective consciousness or intelligence").[416] A central computer, known as The Collective, guides each of the Borg's thoughts and actions. Likewise, all Borgs are connected to one another, so that each of them is aware of and registers the thoughts and actions of all other Borgs at all times. The hostile aim of these imagined cybernetic organisms is to assimilate other alien species in order to appropriate their acquired knowledge and technological capabilities and thus take over the universe. Is this doomsday scenario not reflective of a reality already in progress?

Consider the children being brought up in today's developed world, the future of our species. They are living with huge and terrifying fears that my generation of youth could never even have fathomed. As a child growing up in the 1960s and 1970s (I was born in Canada in 1962), I can distinctly remember the fear in my gut at the nuclear threat looming over us during the Cold War between the United States and the Soviet Union. This doomsday scenario has not, of course, been resolved since this time (we are now only 100 seconds away from midnight on the doomsday clock)[417] because the threat of widespread nuclear destruction has been increasing daily after the catastrophic presidency of Donald Trump who found it fitting somehow to pull out of the 1987 nonproliferation pact with the Russians).[418] But I can also remember growing up in a period of optimism in 1970s North America (after the war in Vietnam) when youth – male and female – strove to assimilate, improve and move beyond the values achieved from society's freeing itself from the conservative constraints imposed by previous generations (following the social revolutions of the Baby Boomers) turning optimistically toward the future: get an education, land a job, plan a family, buy a home, have children and grandchildren, retire comfortably. Today's youth are struggling to survive in the midst of proportionately far greater fears engendered, perhaps, by this irresponsible race to success played out by preceding generations regardless of the costs to the environment. Today's generation of youth is paying the price. They are living not only with the fear of total destruction of the planet by a horrific nuclear arms war but also with the impact of pollution and the raping of the Earth; the daily global extinction of plants and animals; uncontrolled viral pandemics; the fear of terrorist attacks anytime, anywhere; the uncertainty of our own continuity as a species. So why bother planning? What is the point of having children in an uncertain world, why pursue an education when there are no jobs out there anyway? My own experience as a mother and as a teacher suggests to me that our youth has stopped planning for their future. They simply cannot assume the disproportionately huge responsibility for the gigantic mess that millennia of anthropogenic transformations have left since the Late Pleistocene.[366] From my own experience, I have found that today's youth are living entirely in the present, asking only for some escape from their fears in the form of fleeting digital pleasures. By entering into their telephone screens, it seems that our children are already being assimilated into the Collective, giving credence to the Borg motto: "You will be assimilated; resistance is futile." This situation has resulted in a world of individuals who thrive in their own constructed realities absorbed into massive communication networks. The "me generation" or "millennials" use technology to manufacture their own (fleeting, changeable) identities, shaping them into whatever they fancy without ever leaving the comfort of their own sofas:

> Millennials consist, depending on whom you ask, of people born from 1980 to 2000. To put it more simply for them, since they grew up not having to do a lot of math in their heads, thanks to computers, the group is made up mostly of teens and 20-somethings. At 80 million strong, they are the biggest age grouping in American history. Each country's millennials are different, but because of globalization, social media, the exporting of Western culture and the speed of change, millennials worldwide are more similar to one another than to older generations within their nations. Even in China, where family history is more important than any individual, the Internet, urbanization and the one-child policy have created a generation as overconfident and self-involved as the Western one. And these aren't just rich-kid problems: poor millennials have even higher rates of narcissism, materialism and technology addiction in their ghetto-fabulous lives.[419]

WHAT FUTURE FOR STUDIES OF THE PAST?

Today, individuals process huge masses of information thanks to different types of computerized tools while dwelling mainly inside a relatively limited spatial-temporal range (of immediacy). Anesthetized by the complexity of existence (and survival) in the twenty-first century, people rarely employ modern technologies to delve into real, conscious reflection about the distant past, only exceptionally moving beyond customary temporal referents. Yet these very same technological agencies are at our disposal to discover and explore the events marking our evolutionary trajectory and can be used to help us shape better pathways into the future. By turning our gaze, even occasionally, back to the past, we can familiarize ourselves with true (rather than fabricated) evolutionary processes, and this will help our species to finally end the spiral of destructive practices by overcoming manufactured categorizations pigeonholing peoples in accordance with constructed and imaginary divisions. The field of prehistory, dealing necessarily and constantly with questions relating to origins, addresses the gnawing questions commonly posed (publicly or privately) by all peoples: How, why and where did humanity commence? What is our role on the planet? What is our individual and collective responsibility toward the other living beings with which we share the Earth? How can we preserve life – a life worth living – in the face of the incredible power of our technologies that has given us unprecedented demographic growth and power?

Except for the important lessons of evolutionary contingency that humble our species to recognize its story as one that could just have easily been written very differently, evolutionary theory also teaches us that diversity – be it genetic, social or cultural – is favorable to resilience. Our prehistoric ancestors certainly possessed different means by which to grasp and share lessons from the past that aided them in dealing with their lives as they moved into the future: lessons made possible by opting to develop extrasomatic manipulative technologies facilitating resource acquisition and freeing time for innovative behaviors. Growing technological complexity in turn engendered the necessary development of abstract symbolic behaviors and customs that we progressively transformed into human culture. This shared human consciousness still forms an essential part of our existence today. It constitutes a database indispensable for the survival of each individual in the present and ensures the endurance of our species into the future. If we are to move positively into the future in the globalized world we now live in, it is essential for our species to preserve cultural diversity, to accept cultural differences between and among peoples for what they are in essence: a communicative system of shared symbolic constructions. Before moving on, we must address the seemingly paradoxical relationship between religion and culture. A colleague of mine once commented that without the world's religions, humans would never have created the tremendous monuments we preserve and cherish – those formal expressions of spiritualism that, as culture, continue to inspire awe and respect in most human beings. In this view, a world devoid of religious fervor would also lack the creative sociobehavioral traditions marked by colorful rituals that provide societies with a framework within which they can function as a unit, centering themselves in important values of community, identity and belonging. Accordingly, the richness of culture, which I have shown was created during the Oldowan and developed into the Acheulian and was perpetuated throughout the Middle Paleolithic and beyond, has been passed on and elaborated on generation after generation, year after year after year, since the dawn of humanity. This evolutionary picture shows us that the richness that we call "culture" does not, in fact, need to be dictated by any fixed and imposed religious precepts: it does not depend on any rigid human establishment, but rather, it is founded in human curiosity and wonder and in our cerebral necessity to explain the unexplainable, in our deeply rooted fears sharpened through time by our symbolic thought processes and, finally, in our need to exist as social animals. Human spirituality thus engendered is perceptible in the cave paintings of the Upper Paleolithic, in the monumental constructions of the Bronze Age and later social groupings, in the ritualistic gatherings practiced today by virtually every civilization in the world. In response, therefore, to the viewpoint expressed by my university colleague, I contend that humanity has always invented ways to exteriorize the symbolic universe existing within each of us and so, even in the absence of "religion" as such, has always created culture. In this way, the role of culture is twofold: first, it allows us to meld with the collective consciousness of events from our past that have made us what we are today, and second, it provides us with a unifying social force. In the preceding chapters, I explained how some of the dangers inherent in the imposition of dogmatic and institutionalized religious doctrines have impeded the advancement of science by silencing alternative viewpoints (even through violent means). Although we have learned this lesson from the past at the expense of many lives, this scourge continues to plague modern societies today. Especially now, when our species has achieved such huge technological powers and the responsibility of all life on the planet lies in our hands and we are called on for decision making that will affect the future of our planet, we cannot allow narrow religious doctrines to interfere in the formulation of reasonable scientific hypotheses (based on objective interpretations of factual and provable evidence).

Imposing strict religious precepts on individuals is simply contrary to all of the advances that have been made in human societies as a whole. So, we must not equate culture with institutionalized religion. I think that given the present-day situation of our species, it is essential to be keenly aware of the separation between these two concepts. As societies strive to free themselves from the shackles of imposed ideologies, individuals have the right to preserve their own form of spiritual enlightenment and to share it through tradition and ritual as ways to maintain the cultural constructions that through time have become so closely knitted into the human survival strategy. All peoples therefore have the right to preserve and perpetuate their cultural constructions because they play a much-needed role in the very scary world in which we presently live. As social animals, humans need to nurture their sense of belonging to some type of stable entity and have invented culture to fill this need. Culture provides a reliable (because it is fixed) mental template, guiding daily lives and helping us to reign in the negative aspects of our basal instincts (sexual drive, violent and murderous tendencies, greed, apathy). Culture therefore facilitates survival in the huge social units that our species through time has opted to live in, allowing individuals to take refuge in such seemingly immutable social paradigms as family, neighborhood or community. It provides reliable seasonal rituals that occur rhythmically on a yearly basis and whose role it is to reinforce these comforting concepts by strengthening the abstract (invented) notions of identity and belonging.

Prehistoric archeology provides indisputable scientific proof that we are one species derived on The Tangled Tree of Life[420] from a (bushy) series of common ancestors, annulling finally and immutably any arguments supporting racist, nationalist or fascist tendencies. Using this knowledge, we must now strive to terminate the suffering and clashes between ethnocentric societies occurring cyclically in every known historical era.[298] Populations grouped together under their constructed common identities compete with one another, striving like the Borg to bound forward by assimilating the know-how acquired from other existing civilizations. So we have moved into the globalized world. We must accept this assimilative process and provide equal lives to all members of our species now that we have acquired the technological capacity to do so. As keepers of the planet's equilibrium, we must use our technologies to stop the degenerative and horrific state in which we keep the living organisms with which we share the planet and recognize their right to live decent lives. We may regret the assimilation process characterizing our global existence, but it is our reality. Yes, languages and cultural differences are disappearing; yes, mass communication networks linking more and more peoples in all geographical areas of the world have bestowed the same yearnings on all peoples living on the planet: to live on equal footing, to have equal access to resources and health care, to live with an optimistic outlook toward the future. And so we have a difficult balancing act to perform: embrace all of humanity on par with one another while preserving the genial aspects of each of the regionally constructed cultural identities.

Only the reality of events that have occurred in the past can explain what we are today. But what are the real facts and how can we understand the transformations, whether sustained or deliberately provoked, of human society? Since its earliest foundations, science has sought to objectively understand reality. There is still so much to learn. Scientific methodologies allow us to observe the physical manifestations of past realities in the form of archeological data. But because there is no observation without interpretation, our struggle is to escape our own subjectivity and to avoid anachronisms imposed on us by our own historical contextualization. Following the course of events through time tells us that the drastic climatic events and the demise of numerous plant and animal species that we are witnessing all around us today are the direct result of climate change caused and accelerated by modern human activity. As a single global unity, we must now deal with the reality of climate change and the resulting environmental scourges as our most urgent challenge. We need to accept the fact that our species has forced the atmospheric equilibrium of our planet past the "tipping point" and that we are exceeding the limits of environmental sustainability. In spite of the fact that this is now a proven scientific circumstance, mass media often feeds us a different, more optimistic prognosis: that human life expectancy has grown to be longer than ever before; that more people are gaining daily access to clean water, medication and education than before; that fewer people are dying of violent deaths; that there are fewer wars than before; that homophobia is on the decline; that women's rights movements are gaining momentum; and so on. All suggest that we must truly be a remarkable and unique Darwinian success story. We can indeed strive to uphold these progressive outcomes once they belong in truth to the human species as a whole.

NEW PERSPECTIVES ON OLD PARADIGMS

In order to put the human condition into perspective, it is essential that we review our present position from an evolutionary standpoint. Where do we come from, how and why have we attained such evolutionary imperialism and where will all of this lead? To do this in any coherent way requires us to look back to the dawn of human origins, thus employing a thought mode that allows us to cover a long temporal scale. In order to share data from the wide range of disciplines now connected with prehistoric archeology and their associated technologies, we must do our best to provide accurate perceptions of the conditions of human life hundreds, thousands or even millions of years ago, transcending the conceptual barrier represented by large-scale inverse chronology. Ideally, the apprenticeship of reverse conceptualization generates images from humanity's past that may help to explain behavior observed in the modern populace. We have to do so avoiding the trap of storytelling by using science to provide us with factual versions with which we may endeavor to elaborate reasonable interpretations of past and present phenomena and hypotheses for the future. As a science-based civilization, it is our responsibility to translate accumulated data into common knowledge so that we can advance, modeling behavior along realistic, positive and durable patterns. Thus, the enlarged cognitive processes nascent in our prehistory provide an original world vision that may even lead us to implement new ways to face up to today's greatest challenges in hopes of building a more acceptable future scenario, not only for ourselves, but also for all forms of *Wonderful Life*[414] on the planet. The survival of our species depends on it.

The future of our species lies in the widening of our reflective horizons based on new, globalized thought processes diffused through communication technologies. In order to access the new and enlarged reference database available to us through technology, we ought to explore the possibilities opened for us to by tools of our own creation, for these tools will remain useless for advancing human development in a positive way if our intellectual capacities continue to stagnate on familiar references. Our capacity to solve the increasingly complex global problems facing us today depends on our ability to reference and exploit the information latent in our subconscious minds, now transposed into computer systems enabling us to significantly enlarge our memory-reference capacity. The foundations of this common database, mirror of our collective consciousness, is built on shared past events. It constitutes the elements uniting us today as social beings within a system created and continuously renewed by each and every one of us as representatives of an accumulative process begun so long ago. The past belongs to all of us; it is the root of all things. It has molded us and will continue to define us. The past exists in perpetual motion, eternally and diachronically creating new forms of human expression. All our thought processes are ruled by a myriad of unconscious laws, which are so natural and spontaneous that we are not aware of the steps leading to their construction. In these processes lies the value of studying the past and of our obligation to analyze it in its innermost detail because somewhere along the way, we have lost the filament connecting us to the reality of our existence. Reviving our past may be the only way to fully understand present-day behavior and to modify it in a durable fashion in order to improve the chances for survival of our species and, by extension, other living beings; this is a goal worthy of our level of cognition. New perspectives are being defined for improving large-scale socialization through evolutionary theory. As a first step, we must stop the use of technology as a means to create false desires to nurture capitalist values. Today, we no longer support living as mere spectators while we would like to be who we are: the protagonists of our own historical movement.

NOTES

1 Sagan (1980).

2 Eller (2009).

3 The word *hominization* originated in ancient Greece from the Aristotelian belief that infants obtained their souls only after forty days of life. It was also adapted in later theological works to explain how humans obtained souls. Today, it can be found in texts relating to prehistoric archeology as a concept explaining the evolutionary milestones that led early hominins to their modern condition.

4 Brunet et al. (2002).

5 Although it was banned at first, de la Peyrère's book Praedamitae (1642–1643) circulated secretly in Europe until it was finally printed and distributed. www.jewishvirtuallibrary.org/la-peyr-x00e8-re-isaac

6 G. L. Leclerc, Compte de Buffon, published his L'Histoire Naturelle in thirty-six volumes between 1749 and 1789 with the Imprimerie royale in Paris.

7 www.britannica.com/biography/Carolus-Linnaeus

8 www.britannica.com/biography/Jean-Baptiste-Lamarck

9 Darwin (1859).

10 Raby (2002).

11 Mendel (1869).

12 Darwin (1871).

13 Marx (1867).

14 Marx and Engels (1859).

15 www.britannica.com/biography/Charles-Lyell

16 https://fr.wikipedia.org/wiki/Paul_Tournal#Biographie

17 Tournal (1827).

18 www.britannica.com/biography/Jacques-Boucher-de-Perthes

19 www.stratigraphy.org/

20 Wood, Henry and Hatala (2015).

21 Periodic changes in the Earth's orbit around the Sun over time are called Milankovitch cycles. They alter the patterns of solar influence received by the Earth, affecting climate over time.

22 Hublin et al. (2017).

23 Villmoore et al. (2015).

24 Harmand et al. (2015).

25 Semaw (2000).

26 Braun et al. (2019).

27 Crutzen and Stoermer (2000).

28 https://quaternary.stratigraphy.org/workinggroups/anthropocene/

29 Smith and Zeder (2013).

30 Doughty, Wolf and Field (2010).

31 Ruddiman and Thomson (2001).

32 Ruddiman (2003).

33 Fuller et al. (2011).

34 Zalasiewicz et al. (2010).

35 After graphs first published by Steffen et al. (2004) monitoring indicators of human activities and their effects on a selected range of features of the Earth's systems.

36 Zalasiewicz et al. (2008).

37 Castro-Curel and Carbonell (1995).

38 Sano et al. (2020).

39 Challis (2014).

40 Barsky (2013).

41 Rodríguez et al. (2011).

42 Barsky et al. (2015a).

43 Vendetti et al. (2019).

44 The word hominin refers to modern Homo and its ancestral forms (Australopithecus, Paranthropus, Ardipithecus).

45 Carbonell and Hortolà (2013).

46 Diamond (1997).

47 Cavalli-Sforza and Feldman (1981).

48 Boyd and Richardson (1985).

49 Radiometric or radioisotopic dating refers to methods used in determining age for archeological contexts based on the principle of known decomposition rates or transformation relationships of some isotopes (for example, uranium-thorium or potassium-argon).

50 Regarding the rise and fall of the earth's lithosphere, continental plates are mobile and sink deeper when burdened by heavy ice sheets during cold climatic phases. Inversely, during interglacial periods, water is released from the ice sheets into the oceans, causing continental plates to adjust by floating upward (isostatic rebound).

51 Allopatric speciation occurs when part (or all) of a species' population is physically isolated by a geographical barrier for a period of time long enough for sexual selection to physically alter the features of that species to fit the new environmental and reproductive conditions. Eventually, this process can produce new species.

52 Barsky (2014).

53 Pedogenesis refers to climate-driven formation processes at work in creating specific kinds of soils.

54 Renfrew and Bahn (2016).

55 Schick and Toth (1994).

56 Bordes (1961).

57 de Sonneville-Bordes (1953).

58 Laplace (1972).

59 Carbonell et al. (1992).

60 Leroi-Gourhan (1943).

61 Morgan et al. (2015).

62 Stout et al. (2005).

63 Oldowan is an eponymous term invented by L. Leakey from Olduvai Gorge (Tanzania) where deposits have revealed numerous archeological sites covering a long period of time and have yielded a rich faunal and artifact record. Oldowan tools come from the denominated "Bed I" sites, dating to nearly 1.8 million years ago. The tools are characterized mainly by knapping waste such as small cores and flakes as well as simple and nonstandardized cobble tools (chopper-cores).

64 Leakey, Evernden and Curtis (1961).

65 Leakey (1971).

66 Barsky et al. (2015b).

67 Stout and Semaw (2006).

68 Barsky et al. (2013).

69 The word *Acheulian* was coined by G. de Mortillet in 1872 to designate a cultural complex in which hominins made symmetrical stone tools called handaxes (or bifaces). The eponymous denomination was used for discoveries made in the middle alluvial terraces of the Somme River at Saint-Acheul. The Acheulian follows the Oldowan cultural complex.

70 www.greencorridor.info/en/index.html

71 www.fromthegrapevine.com/nature/animals-use-tools

72 Slon et al. (2017).

73 www.sciencemag.org/news/2016/05/humans-are-still-evolving-and-we-can-watch-it-happen

74 Mesoudi, Whiten and Laland (2006).

75 Sockol, Raichlen and Pontzer (2007).

76 Arsuaga and Martínez (1998).

77 Kortlandt (1972).

78 Coppens (1994).

79 Ward and Underwood (1967).

80 Wheeler (1984).

81 Wheeler (1985).

82 Wheeler (1991).

83 Best and Kamilar (2018).

84 Rodman and McHenry (1980).

85 Chaplin, Jablonski and Cable (1994).

86 Williams and Callaghan (2020).

87 Okerblom et al. (2018).

88 Johanson and Taieb (1976).

89 Johanson, White and Coppens (1978).

90 Lieberman (2015).

91 Leakey and Hay (1979).

92 White (1980).

93 Leakey et al. (1995).

94 Haile-Selassie (2001).

95 Zollikofer et al. (2005).

96 Brunet et al. (1995).

97 Reynolds, Bailey and King (2011).

98 Pickford and Senut (2001).

99 Roche et al. (2013).

100 Pickford et al. (2002).

101 Haile-Selassie, Suwa and White (2004).

102 Lovejoy et al. (2009).

103 White, Suwa and Asfaw (1994).

104 Leakey et al. (1998).

105 Ward, Leakey and Walker (1999).

106 White et al. (2006).

107 Haile-Selassie et al. (2019).

108 Dart (1925).

109 Clarke and Tobias (1995).

110 Kuman and Clarke (2000).

111 Leakey et al. (2001).

112 Broom (1938).

113 Leakey (1959).

114 Arambourg and Coppens (1968).

115 Asfaw et al. (1999).

116 Goodall (1999).

117 Shumaker, Walkup and Beck (2011).

118 Carbonell et al. (2018).

119 Semaw et al. (1997).

120 Semaw et al. (2003).

121 Semaw, Rogers and Stout (2009).

122 De la Torre et al. (2013).

123 Caruana et al. (2014).

124 Monnier and Bischoff (2014).

125 Yustos et al. (2015).

126 Barsky (2009).

127 Hay (1976).

128 https://olduvai-paleo.org/current-field-research/

129 Howell, Haesaerts and de Heinzelin (1987).

130 Kuman and Clarke (2000).

131 Potts (1998).

132 Zink and Lieberman (2016).

133 Domínguez-Rodrigo, Bunn and Yravedra (2014).

134 Bunn and Pickering (2010).

135 Lumley and Beyene (2004).

136 Toro-Moyano et al. (2013).

137 Arzarello et al. (2012).

138 Carbonell et al. (2008).

139 Álvarez et al. (2015).

140 Michel et al. (2017).

141 Boëda, Hou and Huang (2011).

142 Roebroeks and Van Kolfschoten (1994).

143 Chauhan et al. (2017).

144 Lumley et al. (1988).

145 Gabunia et al. (2000).

146 Gabunia et al. (2002).

147 Vekua et al. (2002).

148 Ferring et al. (2011).

149 M.-A. Lumley (2006).

150 Lumley et al. (2005).

151 Antón (2003).

152 Swisher et al. (1994).

153 Toro-Moyano, Agustí and Martínez-Navarro (2003).

154 Martínez-Navarro et al. (1997).

155 Agustí et al. (2015).

156 Agustí et al. (1996).

157 Oms et al. (2000a).

158 Oms et al. (2000b).

159 Duval et al. (2011).

160 Duval et al. (2012).

161 Toro-Moyano et al. (2010).

162 Barsky et al. (2010).

163 Carbonell et al. (1995).

164 Parés and Pérez-González (1999).

165 Duval et al. (2018).

166 Bermúdez de Castro et al. (1997).

167 Gibert (1999)

168 Carbonell et al. (2009).

169 Stout and Chaminade (2013).

170 Beyene et al. (2013).

171 http://humanorigins.si.edu/evidence/human-fossils/species/homo-erectus

172 Vallverdú et al. (2014).

173 Schoetensack (1908).

174 Pappu et al. (2011).

175 Lumley and Tianyuan (2008).

176 Barsky, Carbonell and Sala Ramos (2018).

177 Lepre et al. (2011).

178 Herries and Shaw (2011).

179 Bar-Yosef and Goren-Inbar (1993).

180 Despriée et al. (2016).

181 Sharon (2009).

182 Li et al. (2017).

183 Lumley and Barsky (2004).

184 Rodríguez-Hidalgo et al. (2017).

185 Barroso-Ruíz et al. (2011).

186 Roebroeks and Villa (2011).

187 Berna et al. (2012).

188 Gowlett (2016).

189 Gowlett et al. (1981).

190 Brain and Sillent (1988).

191 Bellomo (1994).

192 Rolland (2004).

193 Alperson-Afil (2012)

194 Goren-Inbar et al. (2004).

195 Preece et al. (2006).

196 Lumley (2006).

197 Ravon (2019).

198 Sanz et al. (2020).

199 Shimelmitz et al. (2014).

200 Karkanas et al. (2007).

201 Gao et al. (2017).

202 Barkai et al. (2017).

203 Chazan (2017).

204 Rosell and Blasco (2019).

205 Parfitt et al. (2010).

206 Barham and Everett (2020).

207 Late Acheulian denominations. The word Acheulian was created by Mortillet in 1872 for tools from the middle alluvial terrace of the Somme river (Saint Acheul, France). Abbevillian, or Chelian (Saint Acheul, Chelles)(G. de Mortillet in 1878). Clactonian (H. Breuil in 1932) describes the Acheulian from the English site of Clacton-on-Sea that does not contain handaxes. The Levalloisian invented by H. Breuil (1931) denotes tools from the lower Seine alluvial terrace (Levallois, near Paris). The Tayacian (first identified by Breuil) from the lower levels of la Micoque (southwestern France) for "pre-Mousterian" tool kits lacking Levallois technology and with few handaxes and retouched tools shaped by a stepped retouch referred to as Quina (another eponymous term). Micoquian (O. Hauser in 1916) for assemblages from la Micoque (Dordogne, France). Pre-mousterian (adopted by G. Bosinsky in 1967) refers to Mousterian-type tool kits that predate the beginning of the Middle Paleolithic in Western Europe. This term describes certain assemblages of central Europe. The Acheulian is currently considered to include a wide variety of production systems and more generally refers to bifacial industries in different parts of the world.

208 Barsky, Moigne and Pois (2019).

209 Meyer et al. (2016).

210 Harvati et al. (2019).

211 Blain et al. (2013).

212 Aouraghe (2006).

213 Martinón-Torres et al. (2019).

214 Krause et al. (2010).

215 Reich et al. (2010.)

216 Otte (2019).

217 Brown et al. (2004).

218 Morwood et al. (2004).

219 Fuhlrott (1857).

220 Schaaffhausen (1857).

221 http://humanorigins.si.edu/evidence/human-fossils/species/homo-neanderthalensis

222 http://humanorigins.si.edu/evidence/genetics/ancient-dna-and-neanderthals/dna-genotypes-and-phenotypes.

223 Marine isotope stages (MIS) (see Chapter 9): 5 (around 80–130 Ka) and 3 (around 60,000 to 27,000 years ago), which were the last interglacial periods preceding the Holocene (11,650 up to and including the present day).

224 Schoetensack (1908).

225 Rightmire (1998).

226 Hershkovitz et al. (2018).

227 Hoffmann et al. (2018).

228 Peresani et al. (2011).

229 Volpato et al. (2012).

230 Détroit et al. (2019).

231 Henshilwood, d'Errico and Watts (2009).

232 Leroi-Gourhan (1988).

233 Finlayson (2008).

234 Green et al. (2010).

235 Krings et al. (1997).

236 Green et al. (2008).

237 Duarte et al. (1999).

238 Sankararaman et al. (2012).

239 Kuhlwilm et al. (2016).

240 Houldcroft and Underdown (2016).

241 www.republicworld.com/world-news/rest-of-the-world-news/covid19-prehistoric-chinese-village-might-hold-clues-first-epidemic.html

242 www.visualcapitalist.com/history-of-pandemics-deadliest/

243 www.worldometers.info/coronavirus/

244 Dannemann, Andrés and Kelso (2016)

245 Friesem, Zaidner and Shahack-Gross (2014).

246 Meignen, Goldberg and Bar-Yosef (2007).

247 Vallverdú et al. (2012).

248 Wrangham (2009).

249 Cnuts, Tomasso and Rots (2017).

250 Stolarczyk and Schmidt (2018).

251 Mousterian cultural facies after Leroi-Gourhan (1988): Acheulian of Mousterian tradition (MTA) (defined at Le Moustier by D. Peyrony 1930 and F. Bordes 1948): Archaic-looking tool kits with relatively small-sized triangular and very symmetrical cordiform handaxes. These were carefully manufactured by numerous invasive removals and then finely retouched. Light-duty tools are similar to the those of the Typical Mousterian but present a high percentage of Upper Paleolithic types (awls, end-scrapers, chisels). Type A: numerous handaxes and scrapers. Type B: rare and poorly manufactured handaxes, backed knives, numerous denticulates or end-scrapers and blades. Geographical extension: Southwestern France, Spain, Italy, Germany. Typical Mousterian (Bordes, 1963, defined at Le Moustier): Equilibrium between the different light-duty tool types. Rare bifacial tools. Levallois and discoid knapping. Geographical extension: Mediterranean and southwestern France and Spain (Carigüela, Cova Negra). Denticulate Mousterien (Bordes, 1963, defined at Combe Grenal, Peche de l'Azé, Chadourne). High frequency of light-duty denticulate tools, many with thick (notched) retouch. Low Levallois index and numerous elongated flakes. Low tool-type variability with some rectilinear scrapers with marginal retouch. Tool kits include chopper tools but no handaxes. Geographical extension: Europe and Near East (Levant). Ferrassie Mousterian (MTF) (Bordes and Bourgon, 1951, defined at La Ferrassie). High Levallois index, numerous scrapers and points. Retouch may be stepped and assemblages sometimes include limaces and scrapers with plano-convex retouch. Geographical extension: Southwestern France, Bretagne, cf. "Micoquien" in Eastern Europe (Germany).Quina Mousterian (also called "Charentien" from the La Charente region, France. Defined by Bordes and Bourgon, 1951, at La Quina). Low Levallois index, short, thick flakes often retouched into distinctive thick, short scrapers with stepped retouch. Denticulate tools, limaces and scrapers with plano-convex retouch. Geographical extension: Southwestern France, Gironde, Vienne, Mediterranean Europe (Italy). Facies oriental (F. Bordes): foliated tools and triangular points (Provence) or backed scrapers with thinned bases (Rhône Valley).

252 Zilhão et al. (2010).

253 Finlayson et al. (2012).

254 Finlayson (2019).

255 Hublin (2009).

256 Rodríguez-Hidalgo et al. (2019).

257 Radovčić et al. (2015)

258 Martínez et al. (2012).

259 Martínez et al. (2018).

260 Roebroeks et al. (2012).

261 Rifkin (2012).

262 Trinkaus (1983).

263 Fiacconi and Hunt (2015).

264 Pomeroy et al. (2020).

265 Binant (1991).

266 Dibble et al. (2015).

267 Rendu et al. (2016).

268 Tappen (1985).

269 Lordkipanidze et al. (2005).

270 Gracia et al. (2009).

271 White et al. (2003).

272 Bar-Yosef and Meignen (2001).

273 Herschkovitz et al. (2021).

274 Bourgeon, Burke and Higham (2017).

275 Holen et al. (2017).

276 Clarkson et al. (2017).

277 Hublin (2013).

278 Cosgrove, Mazure and Staley (2007).

279 Bruner, Manzi and Arsuaga (2003).

280 Hirst (2018).

281 Henshilwood et al. (2011).

282 Bradley and Stanford (2004).

283 Jacobs et al. (2019).

284 Rosso (2017).

285 Mellars and Stringer (1989).

286 Belfer-Cohen and Hovers (2020).

287 Carbonell and Mosquera (2006).

288 Stringer (2012).

289 Bar-Yosef (2002).

290 Gravina et al. (2018).

291 Clottes et al. (1995).

292 Gaudzinski et al. (2005).

293 http://firstlegend.info/thevenuscult.html

294 Martin (1989).

295 Wroe and Field (2006).

296 Firestone et al. (2007).

297 Childe (1936).

298 www.bbc.com/future/article/20190218-are-we-on-the-road-to-civilisation-collapse

299 Olszewski (2008).

300 Bar-Yosef (1998).

301 Grosman (2013).

302 Grosman and Monroe (2017).

303 Svizzero (2018).

304 Harari (2016).

305 Diamond (1999).

306 Breasted (1916).

307 Dietrich (2011).

308 www.nationalgeographic.org/encyclopedia/fertile-crescent/

309 Leach (2003).

310 www.inquiriesjournal.com/articles/538/was-adopting-agriculture-our-biggest-mistake-challenging-the-progressivist-view-of-human-history

311 Goodman et al. (1984).

312 Eshed and Gopher (2018).

313 Theofanopoulou et al. (2017).

314 Legge and Robinson (2017).

315 https://australianstogether.org.au/discover/indigenous-culture/aboriginal-spirituality/

316 Ford (2010).

317 Malthus (1826).

318 Meyer et al. (2015).

319 Shimelmitz and Rosenberg (2013).

320 Clark and Harris (1985).

321 https://fractalfoundation.org/resources/what-are-fractals/

322 https://en.wikipedia.org/wiki/Iron_Age#Europe

323 Dart and Beaumont (1969).

324 Bárez del Cueto et al. (2016).

325 Marro, Bakhshaliyev and Sanz (2010).

326 Akcil (2006),

327 www.crystalinks.com/prehistoric_mining.html

328 Photos (2010).

329 www.makin-metals.com/UserFiles/Images/Infographics/History of Metals Infographic

330 Nigro (2014).

331 Schmandt-Besserat (1999).

332 Bernard et al. (2017).

333 Weart (2011).

334 www.ipcc.ch/

335 Potts et al. (2018).

336 www.nemosgarden.com/about-us/

337 Lumley, H. (2015).

338 Lumley (2014).

339 Lumley, M. A. (2015).

340 Musée de Préhistoire de Tautavel in France.

341 Moigne et al. (2006).

342 Barsky and Lumley (2010).

343 Yokoyama and Nguyen (1981).

344 Yokoyama, Falguères and Quaegebeur (1985).

345 Lumley et al. (1984).

346 Falguères et al. (2004).

347 Falguères et al. (2015).

348 Lebreton et al. (2015).

349 Ollé et al. (2013).

350 www.atapuerca.org

351 Parés et al. (2006).

352 Huguet et al. (2015).

353 Bermúdez de Castro et al. (2011).

354 Carbonell et al. (2005).

355 Bermúdez de Castro et al. (2008).

356 Bermúdez de Castro et al. (2020).

357 Arsuaga et al. (1997).

358 Arnold et al. (2014).

359 Arsuaga et al. (2014).

360 Bermúdez de Castro and Rosas (1992).

361 Arsuaga et al. (1999).

362 Pablos, Gómez-Olivencia and Arsuaga (2018).

363 Vergès et al. (2016).

364 Cáceres, Lozano and Saladié (2007).

365 Rodríguez-Álvarez and Lozano (2018).

366 Boivin et al. (2016).

367 Berger (2002).

368 García-Medrano et al. (2017).

369 Parfitt et al (2010).

370 Arrhenius (1896).

371 www.historyextra.com/period/modern/climate-change-warnings-history/

372 www.earth-policy.org/indicators/C52/carbon_emissions_2004

373 https://climate.nasa.gov/

374 Intergovernmental Science-Policy Platform on Biodiversity and Ecosystem Services (IPBES).

375 www.wri.org/our-work/topics/climate).

376 Global Climate Change: Evidence (2008).

377 https://unfccc.int/process/the-kyoto-protocol

378 https://unfccc.int/cop7/documents/accords_draft.pdf

379 https://unfccc.int/process/the-kyoto-protocol/the-doha-amendment

380 https://unfccc.int/process-and-meetings/the-paris-agreement/the-paris-agreement

381 https://ipbes.net/sites/default/files/downloads/spm_unedited_advance_for_posting_htn.pdf

382 https://cosmosmagazine.com/palaeontology/big-five-extinctions.
   The five great extinctions are the End-Ordovician extinction, 444 million years ago, 86 percent of
   species lost; Late Devonian extinction, 375 million years ago, 75 percent of species lost; End
   Permian, 251 million years ago, 96 percent of species lost; End Triassic, 200 million years ago, 80
   percent of species lost; and End Cretaceous, 66 million years ago, 76 percent of all species lost.

383 Kolbert (2014).

384 Zalasiewicz et al. (2016).

385 Holloway (1996).

386 Toth (1985).

387 Bauman (2017).

388 Robert Barsky, professor of Humanities jointly appointed in law, Vanderbilt University, Tennessee.

389 https://newint.org/blog/2016/11/30/the-dangerous-rise-of-the-right-an-interview-with-noam-chomsky

390 Herman and Chomsky (1988).

391 The World Bank estimates that only around 20 percent of nonanthropized territory remains on the planet.

392 Marx (1867).

393 Fractals are used here as a metaphor to understand how social systems reproduce hierarchical models infinitely. They are interesting in the evolutionary sense because introducing even the slightest modification into such a system will in the long run (and depending on the reproductive rates) result in tangentially major change.

394 Castles (2002).

395 Bobe and Behrensmeyer (2004).

396 Bar-Yosef and Belfer-Cohen (2001).

397 http://accuca.conectia.es/msnbc-02my05.htm

398 Brace (2004).

399 www.nationalgeographic.com/science/article/climate-migrants-report-world-bank-spd

400 www.aljazeera.com/ajimpact/davos-world-prepare-millions-climate-refugees-200121175217520.html

401 Dalley (2000).

402 Dawkins (2006).

403 Nunn (2002).

404 Yves Coppens preface to Defleur (1993).

405 Riel-Salvatore and Gravel-Miguel (2013).

406 Saladié et al. (2012).

407 Bello et al. (2015).

408 Berger and Trinkaus (1995).

409 Sala et al. (2015).

410 Goodall (1990).

411 Lahr et al. (2016).

412 Friedman (2014).

413 www.un.org/development/desa/en/news/population/2018-revision-of-world-urbanization-prospects.html

414 Gould (1989).

415 https://whc.unesco.org/en/list/1388

416 https://en.wikipedia.org/wiki/Group_mind_(science_fiction)

417 www.nytimes.com/2021/01/27/us/doomsday-clock-midnight.html

418 Intermediate-Range Nuclear Forces Treaty.

419 Stein (2013).

420 Quammen (2018).

REFERENCES

Agustí, J., Blain, H.-A., Lozano-Fernández, I., et al. (2015). Chronological and environmental context of the first hominin dispersal into Western Europe: The case of Barranco León (Guadix-Baza Basin, SE Spain). *Journal of Human Evolution*, 87, 87–94.

Agustí, J., Oms, O., Garcés, M. and Parés, J. M. (1996). Calibration of the late Pliocene–early Pleistocene transition in the continental beds of the Guadix-Baza Basin (southeastern Spain). *Quaternary International*, 40, 93–100.

Akcil, A. (2006). Mining history in Anatolia – Part 1. *CIM Magazine*, 1(1),90–92.

Alperson-Afil, N. (2012). Archaeology of fire: Methodological aspects of reconstructing fire history of prehistoric archaeological sites. *Earth-Science Reviews*, 113(S 3-4), 111–19.

Álvarez, C., Parés, J. M., Granger, D., et al. (2015). New magnetostratigraphic and numerical age of the Fuente Nueva-3 site (Guadix-Baza basin, Spain). *Quaternary International*, 389, 224–34.

Antón, S. C. (2003). Natural history of *Homo erectus*. *American Yearbook of Physical Anthropology*, 46, 126–70.

Aouraghe, H. (2006). Histoire du peuplement paléolithique de l'Afrique du Nord et dynamique des interactions entre l'homme et son environnement. *Comptes Rendus Palevol*, 5, 237–42.

Arambourg, C. and Coppens, Y. (1968). Sur la découverte dans le Pléistocène inferieur de la vallée de l'Omo (Ethiopie) d'une mandibule d'Australopithecien. *Comptes Rendus de l'Académie des Sciences*, 265, 589–90.

Arnold, L. J., Demuro, M., Parés, J. M., et al. (2014). Luminescence dating and paleomagnetic age constraint on hominins from Sima de los Huesos, Atapuerca, Spain. *Journal of Human Evolution*, 67, 85–107.

Arrhenius, S. (1896). On the influence of carbonic acid in the air upon the temperature of the ground. *Philosophical Magazine and Journal of Science*, 41(5), 237–76.

Arsuaga, J. L., Gracia, A., Lorenzo, C., Martínez, I. and Pérez, P.-J. (1999). Resto craneal humano de Galería/Cueva de los Zarpazos (Sierra de Atapuerca). In E. Carbonell, A. Rosas and J. C. Díez, eds., *Atapuerca: ocupaciones humanas y paleoecología del yacimiento de Galería*, vol. 7. Zamora: Junta de Castilla y León, 233–35.

Arsuaga, J. L. and Martínez, I. (1998). *La Especie Elegida. La Larga Marcha de la Evolución Humana*. Barcelona: Ediciones Destino.

Arsuaga, J. L., Martínez, I., Arnold, L., et al. (2014). Neandertal roots: Cranial and chronological evidence from the Sima de los Huesos. *Science*, 344(6190), 1358–63.

Arsuaga, J. L., Martínez, I., Gracia, A., et al. (1997). Sima de los Huesos (Sierra de Atapuerca, Spain). The site. *Journal of Human Evolution*, 33(2–3), 109–27.

Arzarello, M., Pavia, G., Peretto, C., Petronio, C. and Sardella, R. (2012). Evidence of an Early Pleistocene hominin presence at Pirro Nord (Apricena, Foggia, southern Italy P13 site). *Quaternary International*, 267, 56–61.

Asfaw, B., White, T., Lovejoy, O., et al. (1999). *Australopithecus garhi*: A new species of early hominid from Ethiopia. *Science*, 284(5414), 629–35.

Bárez del Cueto, S., Baena Preysler, J., Pérez-Gonzàlez, A., et al. (2016). Acheulian flint quarries in the Madrid Tertiary basin, central Iberian Peninsula: First data obtained from geoarchaeological studies. *Quaternary International*, 411, 329–48.

Barham, L. and Everett, D. (2020). Semiotics and the origin of language in the Lower Palaeolithic. *Journal of Archaeological Method and Theory*, 28, 535–79.

Barkai, R., Rossell Árdevol, J., Blasco, R. and Gopher, A. (2017). Fire for a reason: Barbecue at Middle Pleistocene Qesem Cave, Israel. *Current Anthropology*, 58(S16), S314–28.

Barroso Ruíz, C., Botella Ortega, D., Caparrós, M., et al. (2011). The Cueva del Angel (Lucena, Spain): An Acheulian hunters habitat in the south of the Iberian Peninsula. *Quaternary International*, 243, 105–26.

Barsky, D. (2014). North and Saharan Africa Geography and Culture During the Lower Stone Age. In M. Otte and R. Miller, eds., *Encyclopedia of Global Archaeology*, vol. II. New York: Springer, 5454–75.

Barsky, D. (2013). The Caune de l'Arago Stone industries in their stratigraphical context. *Comptes Rendus Palevol*, 12(5), 305–25.

Barsky, D. (2009). An overview of some African and Eurasian Oldowan sites: Evaluation of hominin cognitive levels, technological advancement and adaptive skills. In E. Hovers and D. Braun, eds., *Interdisciplinary Approaches to the Oldowan*. Dordrecht: Springer, 39–48.

Barsky, D., Carbonell, E. and Sala Ramos, R. (2018). Diversity and multiplicity in the Asian Acheulian. *L'Anthropologie*, 122(1), 59–73.

Barsky, D., Celiberti, V., Cauche, D., et al. (2010). Raw material discernment and technological aspects of the Barranco León and Fuente Nueva 3 stone assemblages (Orce, southern Spain). *Quaternary International*, 223–24, 201–19.

Barsky, D., Garcia, J., Martínez, K., et al. (2013). Flake modification in European Early and Early-Middle Pleistocene stone tool assemblages. *Quaternary International*, 316, 140–54.

Barsky, D. and Lumley, H. de (2010). Early European Mode 2 and the stone industry from the Caune de l'Arago's archeostratigraphical levels "P." *Quaternary International*, 223–24, 71–86.

Barsky, D., Moigne, A. M. and Pois, V. (2019). The shift from typical Western European Late Acheulian to microproduction in unit "D" of the late Middle Pleistocene deposits of the Caune de l'Arago (Pyrénées-Orientales, France). *Journal of Human Evolution*, 135(2), 102650.

Barsky, D., Sala, R., Menéndez, L. and Toro-Moyano, I. (2015a). Use and re-use: Re-knapped flakes from the Mode 1 site of Fuente Nueva 3 (Orce, Andalucía, Spain). *Quaternary International*, 361, 21–33.

Barsky, D., Vergès, J. M., Sala, R., Menéndez, L. and Toro-Moyano, I. (2015b). Limestone percussion tools from the late Early Pleistocene sites of Barranco León and Fuente Nueva 3 (Orce, Spain). *Philosophical Transactions of the Royal Society B*, 370(1682), 2014352.

Bar-Yosef, O. (2002). The Upper Paleolithic revolution. *Annual Review of Anthropology*, 31, 363–93.

Bar-Yosef, O. (1998). The Natufian culture in the Levant, threshold to the origins of agriculture. *Evolutionary Anthropology*, 6(5), 159–77.

Bar-Yosef, O. and Belfer-Cohen, A. (2001). From Africa to Eurasia – Early dispersals. *Quaternary International*, 75(1), 19–28.

Bar-Yosef, O. and Goren-Inbar, N. (1993). *The Lithic Assemblage of 'Ubeidiya: A Lower Paleolithic site in the Jordan Valley*. Jerusalem: Qedem 34, Institute of Archeology, Hebrew University of Jerusalem.

Bar-Yosef, O. and Meignen, L. (2001). The chronology of the Levantine Middle Palaeolithic Period in retrospect. *Bulletins et mémoires de la Société d'Anthropologie de Paris*, 13(3–4), 269–89.

Bauman, Z. (2017). *Retrotopia*. Cambridge: Polity Press.

Belfer-Cohen, A. and Hovers, E. (2020). Prehistoric perspectives on "others" and "strangers." *Frontiers in Psychology*, 10(3063), doi: 10.3389/fpsyg.2019.03063

Bello, S. M., Saladié, P., Cáceres, I., Rodriguez-Hidalgo, A. and Parfitt, S. A. (2015). Upper Palaeolithic ritualistic cannibalism at Gough's Cave (Somerset, UK): The human remains from head to toe. *Journal of Human Evolution*, 82, 170–89.

Bellomo, R. (1994). Methods of determining early hominid behavioral activities associated with the controlled use of fire at FxJj20 Main, Koobi Fora, Kenya. *Journal of Human Evolution*, 27, 173–95.

Berger, T. D. and Trinkaus E. (1995). Patterns of trauma among the Neandertals. *Journal of Archaeological Science*, 22, 841–52.

Berger, W. H. (2002). Cesare Emiliani (1922–1995), pioneer of Ice Age studies and oxygen isotope stratigraphy. *Comptes Rendus Palevol*, 1(6), 479–87.

Bermúdez de Castro, J. M., Arsuage, J. L., Carbonell, E., et al. (1997). A hominid from the lower Pleistocene of Atapuerca, Spain: Possible ancestor to Neandertals and modern humans. *Science*, 276 (5317), 1392–95.

Bermúdez de Castro, J. M., Martínez, I., Gracia-Téllez, A., Martinón-Torres, M. and Arsuaga, J. L. (2020). The Sima de los Huesos Middle Pleistocene hominin site (Burgos, Spain). Estimation of the number of individuals. *The Anatomical Record* (Hoboken), 304(7), 1463–77.

Bermúdez de Castro, J. M., Martinón-Torres, M., Robles, A. G., et al. (2011). Early Pleistocene human mandible from Sima del Elefante (TE) cave site in Sierra de Atapuerca (Spain): A comparative morphological study. *Journal of Human Evolution*, 61(1), 12–25.

Bermúdez de Castro, J. M., Pérez-González, A., Martinón-Torres, M., et al. (2008). A new Early Pleistocene hominin mandible from Atapuerca-TD6, Spain. *Journal of Human Evolution*, 55(4), 729–35.

Bermúdez de Castro, J. M. and Rosas, A. (1992). A human mandibular fragment from the Atapuerca trench (Burgos, Spain). *Journal of Human Evolution*, 22(1), 41–46.

Berna, F., Goldberg, P., Kolska Horwitz, L. , et al. (2012). Microstratigraphic evidence of *in situ* fire in the Acheulian strata of Wonderwerk Cave, Northern Cape province, South Africa. *Proceedings of the National Academy of Sciences USA*, 109(20), e1215–e1220.

Bernard, S., Daval, D., Ackerer, P., Pont, S. and Meibom A. (2017). Burial-induced oxygen-isotope re-equilibration of fossil foraminifera explains ocean paleo temperature paradoxes. *Nature Communications*, 1(1134), 1–10.

Best, A. and Kamilar, J. M. (2018). The evolution of eccrine sweat glands in human and non-human primates. *Journal of Human Evolution*, 117, 33–43.

Beyene, Y., Katoh, S., WoldeGabriel, G., et al. (2013). The characteristics and chronology of the earliest Acheulean at Konso, Ethiopia. *Proceedings of the National Academy of Sciences USA*, 110(5), 1584–91.

Binant, P. (1991). *Les sépultures du Paléolithique*. Paris: Errance.

Blain, H. A., Gleed-Owen, C. P., López-García, J. M., et al. (2013). Climatic conditions for the last Neanderthals: Herpetofaunal record of Gorham's Cave, Gibraltar. *Journal of Human Evolution*, 64(4), 289–99.

Bobe, R. and Behrensmeyer, A. K. (2004). The expansion of grassland ecosystems in Africa in relation to mammalian evolution and the origin of the genus *Homo*. *Palaeogeography, Palaeoclimatology and Palaeoecology*, 207, 399–420.

Boëda, E., Hou, Y.-M., Huang, W.-B. (2011). Introduction in the study of Longgupo site (introduction à l'étude du site de Longgupo). *L'Anthropologie*, 115(1), 8–22.

Boivin, N. L., Zeder, M. A., Fuller, D. Q., et al. (2016). Ecological consequences of human niche construction: Examining long-term anthropogenic shaping of global distributions. *Proceedings of the National Academy of Sciences USA*, 113(23), 6388–6396.

Bordes, F. (1961). Typologie du Paléolithique ancien et moyen. l'Université de Bordeaux: Imprimerie Delmas.

Bourgeon, L., Burke, A. and, Higham, T. (2017). Earliest human presence in North America dated to the last glacial màximum: New radiocarbon dates from Bluefish Caves, Canada. *PLoS One*, 12(1): e0169486, doi: 10.1371/journal.pone.0169486

Boyd, R. and Richardson, P. J. (1985). *Culture and the Evolutionary Process*. Chicago: University of Chicago Press.

Brace, L. (2004). *The Politics of Property: Labour, Freedom and Belonging*. Edinburgh: Edinburgh University Press.

Bradley, B. and Stanford, D. (2004). The North Atlantic ice-edge corridor: A possible Palaeolithic route to the New World. *World Archaeology*, 36(4), 459–78.

Brain, C. K. and Sillent, A. (1988). Evidence from the Swartkrans Cave for the earliest use of fire. *Nature*, 336(6198), 464–66.

Braun, D. R., Aldeias, V., Archer, W., et al. (2019). Earliest known Oldowan artifacts at >2.58 Ma from Ledi-Geraru, Ethiopia, highlight early technological diversity. *Proceedings of the National Academy of Sciences USA*, 116(24), 11712–17.

Breasted, J. H. (1916). *Ancient Times, a History of the Early World: An Introduction to the Study of Ancient History and the Career of Early Man*. Boston: Ginn.

Broom, R. (1938). The Pleistocene anthropoid apes of South Africa. *Nature*, 142, 377–79.

Brown, P., Sutikana, T., Morwood, M. J., et al. (2004). A new small-bodied hominin from the Late Pleistocene of Flores, Indonesia. *Nature*, 431(7012), 1055–61.

Bruner, E., Manzi, G. and Arsuaga, J. L. (2003). Encephalization and allometric trajectories in the genus *Homo*: Evidence from the Neandertal and modern lineages. *Proceedings of the National Academy of Sciences of the USA*, 100(26), 15335–40.

Brunet, M., Beauvilain, A., Coppens, Y., et al. (1995). The first australopithecine 2,500 kilometers west of the Rift Valley (Chad). *Nature*, 378, 273–75.

Brunet, M., Guy, F., Pilbeam, D., et al. (2002). A new hominid from the Upper Miocene of Chad, Central Africa. *Nature*, 418(6894), 145–51.

Bunn, H. T. and Pickering, T. R. (2010). Bovid mortality profiles in paleoecological context falsify hypotheses of endurance running-hunting and passive scavenging by early Pleistocene hominins. *Quaternary Research*, 74(3), 395–404.

Cáceres, I., Lozano, M. and Saladié, P. (2007). Evidence for Bronze Age Cannibalism in El Mirador Cave (Sierra de Atapuerca, Burgos, Spain). *American Journal of Physical Anthropology*, 133(3), 899–917.

Carbonell, E., Barsky, D., Bermúdez de Castro, J. M. and Sala Ramos, R. (2018). Archaic lithic industries: Structural homogeneity. *Journal of Historical Archaeology & Anthropological Sciences*, 3(2), 199–203.

Carbonell, E., Barsky, D., Sala, R. and Celiberti, V. (2009). In E. Hovers and D. Braun, eds., *Interdisciplinary Approaches to the Oldowan*. Dordrecht: Springer, 25–37.

Carbonell, E., Bermúdez de Castro, J. M., Arsuaga, J. L., et al. (2005). An early Pleistocene hominin mandible from Atapuerca-TD6, Spain. *Proceedings of the National Academy of Sciences USA*, 102(16), 5674–78.

Carbonell, E., Bermúdez de Castro, J. M., Arsuaga, J. L., et al. (1995). Lower Pleistocene hominids and artifacts from Atapuerca-TD6 (Spain). *Science*, 269(5225), 826–30.

Carbonell, E., Bermúdez de Castro, J. M., Parés, J. M., et al. (2008). The first hominin of Europe. *Nature*, 452(7186), 465–69.

Carbonell, E. and Hortolà, P. (2013). Hominization and humanization, two key concepts for understanding our species. *Revista Atlàntica-Mediterrànea de Prehistoria y Arqueología Social*, 15, 7–11.

Carbonell, E. and Mosquera, M. (2006). The emergence of symbolic behavior: The sepulchral pit of Sima de los Huesos, Sierra de Atapuerca, Burgos, Spain. *Comptes Rendus Palevol*, 5(1-2), 155–60.

Carbonell, E., Mosquera, M., Ollé, A., et al. (1992). New elements of the logical analytical system. *Cahier Noir 6*.Tarragona: Reial Societat Arqueològica Tarraconense.

Caruana, M. V., Carvalho, S., Braun, D. R., et al. (2014). Quantifying traces of tool use: A novel morphometric analysis of damage patterns on percussive tools. *PLoS ONE*, 9(11), e113856.

Castles, S. (2002). International migration at the beginning of the twenty-first century: Global trends and issues. *International Social Science Journal*, 52(165), 269–81.

Castro-Curel, Z. and Carbonell, E. (1995). Wood pseudomorphs from Level I at Abric Romani, Barcelona, Spain. *Journal of Field Archaeology*, 22(3), 376–84.

Cavalli-Sforza, L. L. and Feldman, M. W. (1981). *Cultural Transmission and Evolution: A Quantitative Approach*. Princeton: Princeton University Press.

Challis, D. (2014). "Speculative Phase" of Archaeology. In C. Smith, ed., *Encyclopedia of Global Archaeology*. New York: Springer.

Chaplin, G., Jablonski, N. G. and Cable, N. T. (1994). Physiology, thermoregulation and bipedalism. *Journal of Human Evolution*, 27(6), 497–510.

Chauhan, P. R., Bridgeland, D. R., Moncel, M.-H., et al. (2017). Fluvial deposits as an archive of early human activity: Progress during the 20 years of the Fluvial Archives Group. *Quaternary Science Reviews*, 166, 114–49.

Chazan, M. (2017). Toward a long prehistory of fire. *Current Anthropology*, 58(16), S351–59.

Childe, G. (1936). *Man Makes Himself*. London: Watts.

Clark, J. D. and Harris, J. W. K. (1985). Fire and its roles in early hominid lifeways. *The African Archaeological Review*, 3, 3–27.

Clarke, R. J. and Tobias, P. V. (1995). Sterkfontein Member 2 foot bones of the oldest South African hominid. *Science*, 269(5223), 521–24.

Clarkson, C., Jacobs, Z., Marwick, B., et al. (2017). Human occupation of northern Australia by 65,000 years ago. *Nature*, 547, 306–10.

Clottes, J.-M., Chauvet, E., Brunel-Deschamps, C., et al. (1995). Les peintures paléolithiques de la grotte Chauvet–Pont-d'Arc à Vallon-Pont- d'Arc (Ardèche, France): datations directes et indirectes par la méthode du radiocarbone. Comptes Rendus de l'Académie des Sciences de Paris, 320, (IIa), 50, 1133–40.

Cnuts, D., Tomasso, S. and Rots, V. (2017). The role of fire in the life of an adhesive. *Journal of Archaeological Method and Theory*, 25(4) 839–62.

Coppens, Y. (1994). East side story: The origin of humankind. *Scientific American*, 270(5), 88–95.

Cosgrove, K. P., Mazure, C. M. and Staley, J. K. (2007). Evolving knowledge of sex differences in brain structure, function and chemistry. *Biological Psychiatry*, 62(8), 847–55.

Crutzen, P. J. and Stoermer, E. F. (2000). The Anthropocene. *Global Change Newsletter*, 41, 17–18.

Dalley, S., ed. (2000). *Myths from Mesopotamia: Creation, the Flood, Gilgamesh, and Others*. Oxford: Oxford University Press.

Dannemann, M., Andrés, A. and Kelso, J. (2016). Introgression of Neandertal- and Denisovan-like Haplotypes contributes to adaptive variation in human toll-like receptors. *The American Journal of Human Genetics*, 98(1), 22–33.

Dart, R. (1925). *Australopithecus africanus*: The man-ape of South Africa. Nature, 115(2884), 195–99.

Dart, R. A. and Beaumont, P. (1969). Evidence of iron ore mining in southern Africa in the Middle Stone Age. *Current Anthropology*, 10(1), 127–28.

Darwin, C. (1859). *On the Origin of Species by Means of Natural Selection*. London: John Murray.

Darwin, C. R. (1871). *The Descent of Man, and Selection in Relation to Sex*. Vol. I. London: John Murray.

Dawkins, R. (2006). *The God Delusion*. London: Bantam Books.

Defleur, A. (1993). *Les Sépultures Moustériennes*. Paris: CNRS Editions.

De la Torre, I., Benito-Calvo, A. Arroyo, A. Zupancich, A. and Proffitt, T. (2013). Experimental protocols for the study of battered stone anvils from Olduvai Gorge (Tanzania). *Journal of Archaeological Science*, 40(1), 313–32.

de Sonneville-Bordes, D. (1953). Essai d'adaptation des méthodes statistiques au Paléolithique supérieur. Premiers résultats. *Bulletin de la Société Préhistorique Française*, 50(5-6), 323–33.

Despriée, J., Courcimault, G., Moncel, M.-H., et al. (2016). The Acheulean site of la Noira (Centre region, France): Characterization of materials and alterations, choice of lacustrine millstone and evidence of anthropogenic behavior. *Quaternary International*, 411(Part B), 144–59.

Détroit, F., Mijares, A. S., Corny, J., et al. (2019). A new species of *Homo* from the Late Pleistocene of the Philippines. *Nature*, 568(7751), 181–86.

Diamond, J. (1999, May). The worst mistake in the history of the human race. www.discovermagazine .com/planet-earth/the-worst-mistake-in-the-history-of-the-human-race

Diamond, J. (1997). *Guns, Germs and Steel. A short history of everybody for the last 13,000 years*. New York: W. W. Norton.

Dibble, H. L., Aldeias, V., Goldberg, P., et al. (2015). A critical look at evidence from La Chapelle-aux-Saints supporting an intentional burial. *Journal of Archaeological Science*, 53, 649–57.

Dietrich, O. (2011). Radiocarbon dating the first temples of mankind. Comments on 14C-Dates from Göbekli Tepe. *Zeitschrift für Orient-Archäologie*, 4, 12–25.

Domínguez-Rodrigo, M., Bunn, H. T. and Yravedra, J. (2014). A critical re-evaluation of bone surface modification models for inferring fossil hominin and carnivore interactions through a multivariate approach: Application to the FLK Zinj archaeofaunal assemblage (Olduvai Gorge, Tanzania). *Quaternary International*, 322–23, 32–43.

Doughty, C. E., Wolf, A. and Field, C. B. (2010). Biophysical feedbacks between the Pleistocene megafauna extinction and climate: The first human-induced global warming? *Geophysical Research Letters*, 37(15), L15703.

Duarte, C., Mauricio, J., Pettitt, P. B., et al. (1999). The Early Upper Paleolithic human skeleton from the Abrigo do Lagar Velho (Portugal), and modern human emergence in Iberia. *Proceedings of the National Academy of Sciences USA*, 96(13), 7604–9.

Duval, M., Aubert, M., Hellstrom, J. and Grün, R. (2011). High resolution LA-ICP-MS mapping of U and Th isotopes in an early Pleistocene equid tooth from Fuente Nueva-3 (Orce, Andalusia, Spain). *Quaternary Geochronology*, 6, 458–67.

Duval, M., Falguères, C., Bahain, J.-J., et al. (2012). On the limits of using combined U-series/ESR method to date fossil teeth from two Early Pleistocene archaeological sites of the Orce area (Guadix-Baza basin, Spain). *Quaternary Research*, 77(3), 482–91.

Duval, M., Grün, R., Parés, J. M., et al. (2018). The first direct ESR dating of a hominin tooth from Atapuerca Gran Dolina (Spain) supports the antiquity of *Homo antecessor*. *Quaternary Geochronology*, 47, 120–37.

Eller, J. D. (2009). *Defining Culture*. New York: Routledge.

Eshed, V. and Gopher, A. (2018). Agriculture and life style: A paleodemography of Pottery Neolithic (8500–6500 cal. BP) farming populations in the Southern Levant. *Paléorient*, 44(2): 93–111.

Falguères, C., Shao, Q., Han, F., et al. (2015). New ESR and U-Series dating at the Caune de l'Arago, France: A key-site for European Middle Pleistocene. *Quaternary Geochronology*, 30, 547–53.

Falguères, C., Yokoyama, Y., Shen, G., et al. (2004). New U-series dates at the Caune de l'Arago, France. *Journal of Archaeological Science*, 31(7), 941–52.

Ferring, R., Oms, O., Agustí, J., et al. (2011). Earliest human occupations at Dmanisi (Georgian Caucasus) dated to 1.85-1.778 Ma. *Proceedings of the National Academy of Sciences USA*, 108(26), 10432–36.

Fiacconi, M. and Hunt, C. O. (2015). Pollen taphonomy at Shanidar Cave (Kurdish Iraq): An initial evaluation. *Review of Palaeobotany and Palynology*, 223, 87–93.

Finlayson, C. (2019). *The Smart Neanderthal*. Oxford: Oxford University Press.

Finlayson, C. (2008). On the importance of coastal areas in the survival of Neanderthal populations during the late Pleistocene. *Quaternary Science Reviews*, 27(23-24), 2246–52.

Finlayson, C., Brown, K., Blasco, R., et al. (2012). Birds of a feather: Neandertal exploitation of raptors and corvids. *PLoS ONE*, 7(9), e45927.

Firestone, R. B., West, A., Kennett, J. P., et al. (2007). Evidence for an extraterrestrial impact 12,900 years ago that contributed to the megafaunal extinctions and the Younger Dryas cooling. *Proceedings of the National Academy of Sciences USA*, 104(41), 16016–21.

Ford, A. (2010). *Information Feedback and Causal Loop Diagrams. Modeling the Environment*. Washington, DC: Island Press.

Friedman, R. (2014). *Violence and Climate Change in Prehistoric Egypt and Sudan* (blog). https://blog .britishmuseum.org/violence-and-climate-change-in-prehistoric-egypt-and-sudan/. Accessed October 24, 2021.

Friesem, D. E., Zaidner, Y. and Shahack-Gross, R. (2014). Formation processes and combustion features at the lower layers of the Middle Palaeolithic open-air site of Nesher Ramla, Israel. *Quaternary International*, 331, 128–38.

Fuhlrott, J. C. (1857). Verh. naturhist. Ver. preuss. Rhineland 14, Corr. Bl., 50.

Fuller, D., van Etten, J., Manning, K., et al. (2011). The contribution of rice agriculture and livestock pastoralism to prehistoric methane levels: An archaeological assessment. *The Holocene*, 21(5), 743–59.

Gabunia, L., Lumley, M. A. de, Vekua, A., Lordkipanidze, D. and Lumley, H. de. (2002). Discovery of a new hominid at Dmanisi (Transcaucasia, Georgia). *Comptes Rendus Palevol*, 1(4), 243–53.

Gabunia, L., Vekua, A., Lordkipanidze, D., et al. (2000). Earliest Pleistocene hominid cranial remains from Dmanisi, Republic of Georgia: Taxonomy, geological setting, and age. *Science*, 288(5468), 1019–25.

Gao, X., Zhang, S., Zhang, Y. and Chen, F. (2017). Evidence of hominin use and maintenance of fire at Zhoukoudian. *Current Anthropology*, 58(16), 267–77.

García-Medrano, P., Cácares, I., Ollé, A. and Carbonell, E. (2017). The occupational pattern of the Galería site (Atapuerca, Spain): A technological perspective. *Quaternary International*, 433(Part A), 363–78.

Gaudzinski, S., Turner, E., Anzidei, A. P., et al. (2005). The use of Proboscidean remains in every-day Palaeolithic life. *Quaternary International*, 126–28, 179–94.

Gibert, C. J. (1999). The Hominids and their environment during Lower and Middle Pleistocene of Eurasia (Orce, 1995). In J. Gibert, F. Sánchez, L. Gibert and F. Ribot, eds., *Proceedings of the International Congress of Human Paleontology*. Baza: Imprenta Cervantes, 72.

Goodall, J. (with Phillip Berman). (1999). *Reason for Hope: A Spiritual Journey*. New York: Warner Books.

Goodall, J. (1990). *Through a Window: My Thirty Years with the Chimpanzees of Gombe*. Boston: Houghton Mifflin.

Goodman, A. H., Lallo, J., Armelagos, G. J. and Rose, J. C. (1984). Health changes at Dickson Mounds, Illinois (A.D. 950–1300). In M. N. Cohen and G. J. Armelagos, eds., *Paleopathology and the Origins of Agriculture*. New York: Academic Press, 271–305.

Goren-Inbar, N., Alperson, N., Kislev, M. E., et al. (2004). Evidence of hominin control of fire at Gesher Benot Ya'aqov, Israel. *Science*, 304(5671), 725–27.

Gould, S. J. (1989). *Wonderful Life. The Burgess Shale and the Nature of History*. New York: W. W. Norton.

Gowlett, J. A. J. (2016). The discovery of fire by humans: A long and convoluted process. *Philosophical Transactions B of the Royal Society*, 371(20150164).

Gowlett, J. A. J., Harris, J. W. K., Walton, D. and Wood, B. A. (1981). Early archaeological sites, hominid remains and traces of fire from Chesowanja, Kenya. *Nature*, 294, 125–29.

Gracia, A., Arsuaga, J. L., Martínez, I., et al. (2009). Craniosynostosis in the Middle Pleistocene human Cranium 14 from the Sima de los Huesos, Atapuerca, Spain. *Proceedings of the National Academy of Sciences USA*, 106(16), 6573–78.

Gravina, B., Bachellerie, F., Caux, S., et al. (2018). No reliable evidence for a Neandertal-Châtelperronian association at La Roche-à-Pierrot, Saint-Césaire. *Scientific Reports*, 8(15134), 1–12.

Green, R. E., Krause, J., Briggs, A. W., et al. (2010). A draft sequence of the Neandertal Genome. *Science*, 328(5979), 710–22.

Green, R. E., Malaspinas, A. S., Krause, J., et al. (2008). A complete Neandertal mitochondrial genome sequence determined by high-throughput sequencing. *Cell*, 134(3), 416–26.

Grosman, L. (2013). The Natufian chronology scheme – New Insights and their implications. In O. Bar-Yosef and F. R. Valla, eds., *Natufian Foragers in the Levant*. Ann Arbor, MI: International Monographs in Prehistory, 122.

Grosman, L., and Munro, N. D. (2017). The Natufian culture and the threshold for early farming. In Y. Enzel and O. Bar-Yosef, eds., *Quaternary of the Levant: Environments, Climate Change and Humans*. Cambridge: Cambridge University Press, 699–708.

Haile-Selassie, Y. (2001). Late Miocene hominids from the Middle Awash, Ethiopia. *Nature*, 412 (6843), 178–81.

Haile-Selassie, Y., Melillo, S. M., Vazzana, A., Benazzi, S. and Ryan, T. M. (2019). A 3.8-million-year-old hominin cranium from Woranso-Mille, Ethiopia. *Nature*, 573, 214–19.

Haile-Selassie, Y., Suwa, G. and White, T. D. (2004). Late Miocene teeth from Middle Awash, Ethiopia, and early hominid dental evolution. *Science*, 303(5663), 1503–5.

Harari, Y. N. (2016). *Homo Deus. A Brief History of Tomorrow*. London: Harvill Secker.

Harmand, S., Lewis, J. E., Feibel, C. S., et al. (2015). 3.3-million-year-old stone tools from Lomekwi 3, West Turkana, Kenya. *Nature*, 521(7552), 310–15.

Harvati, K., Röding, C., Bosman, A. M., et al. (2019). Apidima Cave fossils provide earliest evidence of *Homo sapiens* in Eurasia. *Nature*, 571(7766), 500–4.

Hay, R. L. (1976). *Geology of the Olduvai Gorge*. Berkeley: University of California Press.

Henshilwood, C. S., d'Errico, F., van Niekerk, K. L., et al. (2011). A 100,000-year-old ochre processing workshop at Blombos Cave, South Africa. *Science*, 334(6053), 219–22.

Henshilwood, C. S., d'Errico, F. and Watts, I. (2009). Engraved ochres from the Middle Stone Age levels at Blombos Cave, South Africa. *Journal of Human Evolution*, 57(1), 27–47.

Herman, E. S. and Chomsky, N. (1988). *Manufacturing Consent. The Political Economy of the Mass Media*. New York: Pantheon Books.

Herries, A. I. R. and Shaw, J. (2011). Palaeomagnetic analysis of the Sterkfontein palaeocave deposits: Implications for the age of the hominin fossils and stone tool industries. *Journal of Human Evolution*, 60 (5) 523–39.

Hershkovitz, I., May, H., Sarig, R., et al. (2021). A Middle Pleistocene Homo from Nesher Ramla, Israel. *Science*, 372(6549), 1424–28.

Hershkovitz, I., Weber, G. H., Quam, R., et al. (2018). The earliest modern humans outside Africa. *Science*, 359(6374), 456–459.

Hirst, K. K. (2018). Natufian period – Hunter-Gatherer ancestors of pre-pottery Neolithic. www.thoughtco.com/ohalo-ii-israel-paleolithic-site-172038

Hoffmann, D. L., Standish, C. D., García-Diez, M., et al. (2018). U-Th dating of carbonate crusts reveals Neandertal origin of Iberian cave art. *Science*, 359(6378), 912–15.

Holen, S. R., Deméré, T. A., Fisher, D. C., et al. (2017). A 130,000 year-old archaeological site in Southern California, USA. *Nature*, 544(7651), 479–83.

Holloway R. (1996). Evolution of the Human Brain. In E. A. Lock and C. R. Peters, eds., *Handbook of Human Symbolic Evolution*. Oxford: Clarendon Press, 74–116.

Houldcroft, C. J. and Underdown, S. J. (2016). Neanderthal genomics suggests a Pleistocene timeframe for the first epidemiologic transmission. *American Journal of Physical Anthropology*, 160(3), 379–88.

Howell, F. C. Haesaerts, P. and de Heinzelin, J. (1987). Depositional environments, archeological occurrences, and hominids from Members E and F of the Shungura Formation (Omo Basin, Ethiopia). *Journal of Human Evolution*, 16(7-8), 665–700.

Hublin, J.-J. (2013). The Middle Pleistocene record. On the origin of Neanderthals, modern humans and others. In R. D. Begun, ed., *A Companion to Paleoanthropology*. Hoboken: Wiley-Blackwell, 517–37.

Hublin, J.-J. (2009). The prehistory of compassion. *Proceedings of the National Academy of Sciences, USA*, 106 (16), 6429–30.

Hublin, J.-J., Ben-Ncer, A., Bailey, S., et al. (2017). New fossils from Jebel Irhoud, Morocco and the pan-African origin of *Homo sapiens*. *Nature*, 546(7657), 289–92.

Huguet, R., Vallverdú, J., Rodríguez-Álvarez, X. P., et al. (2015). Level TE9c of Sima del Elefante (Sierra de Atapuerca, Spain): A comprehensive approach. *Quaternary International*, 433(Part A), 278–95.

Jacobs, Z., Jones, B. G., Cawthra, H. C., Henshilwood, C. S. and Roberts, R. G. (2019). The chronological, sedimentological and environmental context for the archaeological deposits at Blombos Cave, South Africa. *Quaternary Science Reviews*, 235(105850), 1–22.

Johanson, D. C. and Taieb, M. (1976). Plio-Pleistocene hominid discoveries in Hadar. *Nature*, 260 (5549), 293–97.

Johanson, D. C., White, T. D. and Coppens, Y. (1978). A new species of the genus *Australopithecus* (Primates: Hominidae) from the Pliocene of Eastern Africa. *Kirtlandia*, 28, 2–14.

Karkanas, P., Shahack-Gross, R., Ayalon, A., et al. (2007). Evidence for habitual use of fire at the end of the Lower Paleolithic: Site-formation processes at Qesem Cave, Israel. *Journal of Human Evolution*, 53 (2), 197–212.

Kolbert, E. (2014). *The Sixth Extinction. An Unnatural History*. New York: Bloomsbury.

Kortlandt, A. (1972). *New Perspectives on Ape and Human Evolution*. Amsterdam: Stichting voor Psychobiologie.

Krause, J., Fu, Q., Good, J. M., et al. (2010). The complete mitochondrial DNA genome of an unknown hominin from southern Siberia. *Nature*, 464(7290), 894–97.

Krings, M., Stone, A., Schmitz, R. W., et al. (1997). Neandertal DNA sequences and the origin of modern humans. *Cell*, 90(1), 19–30.

Kuhlwilm, M., Gronau, I., Hubisz, M. J., et al. (2016). Ancient gene flow from early modern humans into Eastern Neanderthals. *Nature*, 530(7591), 429–33.

Kuman, K. and Clarke, R. J. (2000). Stratigraphy, artefact industries and hominid associations for Sterkfontein Member 5. *Journal of Human Evolution*, 38(6), 827–47.

Lahr, M. M., Rivera, F., Power, R. K., et al. (2016). Inter-group violence among early Holocene hunter-gatherers of West Turkana. *Nature*, 529(7586), 394–98.

Laplace, G. (1972). La typologie analytique et structurale: base rationnelle d'étude des industries lithiques et osseuses. *Banques de données archéologiques. Colloques Nationaux du CNRS*. Paris: CNRS Editions, 92–143.

Leach, H. M. (2003). Human domestication reconsidered. *Current Anthropology*, 44(3), 349–68.

Leakey, L. S. B. (1959). A new fossil skull from Olduvai. *Nature*, 184(4685), 491–94.

Leakey, L. S. B., Evernden, J. F. and Curtis, G. H. (1961). The age of Bed I, Olduvai Gorge, Tanganyika. *Nature*, 191, 478–79.

Leakey, M. D. (1971). *Olduvai Gorge: Volume 3, Excavations in Beds I and II, 1960–1963*. Cambridge, UK: Cambridge University Press.

Leakey, M. D. and Hay, R. L. (1979). Pliocene footprints in the Laetoli beds at Laetoli, northern Tanzania. *Nature*, 278, 317–23.

Leakey, M. G., Feibel, C. S., McDougall, I. and Walker, A. (1995). New four-million-year-old hominid species from Kanapoi and Allia Bay, Kenya. *Nature*, 376(6541), 565–71.

Leakey, M. G., Feibel, C. S., McDougall, I., Ward, C. and Walker, A. (1998). New specimens and confirmation of an early age for *Australopithecus anamensis*. *Nature*, 393(6680), 62–66.

Leakey, M. G., Spoor, F., Brown, F. H., et al. (2001). New hominin genus from eastern Africa shows diverse Middle Pliocene lineages. *Nature*, 410(6827), 433–40.

Lebreton, L., Desclaux, E., Hanquet, C., Moigne, A.-M. and Perrenoud, C. (2015). Environmental context of the Caune de l'Arago Acheulian occupations (Tautavel, France), new insights from microvertebrates in Q-R levels. *Quaternary International*, 411 (Part B), 182–92.

Legge, M. M. and Robinson, M. (2017). Animals in indigenous spiritualities: Implications for critical social work. *Journal of Indigenous Social Development*, 6(1), 1–20.

Lepre, C. J., Roche, H., Kent, D. V., et al. (2011). An earlier origin for the Acheulian. *Nature*, 477 (7362), 82–85.

Leroi-Gourhan, A. (1988). *Dictionnaire de la préhistoire*. Paris: Presses universitaires de France.

Leroi-Gourhan, A. (1943). *L'Homme et la Matière*. Paris: A. Michel.

Li, H., Kuman, K., Lotter, M. G., Leader, G. M. and Gibbon, R. J. (2017). The Victoria West: Earliest prepared core technology in the Acheulean at Canteen Kopje and implications for the cognitive evolution of early hominids. *Royal Society Open Science*, 4, 170288.

Lieberman, D. E. (2015). Human locomotion and heat loss: An evolutionary perspective. *Comprehensive Physiology*, 5(1), 99–117.

Lordkipanidze, D., Vekua, A., Ferring, R., et al. (2005). The earliest toothless hominin skull. *Nature*, 434(7034), 717–18.

Lovejoy, O., Suwa, G., Spurlock, L. B., Asfaw, B. and White, T. D. (2009). The pelvis and femur of *Ardipithecus ramidus*: The emergence of upright walking. *Science*, 326(5949), 71–71e6.

Lumley, H. de. (2015). *Caune de l'Arago Tome VI Tautavel-en-Roussillon, Pyrénées-Orientales, France: Individualisation des unités archéostratigraphiques*. Paris: CNRS Editions.

Lumley, H. de. (2014). *Caune de l'Arago Tome I Tautavel-en-Roussillon Pyrénées-Orientales, France*. Paris: CNRS Editions.

Lumley, H. de. (2006). Il y a 400 000 ans : la domestication du feu, un formidable moteur d'hominisation. *Comptes Rendus Palevol*, 5(1-2), 149–54.

Lumley, H. de and Barsky, D. (2004). Evolution of the technological and typological characteristics of the stone tool assemblage from the Caune de l'Arago Cave. *L'Anthropologie*, 108(2), 185–237.

Lumley, H. de and Beyene, Y., eds. (2004). *Les sites préhistoriques de la région de Fejej, Sud-Omo, Éthiopie, dans leur contexte stratigraphique et paléontologique. Association pour la diffusion de la pensée française (ADPF)*. Paris: Editions Recherche sur les civilisations.

Lumley, H. de, Fournier, A., Krzepkowska, J. and Echassoux, A. (1988). L'industrie du Pléistocène inférieur de la grotte du Vallonnet, Roquebrune-Cap-Martin, Alpes- Maritimes. *L'Anthropologie*, 92 (2), 501–614.

Lumley, H. de, Fournier, A., Park, Y. C., Yokoyama, Y., and Demouy, A. (1984). Stratigraphie du remplissage pléistocène moyen de la Caune de l'Arago à Tautavel. Étude de huit carottages effectués de 1981 à 1983. *L'Anthropologie*, 88(1), 5–18.

Lumley, H. de, Nioradzé, M., Barsky, D., et al. (2005). Les industries lithiques préoldowayennes du début du Pléistocène inférieur du site de Dmanisi en Géorgie. *L'Anthropologie*, 109(1), 1–182.

Lumley, H. de and Tianyuan, L., eds. (2008). *Le site de l'homme de Yunxian: Quyuanhekou, Quingqu, Yunxian, Province de Hubei*. Paris: CNRS Editions.

Lumley, M. A. de. (2015). L'homme de Tautavel. Un Homo erectus européen evolué. *Homo erectus tautavelensis. L'Anthropologie*, 119(3), 303–48.

Lumley, M.-A. de. (2006). L'Homme de Dmanisi (*Homo georgicus*), il y a 1 810 000 ans. *Comptes Rendus Palevol*, 5(1-2), 273–81.

Malthus, T. R. (1826). *An Essay on the Principle of Population: A View of Its Past and Present Effects on Human Happiness*, 6th ed. London: John Murray.

Marro, C., Bakhshaliyev, V. and Sanz, S. (2010). Archaeological investigations on the salt mine of Duzdagi (Nakhchivan, Azerbaijan). *TÜBA-AR*, 13(13), 229–244.

Martin, P. S. (1989). Prehistoric overkill: A global model. In P. S. Martin and R. G. Klein, eds., *Quaternary Extinctions: A Prehistoric Revolution*. Tucson: University of Arizona Press, 354–404. https://commons.wikimedia.org/wiki/Special:BookSources/0-8165-1100-4

Martínez, I., Arsuaga, J. L., Quam, R., et al. (2018). Human hyoid bones from the Middle Pleistocene site of the Sima de los Huesos (Sierra de Atapuerca, Spain). *Journal of Human Evolution*, 54(1), 118–24.

Martínez, I., Rosa-Zurera, M., Quam, R., et al. (2012). Communicative capacities in Middle Pleistocene humans from the Sierra de Atapuerca in Spain. *Quaternary International*, 295, 94–101.

Martínez-Navarro, B., Turq, A., Agustí, J. and Oms, O. (1997). Fuente Nueva-3 (Orce, Granada, Spain) and the first human occupation of Europe. *Journal of Human Evolution*, 33(5), 611–20.

Martinón-Torres, M., Bermúdez de Castro, J. M., Martínez de Pinillos, M., et al. (2019). New permanent teeth from Gran Dolina-TD6 (Sierra de Atapuerca): The bearing of Homo antecessor on the evolutionary scenario of Early and Middle Pleistocene Europe. *Journal of Human Evolution*, 127, 93–117.

Marx, K. (1867). *Das Kapital: Kritik der politischen Oekonomie*, Vol. I, 2nd ed. Hamburg: Verlag von Otto Meissner.

Marx, K. and Engels, F. (1975). *Marx-Engels Collected Works (MECW)*, Vol. XL Letters1856–1859. Moscow: Progress Publishers. First published 1922 by F. Lassalle. Nachgelassene Briefe und Schriften, Stuttgart-Berlin.

Meignen, L., Goldberg, P. and Bar-Yosef, O. (2007). The hearths at Kebara Cave and their role in site formation processes. InO. Bar-Yosef and L. Meignen, eds., *Kebara Cave, Mt. Carmel, Israel: The Middle and Upper Paleolithic archaeology*, American School of Prehistoric Research, Bulletin 49. Cambridge, MA: Peabody Museum of Archaeology and Ethnology, Harvard University, 91–122.

Mellars, P. and Stringer, C. B., eds. (1989). *The Human Revolution: Behavioural and Biological Perspectives on the Origins of Modern Humans*. Edinburgh: Edinburgh University Press.

Mendel, G. (1869). Ueber einige aus künstlicher Befruchtung gewonnenen Hieracium-Bastarde (On Hieracium hybrids obtained by artificial fertilisation). Verhandlungen des naturforschenden Vereines. Brünn: Abhandlungen, 26–31.

Mesoudi, A., Whiten, A. and Laland, K. N. (2006). *Towards a Unified Science of Cultural Evolution*. Behavioral and Brain Sciences 29. Cambridge: Cambridge University Press, 329–83.

Meyer, C., Lohr, C., Gronenborn, D. and Alt, K. W. (2015). The massacre mass grave of Schöneck-Kilianstädten reveals new insights into collective violence in Early Neolithic Central Europe. *Proceedings of the National Academy of Sciences USA*, 112(36), 11217–22.

Meyer, M., Arsuaga, J., de Filippo, C., et al. (2016). Nuclear DNA sequences from the Middle Pleistocene Sima de los Huesos hominins. *Nature*, 531(7595), 504–7.

Michel, V., Shen, C.-C., Woodhead, J., et al. (2017). New dating evidence of the early presence of hominins in Southern Europe. *Scientific Reports*, 7(10074), doi: 10.1038/s41598–017-10178-4

Moigne, A.-M., Palombo, M. R., Belda, V., et al. (2006). An interpretation of a large mammal fauna from la Caune de l'Arago (France) in comparison to a Middle Pleistocene biochronological frame from Italy. *L'Anthropologie*, 110(5), 788–831.

Monnier, G. F. and Bischoff, E. (2014). Size matters. An evaluation of descriptive and metric criteria for identifying cut marks made by unmodified rocks during butchery. *Journal of Archaeological Science*, 50, 305–317.

Morgan, T. J. H., Rendell, L. E., Chouinard-Thyly, L., et al. (2015). Experimental evidence for the co-evolution of hominin tool-making teaching and language. *Nature Communications*, 6(6029), doi: 10.1038/ncomms7029

Morwood, M. J., Soejono, R. P., Roberts, R. G., et al. (2004). Archaeology and age of a new hominin from Flores in eastern Indonesia. *Nature*, 431(7012), 1087–91.

Nigro, L. (2014). An absolute Iron Age chronology of the Levant and the Mediterranean. *ROSAPAT*, 11, 261–69.

Nunn, P. D. (2002). On the convergence of myth and reality: Examples from the Pacific Islands. *The Geographical Journal*, 167(2), 125–38.

Okerblom, J., Fletes, W., Patel, H. H., et al. (2018). Human-like Cmah inactivation in mice increases running endurance and decreases muscle fatigability: Implications for human evolution. *Proceedings of the Royal Society B*, 285(1886), 20181656.

Ollé, A., Mosquera, M., Rodríguez, X. P., et al. (2013). The Early and Middle Pleistocene technological record from Sierra de Atapuerca (Burgos, Spain). *Quaternary International*, 295, 138–67.

Olszewski, D. (2008). *Mesolithic Cultures. Encyclopedia of Archaeology*. New York: Elsevier Academic Press, 848–53.

Oms, O., Agustí, J., Gabàs, M. and Anadón, P. (2000a). Lithostratigraphical correlation of micromammal sites and biostratigraphy of the Upper Pliocene to Lower Pleistocene in the Northeast Guadix-Baza Basin. *Journal of Quaternary Science*, 15(1), 43–50.

Oms, O., Pareés, J. M., Martínez-Navarro, B., et al. (2000b). Early human occupation of Western Europe: Paleomagnetic dates for two Paleolithic sites in Spain. *Proceedings of the National Academy of Sciences USA*, 97(19), 10666–70.

Otte, M. (2019). Denisova and the Paleolithic traditions in Central Asia. *L'Anthropologie*, 123(2), 452–77.

Pablos, A., Gómez-Olivencia, A. and Arsuaga, J. L. (2018). A Neandertal foot phalanx from the Galería de las Estatuas site (Sierra de Atapuerca, Spain). *American Journal of Physical Anthropology*, 168(1), 222–28.

Pappu, S., Gunnell, Y., Akhilesh, K., et al. (2011). Early Pleistocene presence of Acheulean hominins in South India. *Science*, 331(6024), 1596–1599.

Parés, J. M. and Pérez-González, A. (1999). Magnetochronology and stratigraphy at Gran Dolina section, Atapuerca (Burgos, Spain). *Journal of Human Evolution*, 37(3/4), 325–42.

Parés, J. M., Pérez-González, A., Rosas, A., et al. (2006). Matuyama-age lithic tools from the Sima del Elefante site, Atapuerca (northern Spain). *Journal of Human Evolution*, 50(2), 163–69.

Parfitt, S. A., Ashton, N. M., Lewis, S. G., et al. (2010). Early Pleistocene human occupation at the edge of the boreal zone in northwest Europe. *Nature*, 466(7303), 229–33.

Peresani, M., Fiore, I., Gala, M., Romandini, M. and Tagliacozzo, A. (2011). Late neandertals and the intentional removal of feathers as evidenced from bird bone taphonomy at Fumane Cave 44 ky B.P., Italy. *Proceedings of the National Academy of Sciences USA*, 108(10), 3888–93.

Photos, E. (2010). The question of meteoritic versus smelted Nickel-rich iron: Archaeological evidence and experimental results. *World Archaeology*, 20(3), 403–21.

Pickford, M. and Senut, B. (2001). "Millennium Ancestor," a 6-million-year-old bipedal hominid from Kenya – Recent discoveries push back human origins by 1.5 million years. *South African Journal of Science*, 97(1-2), 22.

Pickford, M., Senut, B., Gommery, D. and Triel, J. (2002). Bipedalism in *Orrorin tugenensis* revealed by its femora. *Comptes Rendus Palevol*, 1(4), 191–203.

Pomeroy, E., Bennet, P., Hunt, C. O., et al. (2020). New Neanderthal remains associated with the "flower burial" at Shanidar Cave. *Antiquity*, 94(373), 11–26.

Potts, R. (1998). Variability selection in hominid evolution. *Evolutionary Anthropology*, 7(3), 81–96.

Potts, S. G., Neumann, P., Vaissière, B. and Vereecken, N. J. (2018). Robotic bees for crop pollination: Why drones cannot replace biodiversity. *Science of the Total Environmnent*, 642, 665–67.

Preece, R. C., Gowlett, J. A. J., Parfitt, S. A., Bridgland, D. R. and Lewis, S. G. (2006). Humans in the Hoxnian: Habitat, context and fire use at Beeches Pit, West Stow, Suffolk, UK. *Journal of Quaternary Science*, 21(5), 485–96.

Quammen, D. (2018). *The Tangled Tree of Life: A Radical New History of Life*. New York: Simon & Schuster.

Raby, P. (2002). *Alfred Russel Wallace: A Life*. Princeton: Princeton University Press.

Radovčić, D., Oros Sršen, A., Radovčić, J. and Frayer, D. W. (2015). Evidence for Neandertal jewelry: Modified White-tailed Eagle claws at Krapina. *PLos ONE*, 10(3), e0119802.

Ravon, A.-L. (2019). Early human occupations at the westernmost of Eurasia: The lithic industries from Menez-Dregan I (Plouhinec, Finistère, France). *Comptes Rendus Palevol*, 18(6), 663–84.

Reich, D., Green, R. E., Kircher, M., et al. (2010). Genetic history of an archaic hominin group from Denisova Cave in Siberia. *Nature*, 468, 1053–60.

Rendu, W., Beauval, C., Crevecoeur, I., et al. (2016). Let the dead speak... comments on Dibble et al.'s reply to "Evidence supporting an intentional burial at la Chapelle-aux-Saintes." *Journal of Archaeological Science*, 69, 12–20.

Renfrew, C. and Bahn, P. (2016). *Archaeology: Theories, Methods and Practice*, 7th ed. London: Thames and Hudson.

Reynolds, S. C., Bailey, G. N. and King, G. C. P. (2011). Landscapes and their relation to hominin habitats: Case studies from *Australopithecus* sites in eastern and southern Africa. *Journal of Human Evolution*, 60(3), 281–98.

Riel-Salvatore, J. and Gravel-Miguel, C. (2013). Upper Paleolithic mortuary practices in Eurasia: a critical look at the burial record. In S. Tarlow and Nilsson Stutz, eds., *The Oxford Handbook of Death and Burial*. Oxford: Oxford University Press, 303–46.

Rifkin, R. F. (2012). Processing ochre in the Middle Stone Age: Testing the inference of prehistoric behaviours from actualistically derived experimental data. *Journal of Anthropological Archaeology*, 31(2), 174–95.

Rightmire, G. P. (1998). Human evolution in the Middle Pleistocene: The role of *Homo heidelbergensis*. *Evolutionary Anthropology*, 6, 218–27.

Roche, D., Ségalen, L., Senut, B. and Pickford, M. (2013). Stable isotope analyses of tooth enamel carbonate of large herbivores from the Tugen Hills deposits: Palaeoenvironmental context of the earliest Kenyan hominids. *Earth and Planetary Science Letters*, 381, 39–51.

Rodman, P. S. and McHenry, H. M. (1980). Bioenergetics and the origin of hominid bipedalism. *American Journal of Physical Anthropology*, 52(1), 103–6.

Rodríguez, J., Burjachs, F., Cuenca-Bescós, G., et al. (2011). One million years of cultural evolution in a stable environment at Atapuerca (Burgos, Spain). *Quaternary Science Reviews*, 30(11-12), 1396–1412.

Rodríguez-Álvarez, X. P. and Lozano, S. (2018). Gender balance in the scientific production of the Atapuerca archaeological and palaeontological research project. *Journal of Anthropological Sciences*, 96, 1–8.

Rodríguez-Hidalgo, A., Morales, J. I., Cebrià, A., et al. (2019). The Châtelperronian Neandertals of Cova Foradada (Calafell, Spain), used imperial eagle phalanges for symbolic purposes. *Science Advances*, 5 (11), 1–11.

Rodríguez-Hidalgo, A., Saladié, P., Ollé, A., et al. (2017). Human predatory behavior and the social implications of communal hunting based on evidence from the TD10.2 bison bone bed at Gran Dolina (Atapuerca, Spain). *Journal of Human Evolution*, 105, 89–122.

Roebroeks, W. and Van Kolfschoten, T. (1994). The earliest occupation of Europe: A short chronology. *Antiquity*, 68(260), 489–503.

Roebrooks, W., Sier, M. J., Nielsen, T. K., et al. (2012). Use of red ochre by early Neandertals. *Proceedings of the National Academy of Sciences USA*, 109(6), 1889–94.

Roebrooks, W. and Villa, P. (2011). On the earliest evidence for habitual use of fire in Europe. *Proceedings of the National Academy of Sciences USA*, 108(13), 5209–14.

Rolland, N. (2004). Was the emergence of home bases and domestic fire a punctuated event? A review of the Middle Pleistocene record in Eurasia. *Asian Perspectives*, 43(2), 248–80.

Rosell, J. and Blasco, R. (2019). The early use of fire among Neanderthals from a zooarchaeological perspective. *Quaternary Science Reviews*, 217, 268–83.

Rosso, D. E. (2017). Ocher and hair treatment among the Hamar (Ethiopia): An ethnoarchaeological approach. *PYRENAE*, 48(2), 123–49.

Ruddiman, W. F. (2003). The Anthropogenic greenhouse era began thousands of years ago. *Climatic Change*, 61, 261–93.

Ruddiman, W. F. and Thomson, J. S. (2001). The case for human causes of increased atmospheric CH4 over the last 5000 years. *Quaternary Science Reviews*, 20, 1769–77.

Sagan, C. E. Writer. (1980). *Cosmos: A Personal Voyage. Episode 2, One Voice in the Cosmic Fugue. Aired October 15,* 1980. Arlington, VA: Public Broadcasting Service.

Sala, N., Arsuaga, J. L., Pantonja-Pérez, A., et al. (2015). Lethal interpersonal violence in the Middle Pleistocene. *PLoS ONE*, 10(5), e0126589.

Saladié, P., Huguet, R., Rodriguez-Hidalgo, A., et al. (2012). Intergroup cannibalism in the European Early Pleistocene: The range expansion and imbalance of power hypothesis. *Journal of Human Evolution*, 63(5), 682–95.

Sankararaman, S., Patterson, N., Li, H., Pääbo, S. and Reich, D. (2012). The date of interbreeding between Neandertals and Modern Humans. *PLoS Genetics*, 8(10), e1002947.

Sano, K., Beyene, Y., Katoh, S., et al. (2020). A 1.4 million-year-old bone handaxe from Konso, Ethiopia, shows advanced tool technology in the early Acheulian. *Proceedings of the National Academy of Sciences USA*, 117(31), 18393–400.

Sanz, M., Daura, J., Cabanes, D., et al. (2020). Early evidence of fire in south-western Europe: The Acheulian site of Gruta da Aroeira (Torres Novas, Portugal). *Scientific Reports*, 10(12053), doi: 10.1038/s41598–020-68839-w

Schaaffhausen, H. (1857). Verh. naturhist. Ver. preuss. Rhineland.14, Corr. Bl., 50–52.

Schick, K. and Toth, N. (1994). *Making Silent Stones Speak: Human Evolution and the Dawn of Technology*. New York: Simon & Schuster.

Schmandt-Besserat, D. (1999). *How Writing Came about*. Austin: University of Texas Press.

Schoetensack, O. (1908). Der Unterkiefer des *Homo heidelbergensis* aus den Sanden von Mauer bei Heidelberg. *Ein Beitrag zur Paläontologie des Menschen*. Leipzig: Verlag von Wilhelm Engelmann.

Semaw, S. (2000). The world's oldest stone artifacts from Gona, Ethiopia: Their implications for understanding stone technology and patterns of human evolution between 2.6–1.5 million years ago. *Journal of Archaeological Science*, 27(12), 1197–1214.

Semaw, S., Renne, P., Harris, J. W. K., et al. (1997). 2.5-million-year-old stone tools from Gona, Ethiopia. *Nature*, 385(6614), 333–36.

Semaw, S., Rogers, M. J., Quade, J., et al. (2003). 2.6-Million-year-old stone tools and associated bones from OGS-6 and OGS-7, Gona, Afar, Ethiopia. *Journal of Human Evolution*, 45(2), 169–77.

Semaw, S., Rogers, M. J. and Stout, D. (2009). Insights into Late Pliocene lithic assemblage variability: The East Gona and Ounda Gona South Oldowan archaeology (2.6 Million Years Ago), Afar, Ethiopia. In K. Schick and N. Toth, eds., *The Cutting Edge: New Approaches to the Archaeology of Human Origins*. Bloomington: Stone Age Institute Press, 211–46.

Sharon, G. (2009). Acheulian giant core technology. A worldwide perspective. *Current Anthropology*, 50 (3), 335–67.

Shimelmitz, R., Kuhn, S. L., Jelinek, A., et al. (2014). "Fire at will": The emergence of habitual fire use 350,000 years ago. *Journal of Human Evolution*, 77, 196–203.

Shimelmitz, R. and Rosenberg, D. (2013). Dull-edged weapons and low-level fighting in the Late Prehistoric Southern Levant. *Cambridge Archaeological Journal*, 23(3), 433–52.

Shumaker, R. W., Walkup, K. R. and Beck, B. B. (2011). *Animal tool behavior: The use and manufacture of tools by animals*. Baltimore: Johns Hopkins University Press.

Slon, V., Hopfe, C., WeiÔ, C. L., et al. (2017). Neandertal and Denisovan DNA from Pleistocene sediments. *Science*, 356(6338), 605–8.

Smith, B. and Zeder, M. A. (2013). The onset of the Anthropocene. *Anthropocene*, 4, 8–13.

Sockol, M. D., Raichlen, D. A. and Pontzer, H. (2007). Chimpanzee locomotor energetics and the origins of human bipedalism. *Proceedings of the National Academy of Sciences USA*, 104(30), 12265–69.

Steffen, W., Sanderson, A., Tyson, P. D., et al. (2004). *Global Change and the Earth System: A Planet under Pressure*. Berlin, Heidelberg, New York: Springer-Verlag.

Stein, J. (2013, May). The ME ME ME Generation. *Time Magazine*, 1–21.

Stolarczyk, R. E. and Schmidt, P. (2018). Is early silcrete heat treatment a new behavioral proxy in the Middle Stone Age? *PLos ONE*, 13(10), e0204705.

Stout, D. and Chaminade, T. (2013). Stone tools, language and the brain in human evolution. *Philosophical Transactions of the Royal Society B*, 367(1585), 75–87.

Stout, D., Quade, J., Semaw, S., Rogers, M. J. and Levin, N. E. (2005). Raw material selectivity of the earliest stone toolmakers at Gona, Afar, Ethiopia. *Journal of Human Evolution*, 48(4), 365–80.

Stout, D. and Semaw, S. (2006). Knapping skill of the earliest stone toolmakers: Insights from the study of modern human novices. In N. Toth and K. Schick, eds., *The Oldowan: Case Studies into the Earliest Stone Age*. Bloomington, IN: Stone Age Institute Press, 307–20.

Stringer, C. (2012). *Lone Survivors. How We Came to Be the Only Humans on the Earth*. New York: St. Martin's Griffin.

Svizzero, S. (2018). Persistent controversies about the Neolithic revolution. *Journal of Historical Archaeology & Anthropological Sciences*, 1(2) 53–61.

Swisher III, C. C., Curtis, G. H., Jacob, T., et al. (1994). Age of the earliest known hominids in Java, Indonesia. *Science*, 263(5150) 1118–21.

Tappen, N. C. (1985). The dentition of the "Old Man" of La Chapelle-aux-Saints and inferences concerning Neanderthal behavior. *American Journal of Physical Anthropology*, 67(1), 43–50.

Theofanopoulou, C., Gastaldon, S., O'Rourke, T., et al. (2017). Self-domestication in *Homo sapiens*: Insights from comparative genomics. *PLoS ONE*, 12(10): e0185306.

Toro-Moyano, I., Agustí, J. and Martínez-Navarro, B., eds. (2003). *El Pleistoceno inferior de Barranco León y Fuente Nueva 3, Orce (Granada). Memoria científica campañas 1999–2002*. Seville: Junta de Andalucía.

Toro-Moyano, I., Lumley, H. de, Barrier, P., et al. (2010). *Les industries lithiques archaïques du Barranco León et de Fuente Nueva 3, Orce, basin du Guadix-Baza*, Andalousian. En : Monography, CNRS Editions.

Toro-Moyano, I., Martínez-Navarro, B., Agustí, J., et al. (2013). The oldest human fossil in Europe, from Orce (Spain). *Journal of Human Evolution*, 65(1), 1–9.

Toth, N. (1985). Archaeological evidence for preferential right-handedness in the Lower and Middle Pleistocene and its possible implications. *Journal of Human Evolution*, 14(6), 607–14.

Tournal, P. (1827). *Notes sur deux cavernes à ossements découvertes à Bize. Annales des Sciences Naturelles: Physiologie animale et végétale, anatomie comparée des deux règnes, zoologie, botanique, minéralogie et géologie*, t. XII. Paris: Crochard, 78–82.

Trinkaus, E. (1983). *The Shanidar Neandertals*. New York: Academic Press.

Vallverdú, J., Alonso, S., Bargalló, A., et al. (2012). Combustion structures of archaeological level O and Mousterian activity areas with use of fire at the Abric Romaní rockshelter (NE Iberian Peninsula). *Quaternary International*, 247, 313–24.

Vallverdú, J., Saladié, P., Rosas, A., et al. (2014). Age and date for early arrival of the Acheulian in Europe (Barranc de la Boella, la Canonja, Spain). *PLoS One*, 9(7), e103634.

Vekua, A., Lordkipanidze, D., Rightmire, G. P. (2002). A new skull of early *Homo* from Dmanisi, Georgia. *Science*, 297(5578), 85–89.

Vendetti, F., Nunziante-Cesaro, S., Parush, Y., Gopher, A. and Barkai, R. (2019). Recycling for a purpose in the late Lower Paleolithic Levant: Use-wear and residue analyses of small sharp flint items indicate a planned and integrated subsistence behavior at Qesem Cave (Israel). *Journal of Human Evolution*, 131, 109–28.

Vergès, J. M., Allué, E., Fontanals, M., et al. (2016). El Mirador cave (Sierra de Atapuerca, Burgos, Spain): A whole perspective. *Quaternary International*, 414, 236–43.

Villmoare, B., Kimbel, W. H., Seyoum, C., et al. (2015). Early *Homo* at 2.8 Ma from Ledi-Geraru, Afar, Ethiopia. *Science*, 347(6228), 1352–55.

Volpato, V., Macchiarelli, R., Guatelli-Steinberg, D., et al. (2012). Hand to mouth in a Neanderthal: Right-handedness in Regourdou 1. *PLoS ONE*, 7(8), e439492.

Ward, C. Leakey, M. and Walker, A. (1999). The new hominid species *Australopithecus anamensis*. *Evolutionary Anthropology*, 7(6), 197–205.

Ward, E. J. and Underwood, C. R. (1967). The effect of posture on the solar radiation area of man. *Ergonomics*, 10(4), 399–409.

Weart, S. R. (2011). Global warming: How skepticism became denial. *Bulletin of the Atomic Scientists*, 67(1), 41–50.

Wheeler, P. E. (1991). The thermoregulatory advantages of hominid bipedalism in open equatorial environments: The contribution of increased convective heat loss and cutaneous evaporative cooling. *Journal of Human Evolution*, 21(2), 107–15.

Wheeler, P. E. (1985). The loss of functional body hair in man: The influence of thermal environment, body form and bipedality. *Journal of Human Evolution*, 14(1), 23–28.

Wheeler, P. E. (1984). The evolution of bipedality and loss of functional body hair in hominids. *Journal of Human Evolution*, 13(1), 91–98.

White, T. D. (1980). Evolutionary implications of Pliocene hominid footprints. *Science*, 208 (4440), 175–76.

White, T. D., Asfaw, B., DeGusta, D., et al. (2003). Pleistocene *Homo sapiens* from Middle Awash, Ethiopia. *Nature*, 423(6491), 742–47.

White, T. D., Suwa, G. and Asfaw, B. (1994). *Australopithecus ramidus*, a new species of early hominid from Aramis, Ethiopia. *Nature*, 371, 306–12.

White, T. D, WoldeGabriel, G., Asfaw, B., et al. (2006). Asa Issie, Aramis and the origin of *Australopithecus*. *Nature*, 440 (7086), 883–89.

Williams, L. and Callaghan, M. L. (2020). Exploring Our World: Biological and Archaeological Principles of General Anthropology. UCF Created OER Works.

Wood, B., Henry, A. and Hatala, K., eds. (2015). *Wiley Blackwell Student Dictionary of Human Evolution*. : Wiley Blackwell.

World Bank. (2018, March). www.nationalgeographic.com/2018/03/climate-migrants-report-world-bank-spd/

Wrangham, R. W. (2009). *Catching Fire: How Cooking Made Us Human*. New York: Basic Books.

Wroe, S. and Field, J. (2006). A review of the evidence for a human role in the extinction of Australian megafauna and an alternative interpretation. *Quaternary Science Reviews*, 25(21-22), 2692–2703.

Yokoyama, Y., Falguères, C. and Quaegebeur, J. P. (1985). ESR dating of quartz from Quaternary sediments: first attempt. *Nuclear Tracks and Radiation Measurements*, 10(4-6), 921–28.

Yokoyama, Y. and Nguyen, H. V. (1981). Datation directe de l'Homme de Tautavel par la spectrométrie gamma, non destructive, du crâne humain fossile Arago XXI. *Comptes Rendus de l'Académie des Sciences*, 292, 741–44.

Yustos, P. S., Diez-Martín, F., Díaz, I. M. and Duque, J. (2015). Production and use of percussive stone tools in the Early Stone Age: Experimental approach to the lithic record of Olduvai Gorge. *Journal of Archaeological Science*, 2, 367–83.

Zalasiewicz, J., Williams, M., Smith, A., et al. (2008). Are we now living in the Anthropocene? *GSA Today*, 18(2), 4–8.

Zalasiewicz, J., Williams, M., Steffen, W. and Crutzen, P. J. (2010). The new world of the Anthropocene. *Environmental Science and Technology*, 44(7), 2228–31.

Zalasiewicz, J., Williams, M., Waters, C. N., et al. (2016). Scale and diversity of the physical technosphere: A geological perspective. *The Anthropocene Review*, 4(1), 9–22.

Zilhão, J., Angelucci, D. E., Badal-García, E., et al. (2010). Symbolic use of marine shells and mineral pigments by Iberian Neandertals. *Proceedings of the National Academy of Sciences USA*, 107(3), 1023–1028.

Zink, K. and Lieberman, D. E. (2016). Impact of meat and Lower Palaeolithic food processing techniques on chewing in humans. *Nature*, 531(7595), 500–503.

Zollikofer, C. P. E., Ponce de León, M. S., Lieberman, D. E., et al. (2005). Virtual cranial reconstruction of *Sahelanthropus tchadensis*. *Nature*, 434(7034), 755–759.

Webgraphy

http://accuca.conectia.es/msnbc-02my05.htm

http://earth.imagico.de/large.php?site=eafrica

http://firstlegend.info/thevenuscult.html

http://humanorigins.si.edu/evidence/genetics/ancient-dna-and-neanderthals/dna-genotypes-and-phenotypes

http://humanorigins.si.edu/evidence/human-fossils/species/homo-erectus

http://humanorigins.si.edu/evidence/human-fossils/species/homo-neanderthalensis

http://paulbourke.net/fractals/googleearth/

http://unfccc.int/kyoto_protocol/items/2830.php

https://australianstogether.org.au/discover/indigenous-culture/aboriginal-spirituality/

https://climate.nasa.gov/

https://commons.wikimedia.org/wiki/File:Fires_in_Eastern_Siberia_(4860546639).jpg

https://commons.wikimedia.org/wiki/File:Lions_painting,_Chauvet_Cave_(museum_replica).jpg

https://commons.wikimedia.org/wiki/File:Range_of_NeanderthalsAColoured.png

https://cosmosmagazine.com/palaeontology/big-five-extinctions

https://en.wikipedia.org/wiki/Group_mind_(science_fiction)

https://en.wikipedia.org/wiki/Iron_Age#Europe

https://en.wikipedia.org/wiki/Mesolithic

https://fractalfoundation.org/resources/what-are-fractals/

https://fr.wikipedia.org/wiki/Paul_Tournal#Biographie

https://ipbes.net/global-assessment

https://newint.org/blog/2016/11/30/the-dangerous-rise-of-the-right-an-interview-with-noam-chomsky

https://news.nationalgeographic.com/2018/03/climate-migrants-report-world-bank-spd/

https://olduvai-paleo.org/current-field-research/

https://pixabay.com/photos/ethiopia-tribe-ethnicity-4089002/

https://pressbooks.online.ucf.edu/ant2000/chapter/chapter-4/

http://quaternary.stratigraphy.org/working-groups/anthropocene/

https://stars.library.ucf.edu/oer/5

https://theconversation.com/world-politics-explainer-the-twin-tower-bombings-9-11-101443

https://unfccc.int/cop7/documents/accords_draft.pdf

https://unfccc.int/process-and-meetings/the-paris-agreement/the-paris-agreement

https://unfccc.int/process/the-kyoto-protocol

https://unfccc.int/process/the-kyoto-protocol/the-doha-amendment

https://whc.unesco.org/en/list/1388

https://whyfiles.org/2011/climate-simple-beautiful/index.html

www.aljazeera.com/ajimpact/davos-world-prepare-millions-climate-refugees-200121175217520.html

www.atapuerca.org

www.atapuerca.org/en/apartado/1990/atapuerca-project

www.bbc.com/future/article/20190218-are-we-on-the-road-to-civilisation-collapse?

www.britannica.com/biography/Carolus-Linnaeus

www.britannica.com/biography/Charles-Lyell

www.britannica.com/biography/Jacques-Boucher-de-Perthes

www.britannica.com/biography/Jean-Baptiste-Lamarck

www.crystalinks.com/prehistoric_mining.html

www.earth-policy.org/indicators/C52/carbon_emissions_2004

www.flickr.com/photos/timlueddemann/27475894907/in/photostream/

www.fromthegrapevine.com/nature/animals-use-tools

www.greencorridor.info/en/index.html

www.historyextra.com/search/?q=climate+change

www.inquiriesjournal.com/articles/538/was-adopting-agriculture-our-biggest-mistake-challenging-the-progressivist-view-of-human-history

www.ipcc.ch/

www.jewishvirtuallibrary.org/la-peyr-x00e8-re-isaac

www.livescience.com/9761-10-animals-tools.html

www.makin-metals.com/about/history-of-metals-infographic/

www.nationalgeographic.com/science/article/climate-migrants-report-world-bank-spd

www.nationalgeographic.org/encyclopedia/fertile-crescent/

www.nbcnews.com/id/wbna7103668

www.nemosgarden.com/

www.nytimes.com/2021/01/27/us/doomsday-clock-midnight.html

www.republicworld.com/world-news/rest-of-the-world-news/covid19-prehistoric-chinese-village-might-hold-clues-first-epidemic.html

www.sciencemag.org/news/2016/05/humans-are-still-evolving-and-we-can-watch-it-happen

www.stratigraphy.org/

www.un.org/development/desa/en/news/population/2018-revision-of-world-urbanization-prospects.html

www.visualcapitalist.com/history-of-pandemics-deadliest/

www.worldbank.org/en/news/feature/2018/03/19/meet-the-human-faces-of-climate-migration

www.worldometers.info/coronavirus/

www.wri.org/our-work/topics/climate

INDEX